CONVERTIBLES
THE COMPLETE STORY

Also by the Author from TAB BOOKS Inc.

No. 2086 How To Restore & Upgrade Your Vintage Car with Factory Accessories

CONVERTIBLES
THE COMPLETE STORY

BY JOHN "GUNNER" GUNNELL

TAB BOOKS Inc.
BLUE RIDGE SUMMIT, PA. 17214

FIRST EDITION

FIRST PRINTING

Copyright © 1984 by TAB BOOKS Inc.

Printed in the United States of America

Library of Congress Cataloging in Publication Data

Gunnell, John.
   Convertibles : the complete story.

   Includes index.
   1. Automobiles, Convertible. I. Title.
TL154.G86 1984   629.2'222   83-24354
ISBN 0-8306-2110-5 (pbk.)

Cover Photographs
Top: 1981 XP-53 Corvette Replicar. Owned by Exxact Cars, Inc.
Center Left: 1948 MG-TC. Owned by British Motor Corp.
Center Right: 1940 Packard Convertible Sedan. Owned by Volo Museum.

Contents

Preface

As an editor at *Old Cars* Publications in Iola, Wisconsin, I work with a group of outstanding people who staff what amounts to a clearing house for information about collectible cars. Together we research articles, compile current collector-car values and answer inquiries for thousands of automotive hobbyists. By mail, by telephone, or in person, I have visited with approximately 200,000 car enthusiasts over the past five years. A great many automotive enthusiasts are convertible (ragtop) lovers. My experience indicates that more than half own convertibles or plan to buy such a model soon. Naturally, they want to know more about these cars.

Some collectors are interested mainly in the history of convertibles. Others ask for technical facts or information concerning a restoration. There are those interested in values and prices and those seeking advice about buying or selling a car. A frequent request concerns manufacturing production totals. "How many cars like this were made? Is mine a rare car?"

To anyone involved in the automotive hobby field, the vast popularity of convertibles is very apparent. At classic-car auctions, hundreds of convertibles are offered for sale annually. There are also many private sales. With very few exceptions, these cars bring higher prices than other body types of the same line. They can also be sold faster and easier than other models. Convertible owners are also extremely active in participating in hobby events such as ralleys, car shows, and car-club functions. Convertibles are so appealing to enthusiasts that many new carmakers have reinstated ragtops in their lines within the last few years.

Despite such obviously heavy appeal and despite built-in collector interest and despite a great deal of hands-on activity, one thing has been missing. There is currently no standard reference guide providing easy-to-find and easy-to-use facts for convertible lovers. A few excellent books about convertibles *do* exist. They pertain to restoration, history, values, or postwar-model specifications. No single, previous book covers the complete topic from beginning to end. This is my motivation for writing *Convertibles: The Complete Story*. It is designed to provide a data bank of information about all convertibles and to be a book that every convertible lover can use.

Introduction

This book is a source for information on every kind of convertible, while also serving as a guide to additional, more in-depth advice. For example, Chapter 6 outlines all of the work specifically involved in refurbishing a car to its original condition and then directs the reader to sources of tools, parts, technical tips, and specialized services that will be of help when hands-on operations begin. The same approach and a similar level of factual completeness is presented in additional chapters dealing with related topics. Everything that the convertible lover might want to know is touched upon. You will see how classic-car auctions operate, what an Indy pace car convertible is, and the procedures to follow in locating and joining car clubs. Photos reveal facts about convertibles and about collecting cars. Tables and charts reveal production figures and the rarity of convertibles.

In 1928, the use of the term convertible became standardized in the auto industry. Before that time there were roadsters, runabouts, and touring cars, which are somewhat similar to—but not quite as special as—convertibles. You'll see why this was so. Plus there is information on some of the new ragtops available such as the 1982 Chrysler LeBaron, the 1982 Buick Riveria, the 1983 Mustang, and the 1983 Pontiac 2000 Sunbird convertibles.

There are special sections within this book designed to make it more useful to today's car collector! The collecting trends of five years ago are not the same as those of the '80s. The popularity of certain types of cars—and their collector values—are constantly changing. Whether your car was built in 1928 or 1983, whether imported or domestic, one of a kind or one of 25,000, or fully restored or in need of much work, this book will answer many of your questions.

PART 1
Collectibles

THE 1976 CADILLAC ELDORADO WAS SUPPOSEDLY THE LAST REGULAR PRODUCTION CONVERTIBLE BUILT IN AMERICA. IN announcing the car, Cadillac originally projected building about 8000 cars. Later, the company stated that it's production run of '76 Eldorado ragtops would be increased to accommodate an anticipated jump in demand for the "last convertible."

This move proved to be based on sound thinking. By 1977, *Ward's Automotive Yearbook* noted that used convertibles—of all model years, in good condition—were attracting much attention and high prices at dealer auctions. Some dealers staged special "convertible day" sales.

The revival of the convertible's popularity to car buyers was a clear indication that convertibles were coming to be viewed as collectors' items.

1. The Mystique

The term *convertible* was first adopted as a standard, automobile body-style designation, by the Society of Automotive Engineers (SAE), in 1928. During the 1930s, this type of car became widely popular with American buyers. The convertible reached the height of its popularity—as gauged by its share of the automobile market—in 1963. Thereafter, sales of this body style began to decline. By 1970, the convertible's market penetration level fell to 1.7 percent of total industry output. Many manufacturers deleted the ragtop from their regular lines. Today the trend is reversing, with more convertibles offered each season since 1981 and sales on the upswing again. The main reason the ragtop almost became extinct was its impracticality. But a factor called the convertible mystique led to the style's survival.

Some say the mystique surrounding the convertible stems from the following factors: driving fun, romance, sexiness, crowd appeal, sportiness, pleasure, environmental harmony, association with success, and just the sheer thrill of having all of these factors combined in one kind of vehicle.

Convertible expert Charles Webb identifies the convertible as one of three elements found in the dreams of many people—romance; riches, and ragtops. He calls these elements "the three Rs."[1] Burt Mills, another expert, talks of the convertible as a dashing and swanky type of car with lots of verve.[2] As you can tell, the basic appeal of this type of car is emotional. People don't merely ride in or drive convertibles; they live out their fantasies in them.

There are several fantasies—or basic misconceptions—that society has formed about convertibles. For one thing, many people believe that most convertible owners live where the weather is warm and sunny all year round. For another, many picture the typical convertible owner as being carefree and irresponsible. A major mistake is the view that convertibles have primarily masculine appeal.

According to L.R. Windecker, a Ford Motor Company spokesman, convertibles were actually most popular in Northeastern localities where the foldaway top meant cool sailing in the summer. They were less popular in the Sun Belt, where intense summer heat made top-down operation uncomfortable and contributed to rapid deterioration of convertible roof fabrics. Moreover, the average convertible buyer was a young, single, well-educated female holding a good, solid job.

The misconceived images surrounding the convertible, while common, do not change the fact that its sales were frequently inspired by emotions. Quite the contrary. Practicality played little or no part in the purchase of convertibles.

While it might be wise to own such a car as an investment today, this wasn't true years ago. When new, convertibles did not represent the best way to spend money on an automobile. Other body styles provided much more value as basic transportation vehicles. Sedans offered extra roominess, added safety and better driving convenience. If sportiness was desired, a coupe was the logical type of car to buy. It combined convertible like styling with most advantages (other than space) found in sedans. Buyers seeking luxury and prestige could more readily find such qualities in the limousine, a larger and more lavish variation of the sedan. Actually, the only models less practical than convertibles were roadsters and touring cars. Both of these styles died out shortly after the first true convertibles appeared.

Over the short run, a convertible wasn't practical from a pricing standpoint either. In the early 1930s, a convertible (or convertible cabriolet) sold for higher prices than roadsters and most closed-body cars in the same line (although Deluxe sedans and limousines were slightly costlier). The ragtop, however, depreciated much faster than other models, according to figures from old used-car price books.

As you can see in Table 1-1, open-body '34 Chevys lost value (depreciated) much faster than closed models. The same situation held true even for Chevys made in the mid-1960s, when convertible popularity was at its peak. In 1966, a five-year-old Impala convertible, four-door hardtop or two-door hardtop coupe, were all equally valued at $710 despite the fact that the ragtop sold for

$185 to $250 above the others when all were new. By 1973, the value of a five-year-old Impala ragtop had actually declined to the point where it was worth $50–150 *less* than any other Impala of the same vintage, including four-door sedans. Such figures show that buying a convertible was not at all practical, from a value standpoint, prior to the time that collectors became interested in ragtops.

The main reason convertibles depreciated faster than closed cars was that they tended to deteriorate more rapidly. This was due to their lower levels of body integrity and weather tightness. Ragtops had no sturdy, fixed upper structure to help maintain body-panel alignment. Fabric tops rarely stayed in good condition for very long. A leaky roof would allow rust to form or moisture to ruin an interior. In addition, convertibles had certain intrinsic shortcomings such as a lack of luggage space, less interior headroom (due to intruding top mechanisms), and poor fuel economy (due to heavier curb weight). To car buyers able to control their emotions, convertibles indeed seemed very impractical.

Yet for over fifty years the convertible has managed to survive and even fight off the threat of virtual

Table 1-1. 1934 Chevy Values 1934–1940.

Model	1934 Price	1940 Value	Percent of original value in 1940	Percent of value lost in 6 years
Roadster	$540	$125	23.2	76.8
Coupe	$560	$140	25	75
Sport Coupe	$600	$145	24.2	75.8
Convertible (Ccabriolet)	$665	$155	23.3	76.7
Coach	$580	$160	27.6	72.4
Sedan	$640	$170	26.6	73.4
Town Sedan	$615	$160	26	74
Sport Sedan	$675	$170	25.2	74.8

Changing values of different models in the 1934 Chevrolet Master series between 1934 and 1940. Source of original prices: *Official Blue Book New & Used Car Guide,* Vol. 29, No. 122, 1934. Source of 1940 value appraisals: *National Used Car Market Report,* March-April 1940 edition.

extinction. Automotive journalist Linda Clark, writing in *Old Cars Price Guide*, summed-up this appeal with the following passage: "A summertime jaunt with the wind in your face, the sun on your arms and the exhaust notes burbling contentedly in your ears is a sure-fire way to live up to the giddy side of one's nature."

TOP-DOWN DRIVING

Collectors, as a general group, do not evoke images of giddy behavior and open-air activity. It's hard to picture the philatelist as a philanderer; he's more likely to be caught kissing stamps than kissing women. A numismatist, in the public eye, might be found polishing off coins instead of a quick lap around the swimming pool.

I can't agree with stereotypes, but no one can deny they exist. Ragtop collectors, on the other hand, are often stereotyped as men with tan arms and wind-blown hair who build strong arm muscles by raising and lowering convertible tops at the mere hint of sunshine.

Here again is a stereotype that's far from accurate. There are many collectors who never lower their convertible roofs. They prefer keeping them up all the time so their ragtop doesn't get ragged.

Still, there *are* certain perceptions and a definite image that go along with owning an open car, and I'd have to agree that many sales and a lot of ragtop love affairs are inspired by the mental associations linking convertibles with very active lifestyles. Whether real or imaginary, this image does exist.

This fact was not overlooked by the Hertz Rent-A-Car System's advertising department, in 1954, when a magazine ad showing a red Chevrolet convertible was prepared. Although actual statistics aren't available, automotive historians agree that these models were available mainly as a promotional gimmick. Hertz probably had very few ragtops in its nationwide fleet of rental cars. One such car was used in the ad because it went well with the overall theme "See more. . .do more. . .have more fun. . .the Hertz Rent-A-Car Way!" Illustrating a convertible in the ad played on the value of perceived images and the very common association of top-down driving with people leading active lives.

This perception still exists and is one reason that convertibles are sought after by collectors. Some might already be active people hoping to find even more fun; others are seeking to fight off boredom with a new ragtop. Then there are those who feel only a ragtop will suit their on-the-go personality. All this is part of the top-down driver stereotype.

There is also an emotional side to top-down motoring because riding in an open-car brings certain feelings and sensitivities into play. In an antique convertible (one more than 25 years old), I've had impressions like those felt riding on the outside deck of the Staten Island Ferry: the wind whistling under and around a flat, flimsy windshield; the rocking and rumbling of a relatively

unsophisticated internal combustion engine; and the slow traveling speeds made me think of a ferryboat while driving such a car.

In a stripped-for-racing, roll-bar-equipped '57 Corvette—with a lead-footed test driver at the wheel—top-down driving seemed totally different. It made me think back to a ride on the Cyclone at Coney Island. Roller-coasting over Wisconsin's winding backroads in a 110 mile-per-hour sports car isn't much different than bronco-busting Brooklyn's amusement park Cannonball.

Then there was the Lincoln four-door convertible, a silver grey, ghost-of-the-past, type of car that seemed like an open-air bus ride. "Settle back and leave the driving to us," said those rich leather seats. As you might guess, this ride was pure relaxation; it was the type of cruise where you spin the wheel with one finger and just watch the scenery glide by. The Lincoln was a real joy to operate.

Your own top-down driving will leave more personalized impressions—like riding in a Hovercraft, cruising in a 30-foot yacht, sailing up a mountain on a ski lift—but one thing's for sure, you won't end the trip without a few long-lasting memories. This is the purely emotional side of driving in a convertible with the "canvas" lowered. It's great. No wonder so many collectors are doing it!

ROMANCE ON WHEELS

Ragtop romance is as real as the rush you receive when a warm springtime breeze blows over an April evening picnic. It has nothing to do with flip-top "sex shops" parked near dark beaches on sultry summer nights. Romance and sex land at different points on the automotive emotional spectrum. You will often see romance reflected in magazine ads where straight sexual suggestiveness is hardly ever found (at least above a subliminal level).

Consider, for example, the Pontiac advertising and publicity photo (Fig. 1-1) showing a 1966 GTO convertible being approached by a young, hand-holding couple. They are running across an immense, well-manicured lawn, away from a very large, modern home perched on a hillside. Isn't this the American dream of romance, riches, and a ragtop?

Car ads can even be romantically written, and this is especially true where open-body models are concerned. Check out the following words that came from the immortal pen of Ned Jordon—a real poet among ad copywriters of the 1920s and 1930s: "The Jordon Playboy. Some day in June, when happy hours abound, a wonderful girl and a wonderful boy will leave their friends in a shower of rice and start to roam."

Yes, it's true that the 1928 Jordon Playboy that inspired these words was a roadster, but that's not the important thing here. The main point is that an open-body car can provoke such an outflow of flowery prose. Rarely are words such as these used in promoting coupes

Fig. 1-1. This promotional photograph depicts the 1966 Pontiac GTO convertible as a part of the American picture of success: romance, riches, and ragtops. (Courtesy Pontiac Motor Division)

or sedans. In later years, after his own company folded during the Great Depression, Ned Jordon wrote ads for other brands of cars. He usually continued to dwell on open models, stressing their romantic character with lines reading like an industrial age version of *Romeo and Juliet.*

Romance remained part of ragtop sales promotions until the bitter end, when Cadillac's "Last Convertible" appeared. The Cadillac sales brochure for 1976 showed a swashbuckling young couple, posed in a boatyard, with a Crystal Blue Eldorado convertible (complete with Antique Light Blue leather interior option). Although they are pictured in a moment of serious discussion, there is definitely that traditional touch of ragtop romance in the air.

Compare this scene with a DeVille sedan ad photographed in an entirely different manner. There were no boats to suggest wealth, no lady to hint of romance, and, most obvious of all, no rag top. For sedan buyers, the ad implied the silence and solitude that the company wanted to stress most of all

In the auto sales business, the planning of advertising, publicity, and sales-brochure photos is very close to a science. It's been highly refined to capture a car's most appealing traits on film. In reality, a convertible might well be used for everyday commuting or lugging groceries home from a supermarket. But the image that *sells* the car (and that can also influence collectors) will often be one filled with romance.

SEX APPEAL

Convertibles have been associated with sexuality and for a good deal longer than some people might guess. The same Ned Jordon who wrote like a romanticist also used sex to sell a few cars now and then (which might be why he called them Playboy roadsters).

According to automotive writer Bill McBride, who specializes in researching automotive advertising history, "Ned's audience for most ads was the wonderous female gender, that subtly powerful sex who not only knew what it wanted, but knew how to get it as well. Yet Jordon's copy could be asexual enough to say things any man would agree with.[3]

McBride's observations are interesting not only in that they suggest that Jordon switched styles according to audience gender (sexual for women; more romantic for men), but also in that the nature of the switch compliments Ford Motor Company's profile of typical convertibles buyers.

In another of his many articles about auto ads—this one focusing on red convertibles—McBride talks about the convertible's sexual image more directly. After discussing red as a color symbolically associated with royalty, heat, love, and affection (i.e., red carpet, red-hot, and red-hot-mamma), he suggests that such associations form the rationale for the immense popularity of ruby-colored ragtops and states, "All the associations go right along with the sexual appeal, male appeal and youth appeal of a red convertible."[4]

Does this mean the sexuality factor surfaces only with red convertibles? Of course not! Look at the photo of a pink Thunderbird convertible (with removable hard-top in place) appearing at a 1982 car show in Berlin, Germany. This car's original owner was actress Marilyn Monroe—America's sex goddess of the mid-1950s. As seen on exhibit (Fig. 1-2), it was backdropped by photos of Marilyn that served to symbolically tie her sexuality with that of the machine. What if the actress had driven a pink Rambler sedan? Would it fit the same image? Naturally the answer is no. Even a red Rambler would not do the trick.

SPORTINESS

The 1971 Cadillac Eldorado ragtop qualifies as a luxury-level machine. It's richly appointed, tastefully trimmed, elegantly styled and high priced. It's a huge car perched on a 126.3-inch wheelbase and measuring 221.6-inches overall. Under the hood is a massive 500-cubic-inch, 365-horsepower V-8, but its top speed won't win a drag race. Automatic transmission is standard equipment and this, combined with a weight of 4690 pounds, puts the Eldorado ragtop out of the sports car class. So does the fancy hood ornament.

The Eldorado isn't a sports car, but its image is certainly sporty. This applies to all convertibles to one degree or another. The variety of sport and the brand of car do change. A Mustang convertible for a rodeo rider or an Olds Cutlass ragtop for a swordsman or a drop-top Dodge Dart for a mile runner seem like a few natural pairings. Also a "natural" is sportiness as part of the ragtop's general character. This type of appeal is felt by collectors as well as other purchasers of convertibles.

DRIVING PLEASURE

The enjoyment to be found in driving a convertible on either a short or long pleasure cruise (preferably long) is not the same as the highly charged, emotional reactions of top-down driving appeal. The sensations involved in the driving experience—wind-blown hair, bugs in your face, and other, similar gutsy feelings—are different than the deeper, more soothing and relaxing feelings that ragtop operation can bring.

Fig. 1-2. Actress Marilyn Monroe was the first owner of this hot pink Thunderbird shown here at a German auto show. Two-seat Thunderbirds were built from 1955 through 1957 and came with an optional, removable hardtop. In this case, the car complimented the owner's status as an American sex symbol. (Courtesy Veedol Starparade)

On a vacation trip in a convertible going across the country at moderate speeds you see things that are usually shut out in closed-body cars. This can include the beauty of a rainbow in the sky, a sunset, or the intricate architectural details of tall buildings in a city. In other words, those things often hidden from view in sedans, coupes, and limousines.

Chrysler Corporation did a very good job of capturing this type of driving pleasure in an ad for its 1962 Dodge, Dart, Plymouth, Chrysler, and Imperial convertibles. The ad shows what looks like an average middle-aged, middle-class, middle-American couple (kids all married and moved out) chasing a rainbow in their rare 1962 Dodge Polara 500 ragtop. The tag line refers to the open-air Chrysler products as "Five exciting ways to follow the sun."

I'm sure that many car collectors have also spent time following the sun in a convertible, possibly during a cross-country trip to their car club's national convention. This type of driving is really one of the greatest joys of convertible ownership.

DRAWING A CROWD

Despite the fact that Ford, Pontiac, Buick, Chrysler, Dodge, and Volkswagen are reintroducing semicustom convertibles right now, everyday sightings of ragtops in the streets seem to occur less frequently these days. Whenever a convertible does show up, a crowd usually forms pretty quickly.

This tendency to draw immediate attention in public was nearly always a part of the convertible mystique. This kind of magnetism might be attributed to two somewhat related factors. First, the relatively low production volume of open cars after the late 1920s and, second, the link between convertibles and dreams of riches, romance, and ragtops.

Let me try to pinpoint some of the reasons why convertibles were not purchased by the majority of new car buyers. Price is—and always was—a minor consideration. In 1932, for example, a Ford convertible cabriolet cost $625, the Deluxe coupe sold for $550, and a Fordor sedan cost $600. In 1940, the prices for comparable models were $849, $742, and $808 respectively. By 1950, the Custom Deluxe convertible, Crestliner coupe, and Fordor sedan models were selling at $1,948, $1,711, and $1,637 in order. Ten years later, the Galaxie convertible was $2,973, the Ford hardtop coupe was $2,723, and the Town Sedan was $2,716. In 1970, comparable Galaxie 500s were priced at $3,501, $3,293, and $3,137 respectively.

As you can see, the names of the cars changed, as did the price relationships of different closed models, but the relationship between prices of the most expensive closed cars and convertibles stayed amazingly stable over 38 years! For prewar years, the spread between the two prices was about $100; in postwar times, it was from $250–300. This is certainly not enough of a variation to explain the drastic differences found in body style popularity levels.

A much stronger reason for the convertible's relatively low market penetration level (percent of convertibles in the overall mix of body styles produced) can be related to basic cultural structures. The family unit controls behavior, usually by preventing nonconformity, through delegated responsibilities, community status, fear of criticism, and concern over economic well being.[5] In plain talk, our family structures tend to keep us in line.

Where economics are concerned, the family structure demands a high degree of emotional control on the part of the member(s) charged with making decisions about the disposal of income. Most convertible sales were based on emotions, rather than strictly practical reasons. The convertible is simply not a very logical vehicle for the average family. It is a body style that always had greatest appeal to the nonconformist.

This is true throughout the world. A Mercedes-Benz convertible (Fig. 1-3) on the streets of Cologne, Germany might draw even a bigger crowd than a Cadillac ragtop in "Middletown" America (Muncie, Indiana). The convertible has come to represent something out of the ordinary and, to some degree, a symbol of freedom from social control. All of us seem to have a touch of the Walter Mitty syndrome in our souls, and this is what the ragtop appeals to.

NOTHING BETTER ON A SUMMER EVENING

Another part of the convertible mystique is its seasonal character. Due to the design factors, a convertible is best suited, and very often limited, to warm-weather use. Therefore, many tend to identify this type of car with pleasant climatic conditions (not too hot and not too cold); the most romantic times of the year (springtime and fall); leisure activities (pleasure driving, vacations and car shows); carefree operation (no icy windshields or sub-zero starts); and attractive exterior appearance (no road salt to eat away metal and more frequent washings in warm weather).

In 1952, Ford Motor Company used these common associations in an advertisement designed to sell parts. It illustrated a convertible and a couple, dressed in beachwear, parked next to a boy shoveling snow. An imaginary glass dome protected the car and the couple from the winter elements. The tag line read, "Your Ford won't feel the winter . . . if you use parts that are made right for Fords."

This promotional concept was clever, but wouldn't have been as effective without the associations that go with the convertible's seasonal character. The fact that the ragtop is commonly viewed as a warm-weather car made this a good ad. I'm sure that these same associations surface in the collector's market today. Car enthusiasts

Fig. 1-3. The convertible is the type of car that can draw a crowd almost anywhere in the world. This Mercedes–Benz Cabriolet gathered lots of attention on a street in Cologne, Germany.

view convertibles as a seasonal treat much like summer strawberries, Georgia peaches, and a juicy Thanksgiving turkey. There's no model better suited for a summer's night drive that will make everyday pressures seem temporarily as remote as the chill winds of February.

A SIGN OF SUCCESS

Some 20 years ago, when Tom and Dick Smothers were an overnight success on TV, Pontiac Motor Division was glad to be sponsoring their popular "Comedy Hour." The company had the opportunity to expose its products to a wide audience and to also have the cars associated with the success of these talented performers. Not coincidentally, Pontiac frequently used the show to display its latest convertibles (Fig. 1-4). This was partly due to the ragtop's image as a sign of success.

It did not cost a lot extra to buy a convertible. Yet ownership of such a car seemed to suggest a certain degree of social or financial success. Purchasing a ragtop indicated a buyer could *afford* to be a bit of a nonconformist.

In the language of social scientists, conformity is identified as a norm. According to Broom & Selznick[6], norms are seen as binding rules by most people, but can be evaded by others for a number of reasons that include differences in perception, conflicts (opposing norms), weak enforcement, and differences in etiquette and lifestyle (class). An extension of the latter reason would be a higher degree of financial independence stemming from class differences and allowing the wealthy to "set their own rules." This can include the freedom to make relatively expensive purchases (home, boat, specialty car) on little more than a whim.

It's easy to see why convertibles have long been associated with success—financial or otherwise—that allowed the evasion of norms. It is not the fact that performers like Tom and Dick Smothers could afford the extra $500 to get a ragtop that equates such a purchase with success. Spread over a few year's payments, nearly any car buyer could do the same thing for a few bucks a week. The real sign of nonconformity here is putting out the total of $3,578 (or so) for a car that was obviously impractical; quick to lose value, and satisfying only to a

Fig. 1-4. For many people, convertibles represent a sign of success. During 1964, one of the most successful variety shows in America was the "Smother's Brothers Comedy Hour," and the two entertainers frequently promoted Pontiac ragtops during the program.

buyer's emotional needs. In other words, the freedom to buy a high-price tag item on impulse.

An interesting adjunct to this line of thought is the increase in popularity earned by convertibles between the close of World War II and the beginning of the Vietnam War era. During this period, the economy was strong, the average American's income increased, impulse buying became more common nationwide, and ragtop sales took a big jump.

As measured by market penetration figures, the top year for convertible sales was 1963 (when 6.3 percent of all American cars were ragtops). In years earlier, the same figure stood at 2.6 percent (about the same as the average prewar level), and 10 years later it dropped to 0.5 percent.

As measured by actual unit sales, the top convertible year was 1965 when 507,337 ragtops were sold. This compares to 223,277 in 1955 and 27,983 in 1975. By any yardstick, however, the period from the mid-1950s to the mid-1960s was the crest of the style's popularity. There is a direct relationship between this fact; the economic prosperity of that decade, and the extra purchasing power Americans had because of their bounding economy.

At the end of 1955 (the best automotive sales year in history up to that point), the McGraw-Hill index of business was 150.2 percent of the 1947–1949 average;

personal income of U.S. citizens stood at a record $306 billion, and the Gross National Product registered a healthy $391.5 billion. Ten years later, the Federal Reserve index of industrial production reached 131.8 percent of the 1957–1959 average, personal income was at $484.8 billion, and the GNP was measured at $623 billion. In addition, production and construction activity was strong for nearly the entire decade and prices were exceptionally stable (car prices increased only $10 between 1963 and 1964). Inflation wasn't considered a problem.[7]

In his book *My Years With General Motors*, Alfred P. Sloan, Jr. explained how this prosperity increased the number of multicar families and generated a growing emphasis on sales of specialty cars over standard sedans. This included convertibles, which Sloan classified under "sports cars."[8]

Convertibles began to lose popularity after 1965 for a number of reasons. One reason had to do with constraints placed upon the auto industry by the government and insurance companies. These constraints placed artificial pressure on the market by regulating the character of the product itself. Even the impulse buyer with an exceptionally high income could no longer have *exactly* the type of car that he wanted.

By the early 1970s, it was clear that the convertible's future as a regular production model was doomed. While the auto market operated free of outside constrictions, in a healthy economy, the popularity of the ragtop was clearly and directly related to the level of national economic prosperity. This was another reflection of the convertible as a sign of success.

Footnotes

[1]Charles Webb, *The Investor's Illustrated Guide to American Convertibles and Special-Interest Automobiles 1946-1976.* 1st ed. Cranbury, N.J.: A.S. Barnes and Co., Inc. 1979. Page 11.

[2]Burt Mills, *Restoring Convertibles: From Rags To Riches.* 1st ed. New York: Dodd, Meade & Co., 1977. Page 3.

[3]Bill McBride, "Car Ads That Sing," *Best of Old Cars*, Vol. III. Iola, Wis.: Krause Publications, 1982. Page 434.

[4]Bill McBride, "Ad Infinitum," *Car Exchange*, Oct. 1979. Iola, Wis.: Krause Publications. 1979. Page 17.

[5]Broom & Selznick, *Sociology.* 3rd ed. New York: Harper & Row. 1963. Chapter 10.

[6]Broom & Selznick, *op. cit.*, pages 71-73.

[7]Wilfred Funk, *et. al.*, *New Standard Encyclopedia. 1955 Yearbook. 1964 Yearbook.* (Business Reviews). New York: Wilfred Funk, Inc. 1955, 1964.

[8]Alfred P. Sloane, Jr., *My Years With General Motors.* ed. John McDonald, *et. al.* 4th ed. New York: Macfadden-Bartell, Corp. 1965. pg. 278.

2. The Rarity Aspect

You might have been told that your convertible is a collector's item, but the convertible mystique didn't really prove this. Strong demand alone does not make something collectible. A degree of scarcity must also exist. Collector value comes when something is both popular and relatively rare. The idea of relativity is very important. Supply (as well as demand and value) are never absolute factors in the collector market. All three can vary with numerous outside factors. Here are just three examples:

Supply. There might be thousands of Wartburg convertibles available in East Germany where these cars are built, but they are rare in America because exportation is prohibited.

Demand. Demand for convertibles increases in the summer and drops in the winter. Some dealers feel that it's even hard to sell a convertible on a rainy day.

Value. A collector-car dealer who relies on bank loans to purchase convertibles for his inventory might set his prices for the cars according to recent adjustments in the bank's interest rates.

DETERMINING RELATIVE SCARCITY

A collector car's rarity aspect is based on how few people own another car like it. Gauging this aspect isn't usually an exact science, but different measurements of relative scarcity can be achieved by using various statistics or making estimates based on them. Market penetration statistics will tell us the percentage of convertibles included in the overall mix of different models built during a period of time. For example, from 1928–1976 as a whole, the average market penetration for convertibles was approximately 3.2 percent; that is the lowest for any truly "distinct" body type.[1] Therefore, it can be said that over these 48 years convertibles were generally rarer than other kinds of cars.

Other kinds of statistics can help you determine the relative scarcity of a specific year, make, and model of car. Three of the most useful statistics are:

- ☐ original production totals.
- ☐ survival rates.
- ☐ optional equipment installation rates.

To be useful, rarity determinants must be obtained either from written records supplied by reliable sources or by making extrapolations from documented evidence.

True Rarity

If a car is truly rare, a comparison of the statistics you wind up with against similar statistics for other cars will show that at least one of the following situations exists:

☐ Few (or no) others like it were built (low-production).

☐ Few (or no) others like it survive (low-survival).

☐ Few (or no) others like it were similarly equipped (has rare options).

Stated another way, the statistics will show that the model's availability was low to begin with, that surviving examples are widely distributed (few and far between), or that the car is unusual in character (due to its uncommon equipment features). It will be a comparatively unusual automobile or, in other words, a relative scarcity.

Ragtop Rarity Versus Dollar Value

Rarity in itself is not necessarily related directly to dollar value. There are certain extremely rare cars—including some one-of-a-kind models—that have not been popular since the day they were made. This explains why few sold in the first place. With convertibles, however, I can't think of a single case where rarity is inversely related to value. The convertible mystique seems to have helped create a strong and positive demand for this type of car.

It must be understood that any collectible's value is determined through levels of supply and demand in an existing market. Thus it can be viewed as a fair market value. An item will not have much value as a collectible if a collector's market does not thrive around it.

In the collector-car market, rarity is one of several important factors that affect ultimate dollar value. In the case of convertibles, there's a particularly strong connection between the rarity aspect and fair-market prices. But even here the link is relative to the influence of other variables.

For instance, a limited-production Mustang ragtop might sell for more than a common Mustang ragtop, but this second car might then bring a higher price than an even rarer Studebaker. Collectors would explain this by saying the Mustang market is strong and the Studebaker market is weak.

AVOIDING RIP-OFFS

Rarity measurements can help collectors avoid rip-offs. As in any case, the informed buyer is a better buyer. While rarity does not always justify high pricing, there are many cases where it is used to help move less desirable models. For example, a very rare car of a certain brand that is not enjoying a good market situation at a certain time can still be promoted as a rarity by the unscrupulous seller.

On the other hand, honest appraisals of rarity can also be a legitimate selling point and have helped many hobbyists sell a car. The thing to avoid here is a picture of direct relationship between rarity a price. Such a picture can be painted through false claims, heresay, and guess-work, and can be used to artificially pump-up the value of cars that are not hot in the market..

This kind of unethical salesmanship was a real problem at one time. Today it can usually be avoided by

collectors who take the time to seek out full information concerning a car that they want to buy. There are hundreds of books available today about old cars. Most published in the last few years are well-researched works that give the exact statistics that hobbyists need.

Virtually all cars—by year, brand, type and model—are covered by one title or another. You can often refer to these books to judge a car's rarity aspects and market demand. These factors will help you make wise buying decisions. Or would you rather listen to hubcap Harry when he advertises his 1958 Chevy convertible as one of three left? According to one source providing scientifically extrapolated data, there are 3514 of this particular ragtop surviving today.

BODY STYLE POPULARITY TRENDS

Open-body cars were the predominant type of vehicles sold in the United States before 1925. With few exceptions, these cars weren't called convertibles. The earliest use of the term convertible can't be documented. In 1976, a Cadillac press release in *Wards Automotive Yearbook* claimed the honor for the 1916 Type 53 five-passenger touring car. This claim is not backed-up by Walter M.P. McCall's authoritative history *80 Years of Cadillac-LaSalle,* (Crestline Publishing, Sarasota, Fla. 1982). McCall does note the Type 53 came with an *optional* semi-permanent "Bishop Top," but such a feature wasn't a Cadillac exclusive.

Other makers had similar cars that had "California tops" or "cape tops" or were simply called semienclosed touring cars. Around the same time, several companies also sold closed coupes on which the door pillars were fully removable for an open-air look in the summer. They were also called convertibles.

At this time, the term did not describe an open car, but any body style that could be "converted" in the sense of being changeable to a somewhat different form. The term convertible, as applied to open cars with roll-up windows, was first used in 1927 and standardized by the SAE in 1928.

The most popular and readily available body styles were the runabout (Fig. 2-1), roadster (Fig. 2-2) and touring car (Fig. 2-3). Less common varieties included the raceabout (Fig. 2-4) and speedster (Fig. 2-5). From 1923 on, the proportion of closed-car output to total production began increasing at a very rapid rate. By 1926, the result was that three-quarters of all cars being made in this country were closed-body models.[2]

A year later, the first true convertibles came along. Yes, that's right! By 1927, Buick and Cadillac did have convertibles even though the SAE hadn't standardized the body-style designation.[3] By 1928, five makers—Cadillac, Chrysler, Franklin, LaSalle and Packard—were providing these "roll-up window ragtops." Buick still had such a model, but changed to the term Country

Fig. 2-1. The runabout was a popular type of body style in the early days of automotive history. A folding top was an option and was usually priced in the $50 range. Many car collectors insist that the term convertible should not be applied to runabouts.

Fig. 2-2. An early open-bodied car was the 1925 Model T Ford roadster.

Fig. 2-3. Open bodied, four-door cars were built from the first days of the industry through the late 1960s. Terms applied to them include touring car, convertible sedan, and phaeton. This car would be identified as a touring car by the majority of historians and collectors.

Fig. 2-4. The 1911 Simplex 50 horsepower "speed car" classifies as a raceabout. This was another type of open-bodied model seen in the days of early motoring. Raceabouts were built in smaller numbers than roadsters, touring cars, and runabouts. (Courtesy Long Island Automotive Museum)

Fig. 2-5. Popular in the Teens and the 1920s was a body style called the speedster. Speedsters were essentially cut-down versions of roadsters made for sporting use. In most cases, a maximum of two passengers could be accommodated.

Club Coupe for identifying it. Likewise, the convertible cabriolets offered by several other companies were technically true ragtops.

LONG-TERM POPULARITY

Even using the best scientific methods, it's hard to gauge with accuracy the total number of convertibles produced in the U.S. from 1928–1930. There were about 55 firms building cars in 1927.[4] By 1931, this figure dropped-off to around 40.[5]

Many companies collapsed during the Great Depression and their business records disappeared. As a result, documentation for body-style production totals was lost. Another problem was that, where records were kept, the figures for convertibles were usually lumped with other, open-car totals. This makes it hard to determine the amount of convertibles in the combined figures. Also, because the manufacturers used different names for convertibles (i.e., Buick's Country Club Coupe), it is sometimes difficult to say just what was a convertible and what wasn't.

By 1932, the record-keeping techniques improved. That year the National Automobile Chamber of Commerce (NACC) booklet *Automobile Facts and Figures* started breaking-out production of two-door convertible coupes and four-door convertible sedans separately. The NACC figures for 1931–1935 are shown in Table 2-1.

SURVIVAL

Unfortunately, cases where actual counts of survival of a model can be made are very rare. Usually, the car in question has to be a one-of-a-kind item. For instance, a man that I know is now restoring the 1953 Pontiac Parisienne show car (Fig. 2-6) at his restoration shop in New Jersey. Only one of these was made. The car under restoration has been documented as being the original.

In other cases, even when original production was extremely low, survivors can't be counted. For example, another person I know owns a 1969 Pontiac Trans Am convertible. According to official Pontiac records, only seven others like it were built. About three other Trans Am ragtops are known to survive, but the exact number of these cars still in existence remains a mystery. There might only be the four left or all eight might still be around. Even though this car (Fig. 2-7) can be viewed as an exceptional rarity, it's survival rate cannot be established by actual count.

Several studies have been made in an attempt to develop a formula or system for estimating automobile survival rates with some degree of accuracy. These studies have been based on certain data compiled by the industry statistical journals, combined with the effects of other factors. The different factors have been plotted on a graph that compares the estimated number of cars still in service with the age of the cars. The result is a curve on the graph suggesting what percent of the original output (production total) will still exist after a given number of years. These studies assume that all models (i.e., hardtop, station wagon or convertible) go out of service at the same rate.

The origin of the graph method dates to 1972 when automotive engineer and historian G. Marshall Naul wrote an article entitled "How Rare It Is" for *Special-Interest Autos* magazine. The data base for his study included the following:

☐ Figures pinpointing the average service life of a car.

☐ Charts and graphs showing the average number of used cars still registered in America at a given time.

☐ Charts and graphs showing the average number of used cars scrapped (taken out of service) each year.

Records, charts, and graphs such as these have been published by industry statistical journals for all years that "true" convertibles were built. An example is the figures covering the replacement market statistics of 1930, as published in the 1931 NACC booklet *Facts and Figures of the Automobile Industry* (which later became *Automobile Facts and Figures*). The original intent of compiling these totals was to supply them to automotive product planners, marketing people, and sales executives. Marshall Naul's study use similar information compiled by R.L. Polk & Co.. His effort marked the first attempt at using such data to answer questions for car collectors.

In May 1978, Evans Clagett—a physicist and car collector—authored an article entitled "Investing in Special-Interest Cars" for *Car Collector* magazine (this periodical is now called *Car Collector & Car Classics*).

Table 2-1. NACC Production Figures.

Passenger Car Production by Body Types
United States and Canada

	1931 Number	1931 Percent	1932 Number	1932 Percent	1933 Number	1933 Percent	1934 Number	1934 Percent	1935 Number	1935 Percent
Roadster	111,119	5.45	36,104	3.04	11,952	.73	13,013	.57	8,556	.25
Touring	33,151	1.62	11,349	.96	10,418	.65	14,679	.65	8,587	.25
Convertible Coupe	66,232	3.25	33,293	2.81	21,185	1.30	35,885	1.58	35,027	1.04
Convertible Sedan	19,082	.94	8,810	.74	1,638	.10	3,020	.13	6,890	.20
Coupe	438,215	21.50	257,404	21.70	325,330	19.99	361,800	15.93	504,491	14.89
2-Door Sedan	524,050	25.71	362,660	30.57	533,905	32.80	830,593	36.58	1,299,325	38.35
4-Door Sedan	765,791	37.57	442,168	37.27	686,621	42.18	962,191	42.38	1,448,577	42.76
All other closed cars	65,804	3.23	17,159	1.45	23,002	1.41	5,902	.26	4,214	.13
Chassis..........	14,739	.73	17,262	1.46	13,717	.84	43,483	1.92	72,139	2.13
Total	2,038,183	100%	1,186,209	100%	1,627,768	100%	2,270,566	100%	3,387,806	100%

Number and Percentage of Closed Cars, 1919-1935
United States and Canada

Year	Open	Closed	% Closed	Year	Open	Closed	% Closed
1919*..	1,496,652	161,000	10.3%	1927 ...	466,238	2,617,122	84.9%
1920*..	1,581,610	323,950	17.0%	1928 ...	460,128	3,552,030	88.5%
1921 ...	1,182,576	335,485	22.1%	1929 ...	510,409	4,284,489	89.4%
1922 ...	1,654,909	714,180	30.0%	1930 ...	282,729	2,627,458	90.4%
1923 ...	2,477,635	1,276,310	34.0%	1931 ...	144,270	1,893,913	92.9%
1924 ...	1,883,280	1,420,366	43.0%	1932 ...	47,453	1,138,756	96.0%
1925 ...	1,684,106	2,186,638	56.5%	1933 ...	22,370	1,604,991	98.5%
1926 ...	1,105,505	2,843,338	72.0%	1934 ...	27,692	2,242,874	98.8%
				1935 ...	17,518	3,370,288	99.5%

*United States onl

Fig. 2-6. There are very few cars that can be positively identified as one-of-a-kind vehicles. This Pontiac Parisienne is one of them. It was constructed for show purposes only, in 1953, and was later updated to 1954 model specifications. Today, it is being restored by Al Sico, of New Jersey, for one of his customers. When it is finished, it will be a true automotive rarity. (Courtesy Al Sico)

Fig. 2-7. Even cars that were built in extremely limited numbers can be hard to pin down to an exact survival figure. Only seven Pontiac Trans Am ragtops were ever made—all during 1969. This example, owned by Charles Adams, is one of at least three cars remaining. (Courtesy Ted Cram)

Clagett adopted a modified version of the graph method for his updated study.

The result is a "supply curve" that, in its pure form, suggests that 98 percent of production exists after a model is one year old and that about 1 percent of production survives after 23 years. He noted that the curve starts to flatten out, when a car is about 10 years old, due to collector interest, utility value, etc.

Table 2-2 provides estimates for the survival rates of cars built in different model years (as based on the survival curve updated to 1983). As with both Naul's and Clagett's figures, those used here assume the deterioration of all body styles at the same rate. Remember, however, that ragtops sometimes deteriorate more rapidly than other types of cars. This raises two interesting questions. Can you locate a reliable source of survival data that distinguishes between the survival of convertibles as opposed to other body styles? Also, can you then adjust the survival graph accordingly?

The answer to both questions is a qualified yes. There is one source—the Chrysler 300 Club International, Inc.'s *Registry*—that maintains a record of all Chrysler 300 letter cars (limited-production models) according to serial number. These numbers have been matched against the serial numbers that were originally assigned to letter cars. An amazingly accurate survival

record has thus been achieved for historians. This tells you the original production number of Chrysler 300 coupes and ragtops, the number of each body style surviving in 1983, and the percentage of each body style left.

Of course, a truly scientific statistical study would be based on data derived from more than just one source. In

Table 2-2. Survival Rates.

Survival Per Model Year (As of 1978)
1968–76.8%
1967–66.0%
1966–55.2%
1965–43.5%
1964–32.3%
1963–23.2%
1962–16.0%
1961– 9.4%
1960– 1.0%E
(Original 1978 Figures)
Source: *Car Collector & Car Classics*

this case there is little choice. You can assume that convertibles disappear at the same rate as other types of car or use the Chrysler 300 Club International's records to "adjust" the curve on the Survival Graph.

There are at least three published sources of survival estimates that I know about; two of them are computerized studies. Each of these sources seems to have positive and negative points. There are also some wide variations between the figures in different publications. Here's a brief rundown on each.

The Investor's Illustrated Guide To American Convertibles And Special-Interest Automobiles 1946-1967, by Charles Webb, has a title that pretty well explains the limit on the cars it covers. Listings in the book cover each model and tell you the estimated number of cars existing in 1979. The introductory text indicates the listings are taken from registration figures. They are presented as ballpark estimates that give a general idea of rarity. One problem with this source is that the book is currently out-of-print.

The Automotive Information Clearinghouse, Box 1746, La Mesa, CA 92041, has published three *How Many Are Left?* booklets. One covers cars of the 1940s, a second covers cars of the 1950s, and the third covers cars of the 1960s. All makes, models, and body styles have an estimated survival count as of 1981. Automotive Information Clearinghouse indicates that their figures are drawn from five sources:

☐ United States registrations by make.

☐ United States production figures by make/model per manufacturer.

☐ A comprehensive computer extrapolation of the above factors.

☐ United States salvage (scrappage) figures by state.

☐ Where appropriate, the experience of collectors who use these guides.

This source is highly usable and provides estimates that seem very reasonable in many cases. In some instances, the figures closely approximate those obtainable through use of the graph method.

R.L. Polk & Company publishes a detailed census of cars and light trucks built from the 1966 model year on. This is a computer-generated listing according to make, series, body style, engine size, and model year. The figures seem to be very reliable estimates. Nevertheless, the census is designed for use by automotive manufacturers and access to the data is provided at what might be called corporate rates. Most hobbyists will find the cost prohibitive. Information can be obtained by writing: Motor Statistical Division, R.L. Polk & Co., 431 Howard St., Detroit, MI 48231.

HOW OPTIONS AFFECT RARITY

Not a major factor in the hobby market years ago, options are becoming very important today. There was a time when options on a collector car affected value the same way that extra-cost equipment raises the price of a new car. In other words, the basic year, make, and model of car had a certain value and each item of optional equipment added to it. An air conditioner might have meant the car was worth $500 extra, while a common item like power steering could boost the value as little as $25.[6]

This has changed, in many cases, to the point where options sometimes are considered something that makes the car itself rare. Not all optional equipment has this affect. For example, I can't imagine somebody considering a car with power steering rarer than one without it unless it was the very first car to ever have this feature. In other words, the type of option has to be unusual or uncommon in itself. If it qualifies as a "rare" option, today's collectors feel that it also adds to the rarity of the car. An example would be a 1961 Chevrolet Super Sport convertible with a 409 cubic-inch V-8. Only 142 of these engines were built by Chevrolet that year. Such a motor would make the car that it's installed in a rare car.

Can the Rarity of Options Be Gauged?

The rarity of some options *can* be measured. Chevrolet kept a complete record of the number of 409 engines that were built in 1961. Some manufacturers can supply even more detailed information about optional equipment installations.

There is also another way to estimate the rarity of options. Beginning in the early 1950s and getting more detailed later on, the industry statistical journals published charts showing the percentage rates of optional equipment installations—usually according to the make (by size class) of the vehicle.

For example, such figures might tell you that 10 percent of all 1960 full-sized Fords had dual exhausts. That would be a relatively large number of cars, but a small percentage of Fords. Nevertheless, the same charts do not usually tell you the series (Fairlane, Fairlane 500 or Galaxie) or the body style (Town Victoria, Sunliner, Starliner) to which the figures relate.

By studying the manufacturer's original specifications you might find that only Fairlane 500 Starliners came with dual exhausts in a certain year. This would allow you to relate the 10 percent figure only to this particular model. Few options were this limited. Most were designed to fit many different types of Fords. You can sometimes narrow down the rarity of certain options, but you can't get exact figures in the great majority of cases.

For your car, you should research the statistical journals if you want to find out about optional equipment rarity factors. Most large libraries will have *Ward's Automotive Yearbooks* and *Automotive News*. How close you can get to exact option installation rates for your car by year, make, and model will depend upon the data available combined with special knowledge you have about the car.

Your special knowledge should allow you to narrow the information down. I wouldn't suggest doing this for common options, but if you feel that your ragtop has some uncommon features, why not give it a shot? If you can prove the equipment is rare, your car will also become that much rarer and more valuable to collectors.

Ragtops Are Becoming Rarer

The convertible that you own or want to buy will undoubtedly get rarer as time goes on. The number of others like it will suffer further attrition through misuse, accident, or simply by wearing out. It's amazing how many people think that the day a car hits 10, 15, 20, or 25 years old a rich collector swoops down from the skies to scoop it up and lock it away, forever, in his humidity-controlled, combination garage-and-bank vault. Such notions are bunk! If they were fact, you can bet that an old friend of mine never would have found his ragtop selling for $500 in a local shopper newspaper.

While it's true that the supply curve on the survival graph gets flatter where collector interest starts, it still doesn't stop going down. Unless you are talking about high-dollar Classics like Marmons and Duesenbergs, you can assume there are a few cars like yours that are still seeing thousands of highway-use miles each year. Because of this, you are going to find your convertible

getting even rarer as the years pass. The rarity aspect of old cars is constantly getting higher. As a convertible collector you are going to benefit.

TYPES OF CONVERTIBLES

Although the term convertible has generally been taken to apply to a ragtop with a fixed-position windshield and roll-up side glass, there have been, over the years, many different variations of this body style brought to market. Rather than giving a long-winded description of each variation, it seems better to show photos of 12 types.

☐ Landau Convertible (Fig. 2-8). Note that fixed-position side window frames. These remain erect when the top is lowered. Most versions have landau irons alongside the rear quarter section.

☐ Convertible Cabriolet (Fig. 2-9). The cabriolet is one of the earliest versions of a convertible. In most cases, landau irons were used until about 1932. The side window frames lower with the glass. The top usually folds down to rest upon the rear deck lid.

☐ Convertible Landau Sedan (Fig. 2-10). Landau styling was used on some four-door models. Only the rear section of the roof is made of cloth and lowers down. This was usually seen on expensive classics, but was offered on standard production models, in some lines, for a few years.

☐ Convertible Coupe (prewar, Fig. 2-11). As the name implies, the convertible coupe is a soft-top auto

Fig. 2-8. Landau convertible.

1932 Chrysler.

1932 Pontiac Cabriolet.

1937 Ford DeLuxe Convertible Sedan.

1937 Packard Super 8 Convertible Coupe.

1940 Buick Roadmaster Convertible Sedan.

1940 Ford DeLuxe Convertible Coupe.

1942 DeSoto.

1950 Pontiac Chieftain DeLuxe.

1955 Pontiac Star Chief. Owned by Wally Shotwell.

1956 Ford Sunliner.

1957 Pontiac Bonneville. Owned by Lou Calisibetta.

1958 Chevrolet Impala. Owned by Carl Dollar.

1963 Plymouth Sport Fury. Owned by Glen Burnett.

1965 Pontiac Catalina 2+2. Owned by Marv Minarich.

1966 Ford Mustang.

1967 Plymouth Barracuda.

Fig. 2-9. Convertible cabriolet.

The New Oakland ALL-AMERICAN Six Convertible Landau Sedan

Fig. 2-10. Convertible landau sedan.

Fig. 2-11. Convertible coupe (prewar).

Fig. 2-12. Cabriolet sedan.

Fig. 2-13. Convertible sedan.

Fig. 2-14. Drop-head coupe.

Fig. 2-15. Convertible coupe (postwar). (Photo courtesy of Eric Oxendorf)

Fig. 2-16. Roadster convertible.

Fig. 2-17. Detachable hardtop convertible.

Fig. 2-18. Retractable convertible.

Fig. 2-19. Spyder.

made to look like a coupe when the top is raised. The top is designed to be exceptionally weathertight (like the roof on a hardtop coupe).

□ Cabriolet Sedan (Fig. 2-12). Similar to a convertible sedan, the Cabriolet Sedan is a little fancier with landau irons used on the rear quarter of the roof. This is a two-door version. Four-door versions were also built.

□ Convertible Sedan (Fig. 2-13). The convertible sedan is a four-door convertible with lowerable side windows and a fixed-position windshield frame. A removable support is used at the center of the bodysides to support the top when it is raised.

□ Drop-Head Coupe (Fig. 2-14). Usually a foreign version of the convertible coupe, the drop-head coupe is a little fancier with landau irons and, sometimes, a multiposition roof. The drophead is also used on domestic classics with coachbuilt bodies.

□ Convertible Coupe (Postwar, Fig. 2-15). The main difference between prewar and postwar convertible coupes is the seating layout. The postwar coupe is a five-passenger model with a full rear seat.

□ Roadster Convertible (Fig. 2-16). A blend of sporty roadster styling, the roadster/convertible has the added advantage of roll-up window glass. Small size and simplicity allows creative roof designs like this one.

□ Detachable Hardtop Convertible (Fig. 2-17). Many open sports cars were available with detachable fiberglass roofs either as standard or optional equipment.

□ Retractable Hardtop/Convertible (Fig. 2-18). The hardtop/convertible is a very rare style. The most famous

example is Ford's Skyliner. The hardtop retracts into the rear of the car.

□ Spyder Convertible (Fig. 2-19). The term Spyder is a sports car word and simply describes a small, sporty ragtop—usually with a high-performance engine.

Footnotes

[1]By "truly distinct" body style I mean convertibles; coupes; sedans; hardtops; station wagons; etc. The number of doors/seats/size is not considered. When counted separately by a certain source, two-door station wagons; four-door station wagons with three seats; limousines and four-door convertibles usually came-up with the lowest market penetration rates.

[2]*Automotive Industries*, Feb. 19, 1927. Chilton Class Journal Co., edit. Norman G. Shindle, *et. al.* Philadelphia. p. 232.

[3]*MoToR*, 1927 Show Annual Issue, January 1927, p. 132.

[4]The figure of 55 was obtained by actual count by the author from *N.A.D.A. The Official Used Car Guide* (For District No. 11 Only), July 16, 1934–August 20, 1934, Vol. 1 No. 8. National Automobile Dealers Association. St. Louis, 1934. p. 346–370.

[5]*Facts and Figures of the Automobile Industry*, 1931 Edition. National Automobile Chamber of Commerce. New York City, 1931. p. 91–92. Note: The figure obtained is by the author's actual count of passenger car manufacturers who were NACC members in 1931.

[6]*Old Cars Price Guide*. Spring 1983. Krause Pub. Iola, Wis.

3. The Value Aspect

The most important measure of collectibility is value. In the United States, this is expressed as the collector car's dollar value or price. Some hobbyists are totally against price tagging a collector car. They'll insist it's "invaluable—hasn't got a price—can't be bought." Only the last statement could be true. If somebody owns an item free and clear and refuses to sell it, that's their business. If they do put the car up for sale, a fair market value will soon be set. A fair market value shouldn't be confused with a selling price. A stubborn owner can hold out for more money than the going rate before he will sell his car. The fair market value is the top price the market will bear under existing conditions. In a private transaction it's the final offer. In an auction it's the high bid.

Fair market value determines itself much the same way that a liquid seeks its own level in a container. The container in this case is the collector market, and its size is determined by the current level of supply. The portion of the container supplied with liquid represents fullfilled demand. The empty portion is unfullfilled demand. As long as the supply of liquid stays in the container, it has market value. Any that floods over the top soon loses worth (i.e., once the market was flooded with '76 Eldorado ragtops the price dropped).

Taking this container analogy one step further, the full container will be worth a lot to a thirsty man, but the contents of a half-filled container will become even more valuable to the man dying of thirst! Each measurable unit (ounce of liquid) gains value as the supply drops and the empty portion of the container (unfullfilled demand) grows.

Eventually the supply of liquid will become unreplenishable, with the small amount remaining available selling for extremely high prices. In the car collecting market, fair market value is relative to two things:

☐ Falling supplies of a certain model.
☐ A thirst for just such a car amongst collectors.

UNFAIR FACTORS

The convertible mystique helps to create a thirst for ragtops, but this is an abstract quality and it's very hard to measure. To make matters worse, there are situations that can temporarily exaggerate demand. This makes it hard to gauge the size of the collector market because the extra demand comes from outside the hobby. This was the case with Cadillac's "last convertible" media blitz in 1976.

Let me stress, once again, that the supply of an item available to the collector market can be measured somewhat scientifically. For example, Ford built 1343 Edsel Corsair convertibles in 1958.[1] According to the Automotive Information Clearinghouse, an estimated 416 of these cars are left.[2] Because 80.5 percent of all 1958 Edsels had automatic transmission[3], this option would

27

not make the Edsel ragtop any rarer from a collectible standpoint.

It is often hard to get a fairly accurate picture of things when a temporary spurt in desirability grows outside the collector's market. For example, when the "Real People" television show covered an Edsel club convention there was a sudden splurge of general interest in old Edsels. This had little to do will the real demand for this model in the old-car hobby.

A similar situation occurs almost every time that some identifiable type of car pops up in movies, a TV show or a local newspaper. "Local Man Owns One of Three 1962 Bonneville Convertibles Remaining," claimed an article in one small, southern newspaper that was sent to me. Actually, this headline represents a vast departure from the truth. Some 3400+ of this model are still around. In addition, I've seen more than five examples in a single old-car show.

A little inaccurate publicity can boost the mystique factor of a convertible and temporarily send uninformed buyers rushing out to pay high prices for such a car. What they spend, however, has little to do with the car's real, fair market value. It is simply a case of a larger container being substituted for the true collector market, thereby catching the overflow for awhile. Eventually, the flood will subside and the real market will level itself off again, though possibly in a different-sized container. It is the changing size of the container (market) that makes it impossible to attempt measuring the exact relationship of demand to price by an equation.

HOW TO JUDGE PRICES

The best way to get a good picture of fair market values in any large hobby is by using a *Price Guide* (Fig. 3-1). Unfortunately, within the collector car field there is a tradition of resistence to this concept. This seems to be related to three factors.

□ Many hobbyists come to think the car that they own is virtually priceless. This is because a nice car generates a personal attachment between owner and machine. People do things with cars. While all collectibles have a nostalgia factor, with cars this goes beyond just time and place. Often the vehicle (or one very much like it) participates in the owner's life. A guide can't put a value on this kind of bond (Fig. 3-2).

□ The usefulness of a car sometimes increases its value as compared to other models that can't be used as often. A big boom in the popularity of postwar models occurred six or seven years ago when collectors started to realize that cars built before the late 1930s weren't very practical (or safe) for operation on modern roads. The postwar car became an alternative for collectors. It was old enough to evoke nostalgic feelings, but it was young enough for modern highway use. Prices for cars (Fig. 3-3) built after WWII soon began to climb.

□ Many collectors equate the hobby price guides

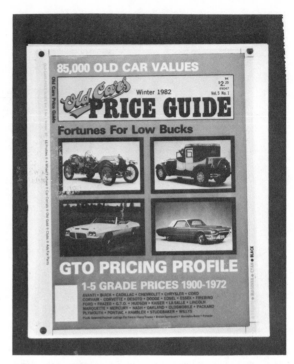

Fig. 3-1. There are no strict formulas to help gauge the value of a collector car. A number of reputable publications such as the *Old Cars Price Guide* (published quarterly) are available to automotive hobbyists.

with *Blue Books* (new/used car price guides) that use an unpopular dual-value system. The steeper value is called the retail price or high book value. The price is the wholesale price, low book value or loan value.

When you buy a car, the new/used car dealer will have it priced at or above high book. If you decide to use the same car as loan colateral, your banker will probably appraise it near low book. The difference between the two is the margin of profit and it can run above $1,000.

Car salesmen, who earn their living from commissions, will often price very good used cars far above high book to increase their take from a sale. Of course, if you're a wise buyer you know this and you will be familiar with both values before you start shopping. Hobby price guides don't use this type of two-value system. Most give a range of different prices for cars in various rated conditions. This is sometimes confused with the high/low book-value system.

The combined affect of these factors is to make the car collector shy away from good hobby price guides. He might say "they don't figure-in my nostalgia." Then he'll add, "This car runs like a new one and ought to be worth more than a showroom fresh non-collectible model." And the usual final argument goes, "The last time that I

Fig. 3-2. One reason that people refuse to place values on their old cars is that they do things with their vehicles. The family fun reflected in a photo like this one is a hard factor on which to put a dollar value.

Fig. 3-3. The usefulness of an automobile plays a role in pricing it. These cars are owned by members of the Milestone Car Society. They are on a tour around the famed Indy Speedway. Seven of the nine cars in the photo are ragtops. (Courtesy MCS)

bought a used car they soaked me for way over book price anyhow." Conclusion: price guides, blah!"

These statements are not really aimed against hobby price guides. Instead, they reject the entire concept of fair market pricing for collectibles. This isn't a very wise policy. In more established fields like coin, stamp, beer can, baseball card, comic book, toys, antiques, and record collecting no hobbyist or dealer would be without a price guide of some type. But with cars, nostalgia, utility, and the high/low book-value syndrome fight the fair market concept.

Luckily, this is changing as the hobby gets more sophisticated. There are now specialty insurance companies and banks that make "customized" collector car loans. This requires the owner or potential buyer of a vehicle to establish a legitimate fair market value for it. A price guide can often be used to establish such a value. Some agents or institutions now require at least one value estimate based on a recognized old car price guide.

Such "official" use of hobby price guides indicates that the data they provide is valid and useful. It also demands a greater responsibility from the publishers of the guides in keeping abreast of the market. These companies (as I know from firsthand experience) do what most individual hobbyists can't. They send representatives to major old-car auctions, obtain direct feedback from private transactions, hire experts to proofread the information, and use computers in assembling the data for print. While not always 100 percent accurate, the guides available today are an extremely good source of fair market values.

GENERAL PRICE RANGES

Having a very broad picture of what cars are worth according to their general appearance can be a big help to you at a car show or auction, or if you're just cruising the streets of your hometown looking for stray convertibles. There are three important things to keep in mind.

□ Some cars (almost all of which are prewar models) are classified as classics. They are worth more than nonclassics. Most of the time, quite a bit more!

□ Some cars built after WWII are classified as milestones and, of course, are more valuable than non-milestones.

□ Some foreign cars can be a lot more valuable than they look.

The 1929 Essex convertible (Fig. 3-4) is an early example of the ragtop body style. Note the windshield that is fixed in position. The upper door edge is quite high; on a roadster it would be cut down. In addition, the windshield would be framed with bright metal and able to fold down flat forward.

This car sold for $895 when new. According to the *Old Cars Price Guide* (the price source used throughout this chapter), it is worth about $15,500 today. That price would apply to a car in perfect condition (or what is generally called Number 1 shape). Naturally, a car in lesser condition would be somewhat less valuable. A five-grade condition code is fairly standardized in the old-car hobby today.

Figure 3-5 shows a 1934 Pontiac with the optional covered sidemount tires. You could also order sidemounts without covers; a single spare on the rear was standard. Notice how it looks more streamlined than the Essex. The fenders are fully skirted and decorated with sculptured "speed-lines." This car sold at $765 when new. In top shape, it's now worth approximately $15,000. In rundown (but restorable) condition, you might need about $2,100 to buy it. These prices are about typical for common convertibles of the same vintage, but not for classics.

A classic would look more like the 1934 Packard convertible shown in Fig. 3-6. It's a bigger, heavier and much more powerful car than a Pontiac. Packards came with straight eights, straight "super" eights, and V-12s under the hood. The more powerful the engine the more they are worth.

They also came with custom bodies in some series and a custom body model is worth more. This one is worth around $120,000 in Number 1 condition. Don't confuse it with mass-produced Pontiacs, Fords, Chevrolets, etc.

The 1938 Buick Century convertible (Fig. 3-7) is styled typical of most cars built from about 1936–1941. After 1939, the headlights started blending into the fenders and the grilles and fenders became a bit more integrated. Overall, there was no major styling break in this period. Most cars came in two or three series back then. Buick had four called Special, Century, Roadmaster, and Limited. Two-door convertibles came in the first two series.

A Special ragtop sold for $1,103 while the Century was $1,359. In top shape, today's values would be $23,000 and $25,000 respectively. Only a four-door Convertible was offered in the Roadmaster line and it's valued at $30,000 now. These four-door phaetons are rarer and worth more than convertible coupes in most—if not all—cases. All 1931–1942 Buick Limiteds are true classics, but other Buicks are not, unless they have special custom-built bodies.

Early postwar cars look a lot like 1940–1942 models. Most automakers continued using their prewar body dies for these 1946–1948 models. Cars were easy to sell after the war ended and there was no need to redesign them (except for changing the trim). Classics were just about gone by this time, although most companies sold sixes and eights.

The eights were usually a couple of inches longer than a six and cost from $60 to $100 more. In today's

Fig. 3-4. A very early example of a true convertible, this 1929 Essex sold for $895 when it was new; is worth about $15,500 in top shape today. Note the fixed-position windshield and high beltline that are characteristics of the first convertibles.

Fig. 3-5. Pontiac's Series 603 cabriolet sold for $765 and weighed 3210 pounds when it was new in 1934. A rumbleseat for extra passenger-carrying room was a standard feature of this model. Note the full-skirted, streamlined look typical of styling from this era. (Courtesy Pontiac Motors)

Fig. 3-6. Some people think that any collector car that isn't an antique is a classic, but this isn't true. Classics are specific cars designated by the Classic Car Club of America (CCCA). This 1934 Packard convertible is one car that is on the Classic car list and is worth about $120,000. (Courtesy Mike Carbonella)

Fig. 3-7. By the late 1930s, convertibles were becoming much more substantial automobiles than ragtops of earlier times. The 1938 Buick Century convertible coupe was priced at $1,359 when new and is worth approximately $25,000 today.

market the eights are usually worth more. This is not the case with a 1946 Oldsmobile Dynamic "66" convertible (Fig. 3-8). Olds' sixes are rarer than eights and this makes the two worth approximately the same. This one, in great shape, is worth about $12,000 in the hobby market.

As far as design goes, early 1950s cars (and many 1948–49) models started showing up with lower hood lines and fenders that were more smoothly blended into the body. This is characterized by the 1950 Oldsmobile convertible (Fig. 3-9). When this car was made, the Olds 88 models were tearing up the tracks in a new form of automotive competition called stock car races.

Olds had taken their biggest engine from the top-of-the-line Olds 98 and added it to the smaller 88 body. This produced the first factory-built, high-performance car of the postwar era. Today this makes the Olds 88 a top collectible. The original price on this shiny example was a mere $2,160, but it's good for around $15,500 today. That's what I call a rapid appreciation rate.

High tailfins and lots of heavy chrome were characteristics of American cars from 1956–57 on. The Chrysler 300-C is a 1957 model. It certainly has tailfins, but the chrome treatment is rather subdued for the day. These models were known as letter cars and were true,

limited-production factory performance cars. Many of them were raced at Daytona Beach.

All Chrysler 300 letter cars built through 1961 are recognized as milestone cars. Unlike classic cars, milestones don't really have a distinguishable look. For example, the 300-C had a general appearance much similar to other 1957 Chryslers. They sure are worth a lot. Figure about $10,000 + for the one shown in Fig. 3-10.

Cars of the early 1960s, like a 1963 Dodge Polara convertible (Fig. 3-11), had a lower and flatter look and more sculptured sheet-metal panels. These were the hot years for ragtop sales, but the Chrysler products weren't doing as well as those from other companies. Dodge only made 5358 convertibles during 1963. They weren't all Polaras either, but that's the closest production total available today. The car shown in Fig. 3-11 isn't in top shape, but it looks pretty good. It would bring around $2,000 to $2,500. A comparable Ford or Chevy would fetch in the $6,000 range because they have more of a market today.

The Coke bottle shape was the new styling craze from 1965 to around 1972. It was well exemplified in the 1968 Buick Wildcat convertible (Fig. 3-12). Selling for around $3,873 when new, a copy in this shape might hit $5,000 in the current marketplace. Those optional mag-

Fig. 3-8. Convertibles built in the early postwar period had styling generally similar to cars from before World War II. This 6-cylinder 1946 Oldsmobile ragtop is one of only 1409 made. In top condition, it might bring about $12,000 in the collector market.

Fig. 3-9. Modern, postwar styling began to appear in 1949, and it is characterized in this handsome 1950 Olds 88 convertible. This car appears to be in top condition and will probably have a fair market value in the range of $15,500. A total of 9127 ragtops were built in this series. (Courtesy Linda Clark)

Fig. 3-10. A member of the "high tailfin" school of design, the 1957 Chrysler 300-C convertible is a true limited-production, high-performance machine. This car—one of just 484 built—belongs to George Cone of Illinois. It has over 289,000 miles on the odometer, has never been restored, and is in nearly perfect condition.

34

Fig. 3-11. This 1963 Dodge Polara represents a good bargain in the hobby market. Examples in top shape can usually be found for prices below $3,000 compared to $6,000 for a Ford or Chevy of comparable age and condition.

Fig. 3-12. The so-called Coke-bottle shape caught on with car buyers in the mid-1960s, and is seen here in a 1968 Buick Wildcat convertible. A total of 3572 of this model were made. It would be valued at about $5,000 today. (Courtesy Buick Motor Division)

styled wheels might add around $200 as a plus-value factor. They don't make the car rarer, however, just better looking and nicer to own.

The last Pontiac convertible was the 1975 Grand Ville version (Fig. 3-13). This might add to its value a bit, but the condition of this car is much more important in the hobby market right now. The "last-one-made" factor will probably become an added benefit in later life. Collector's seem to be paying a top dollar of $3,500 to $4,000 for cars of this sort today. This doesn't seem extremely logical with the 1983 ragtops priced at near $14,000. The '75 is lots more car for the money.

Small sports cars that didn't really sell for high prices when new are starting to get expensive today. A T Series MG (Fig. 3-14) brings about $19,000 in very good shape. Cars of similar character that were more expensive originally—a Jaguar or Mercedes–Benz for example—will easily hit $25,000.

You have to be careful in making general guesses at sportscar prices. Models that don't look a great deal different on the surface can be thousands of dollars apart in price. Sports cars can be roadsters (like the MG-TD) or they might have roll-up windows. It seems like collectors treat them all the same and regard them as a branch of the convertible family.

There are also late-model, specialty ragtops available today. These include semiproduction models, exoticars, replicars, kit cars, and conversions. That's a rather quick-and-dirty look at some generally different types of ragtops. The standardized Condition Code System used by car collectors was devised for the quarterly *Old Cars Price Guide*. It relies on five different categories, each of which gets a name and a number: Number 5—Restorable; Number 4—Good; Number 3—Very

Good; Number 2—Fine and, and Number 1—Excellent. The *Price Guide* describes each category and gives a definitive word description.

Number 1 means the car looks as good and runs as good as the new '83 in the showroom.

The Number 2 car looks as good as those in the front row of the dealer's used car lot, right outside the showroom door. Only the best used cars go in that row and they might look as good as the new ones at first. That is until you drive them a week or two. Then you start to realize why they were traded. No big problems, they are just not perfect cars.

The Number 3 car looks like those on the back row of the dealer's used car lot. You can see problems with these, but they also have their good points.

The Number 4 car looks like the Gray Ghost Peter Falk used to make fun of on the "Columbo" television show. It still runs good.

Your basic Number 5 car looks like the Studebaker in *The Muppet Movie*. Only sometimes it doesn't run. I know you're going to tell me that you loved the car in the movie. Welllll . . . you kind of gotta love a Number 5 car. If nobody loved it, they'd have scrapped it years ago.

You say you have a worse-than-Number 5 car? What's it worth? Probably about $50 or less if it's not a Duesenberg or V-16 Cadillac. In those cases, maybe it's worth $10,000. But only to the guy who's restoring a good one. Chances are that $10,000 to him is like $50 to you and me. Remember, everything in the market is relative.

Once you have a broad picture of the different kinds of cars in the market, plus a Muppet-level understanding of condition classes, there's just one more thing to worry about. I called it plus-value and it's related to a car's equipment. Some kinds of parts and features are pretty

Fig. 3-13. Taking a trophy in a 1976 car show is a 1975 Pontiac Grand Ville convertible. This was the last full-sized ragtop produced by Pontiac. Surviving examples are rapidly finding their way into collector's hands.

Fig. 3-14. One of the first imported sports cars to be brought to this country in large numbers was the T Series MG. During the early postwar years, many of these cars made their way to America with returning servicemen. Valued at approximately $19,000 today, these ragtops are still very popular.

rare. Say that you find one of those 1961 Chevys with a 409 engine. If it's a Number 1 car it's a treasure. You spot it on the street and the owner has it for sale, but he doesn't know the engine is valuable. Pay what he's asking for the car. Don't quibble. It's got plus-value and it's worth it.

If it's a Number 5 car, the engine is still valuable; it might be worth more than the whole car. In any case it's a good buy. There are a lot of options and accessories that can add plus-value. It depends what model they fit and how rare they are in that type of car. TAB book No. 2086, *How To Restore & Upgrade Your Vintage Car With Factory Accessories* gives about 240 pages to the subject. It covers plus-value in great detail from A to Z.

ARE RAGTOPS A GOOD INVESTMENT?

If you can purchase a convertible today at its fair market price or a lower price, it will be worth more than that amount when you sell it in the future. That is assuming that you keep it in the same condition.

Due to economic cycles, it's impossible to say that convertibles will always be good investments. Fair market prices seem sure to go up and almost definitely will not go lower than they are right now. Yet, that does not make the purchase of a convertible a good investment.

One more factor you have to think about is your personal interest and involvement as a car collector. Are you interested in convertibles because you like cars or because you want to make profits? Are you involved with buying and selling cars regardless of slumps in the market?

If you are a car enthusiast and hobbyist, you've probably got motor oil in your veins. Cars are something special to you and the satisfaction you get from automobiles counts as part of total picture. Therefore, a convertible is a good type of car to own. Not because it's a sure thing that can't go up and down in price, but because economic cycles will affect it less than other models when there are downward fluctuations and more than other models when they move upward. This makes the ragtop a good investment without regard to the economy. The investor, on the other hand, will probably regard it mostly as a sometimes item.

Footnotes

[1]*Standard Catalog of American Cars 1946-1975.* Ed. John Gunnell, *et. al.* First Edition. Iola, Wis.: Krause Publications. 1983. pg. 312–313

[2]*How Many Are Left? Autos of the 1950s.* Automotive Information Clearing House. Op. Cit.

[3]*Standard Catalog of American Cars 1946-1975.* Op. Cit. pg. 313

4. Market Trends

When the 1976 Eldorado convertible seemed like it might be the last convertible built in America, there was quite a bit of ragtop speculation going on. Hundreds of these cars were being purchased solely on the premise that serious collectors would be beating down doors to get them after a short while. That didn't happen. Today it's pretty common to hear these once-upon-a-time investors sqawking about how they got burned by buying a car when prices were high. "Why I paid $20,000 for that piece of junk," they will say, "now I'm lucky to get $9,000 for it.

An Eldorado convertible isn't a piece of junk; it's a high-quality automobile. What really happened to these get-rich-quickers is that they sadly misjudged hobby market trends. Some of them felt that car collecting represented a magical, million-dollar pastime that was immune from everyday economics. They were wrong.

JUDGING TRENDS

Experienced and knowledgeable collectors can make some reasonably accurate predictions. Aimed with proper knowledge and a realistic point of view, the person who knows cars and understands that supply, demand, and value are relative factors can make some very solid judgements about how things will go in the hobby car market during the next few years.

Those of us who monitor the automotive collectibles field on a regular basis agree that a very strong future seems to be shaping-up for both the convertible and the car collecting hobby as a whole.

As strange as it might seem, a jump in new-car sales usually brings increased activity in the old-car market as well. For one thing, it means that people are out looking for cars and that often leads to more general interest in automobiles. Some new car buyers will find satisfaction

with Detroit's latest products (even those new, semi-production convertibles built by specially modifying brand new coupes). In other cases, the shoppers will find nothing that they like. This second group will often turn to low-milage used cars or even collector cars.

Another crucial factor is also related—at least partly—to those all-new convertibles and some of the new high-performance cars. In case you haven't heard, Detroit is starting to put a little excitement back into its products by building such items as Turbo Mustangs, Charger 2.2s and special Trans Am MSE (Motor Sports Edition). This means that some of the people who hoarded older convertibles and muscle cars for the last decade or so will now be tempted to buy something new. In some cases, the old cars will become part of a permanent collection. In other instances, they will be recycled into the used car/collector car markets.

RAGTOP REVIVAL

Detroit's current ragtop revival is a very strong sign that the convertible mystique is alive and well and ready for a comeback in more ways than one. In the first place, these cars are already reminding many people of the fun they've been missing since 1976—the old excitement of top-down driving. These cars have already received wide public exposure in magazine articles, automobile shows, and on showroom floors. They are rekindling a very strong desire to own a convertible in the hearts of many enthusiasts. Not everyone, however, can afford to get one of them right now.

Take the Buick Riviera (Fig. 4-1) for example. This car was brought out as a mid-1982 model. It is a genuine ragtop, custom conversion created by American Sunroof Corporation to Buick specifications. This car (Model Z67) was picked as pace car for the Indianapolis 500. As you can guess, it's a highly desirable item, but the cost of ownership is on the steep side too. With a manufacturer's suggested retail price of $23,994.25, the all-new Riviera convertible is out of the reach of many people.

This doesn't mean that the person inspired to own a convertible can't have his wish. Many older convertibles, in good condition, can still be obtained for anywhere between $3,500 and $9,000. Thanks to the convertible revival, we are seeing a renewed interest in moderately priced convertibles for sale in the hobby market. It seems clear that, as more of the new ragtops hit the streets, interest in used models is also bound to pick-up.

KIT CARS

About the same time that convertibles started disappearing in Detroit, hundreds of companies began manufacturing soft-top kits that were usually designed for installation on Volkswagen Beetle or Ford Pinto chassis. Many of these kits featured fiberglass bodies with "old-fashioned" (neo-classic) styling. They were made to look like generic antiques or sports cars.

Other kits resembled original collector-car models such as T-Series MGs, Jaguars, Mercedes–Benzes, and 1955–1957 Thunderbirds. They are not exact replicas of such cars because certain proportions had to be changed to accommodate the modernized running gear. Prices for

1982 BUICK RIVIERA CONVERTIBLE

Fig. 4-1. After curtailing convertible production in 1976, several manufacturer's began offering ragtops again in 1982. These cars are built by specialty companies on the same platform as coupes of the same line and sold through franchised new-car dealers. They are technically semiproduction models and carry rather steep price tags. This 1982 Buick Riviera convertible has a base price of nearly $24,000. (Courtesy Buick Motor Division)

Fig. 4-2. Gaining in interest with collectors are some of the "kit car" convertibles offered in the late 1970s and early 1980s. This Prestige Classics XK140 Jag kit seemed to disappear from the market in the fall of 1982, and the few that were sold will surely become collector's item.

Fig. 4-3. While new car sales have dropped in the last few years, interest in old cars has risen. Note the Cadillac, Lincoln, and Packard ragtops on display at this well-attended event.

most disassembled kits ranged from $5,000 to $9,000. Others could be purchased in fully built-up form for $10,000 to $20,000. In most cases, these were assembled by certified builders (factory-approved independent contractors).

At first there was only minor collector interest in such cars and they weren't viewed as collectibles. At several auctions that I have attended, kit cars failed to draw bids high enough to clinch a sale. In most cases, the bidding stalled at $1,000 to $2,000 below the original cost of the vehicle!

Now things are starting to change. First of all, collectors are beginning to sort out the wide variety of kit cars according to quality. They are realizing that some of them are truly interesting machines. In addition, a degree of rarity seems to be evolving for select models. A great number of kit car firms could not survive the weak economic conditions of the 1976–1982 period. They were forced to withdraw from the market. Today, some of the kits made by these firms are already getting rare.

Some of my recent contacts with hobbyists seeking price information indicates a growing future trend toward more sales (and appreciating prices) where the higher-quality kit cars are concerned. The 1952 XK140 Jag kit—marketed, until recently, by Prestige Classics (Wayzata, MN)—is one low seller that seems to have a lot going for it at a future collectible (Fig. 4-2).

THE HOBBY SEEMS STRONG

Despite the various effects of inflation, high interest rates, and unemployment problems in the last few years, the old-car hobby has remained remarkably strong. Old car shows and events across the nation have been drawing the largest crowds ever seen at such events (Fig. 4-3). It also appears that more new participants are entering the hobby. The summertime "Calendar of Upcoming Events," which is published in each issue of *Old Cars Weekly*, used to fit nicely in two to three pages when I began working for the newspaper. Now we are seeing a list of happenings (*excluding* auctions and 100 percent commercial events) that often covers five to six tabloid pages. Each activity held in a certain region seems to spur new interest and triple the amount of activities scheduled for the next season. Even with this kind of growth, most shows seem to be successful in the end.

One show that I have been involved with is the Iola Car Show. It is held in my home town the first weekend of each July and is one of the three largest shows in the country. Five years ago, when I moved here, the show drew just over 1500 cars and 20,000 people. At the 1983 event, there were 4000 collector cars and 50,000 people.

═ PART 2 ═
Ownership

THERE ARE THREE ASPECTS TO OWNING A CAR WHETHER IT'S A COLLECTIBLE MODEL OR THE BUGGY THAT TAKES YOU TO work everyday. The first aspect involves obtaining the vehicle. The second relates to maintaining it. The third is connected to retaining (or deciding not to retain) the car.

Where convertibles and collector cars are concerned there are some special considerations. They include deciding upon the type of car that you want and knowing how much you should pay for it. In addition, you'll want to know where to locate older ragtops and, possibly, how you can get a nonoperable car back home. Maintaining such a model can involve more than washing the car and changing the oil. A full restoration might be required to put the car back on the road. When you have finished the job, you might be totally happy or you might decide to sell the car or trade it for an even fancier ragtop.

5. Making the Purchase

Despite what the Model A Ford Club display shown in Fig. 5-1 suggests, most convertibles selling today are not bought at new car sales agencies. The first step in obtaining a car the smart way is to start by creating a plan of action. Ask yourself four very basic questions and write down the answers.

Why Do I Want a Convertible? For show purposes only? Strictly for driving? Perhaps for both show and go. The way you plan to use the car affects your choice of types and models.

What Do I Know about Cars? Can you rebuild an engine? Take a dent out of a fender? Recover a seat? Or maybe you're the kind of person who's never changed a spark plug. Be honest about your abilities; the car you pick should fit your level of skills.

What Is My Price Range? Are you short of the money needed to get a nice ragtop? Can your credit union help? How about arranging a bank loan? Do you want to buy only the best regardless of price? You can't buy intelligently without considering price, value, and finances.

What Kind of Car Do I Really Want? A Ford? Possibly any pre-war antique. Or did you have your mind set on a fully loaded, high-performance model? There are thousands of different types to pick from, but there's only certain cars that will match your own preferences.

When these things are written down, you'll have a complete picture of your preferences, purposes, and level of technical skills. This might prevent you from buying the wrong type of car. For instance, you won't be happy with a long-term, project car (Fig. 5-2) if you actually need something to drive.

Don't think the convertible mystique hasn't got the better of more than a few people. Some hobbyists are so anxious to obtain a ragtop that they jump at the first one they see. It doesn't take long to regret such a hasty decision. For example, writer Roger Mease did an article called "The 'X' Factor" in which he recounted an actual case. A friend of Mease's who was an inexperienced

hobbyist, had developed a passion for a certain '57 DeSoto ragtop. According to Mease, "the car had a tattered top, rusty body, ripped seats and non-functional power steering system. It must have been a love of tall tailfins that made this young man buy the car, because it fell far short of his need for everyday transportation. Truth is the clapped-out DeSoto hasn't moved since he trailored it home, although his wife would sure like to see it gone."

This is a good example of what can result from a lack of good planning. Now, don't get me wrong, cars in just about any condition can be—and often are—brought back to a useful existence through a total restoration. This is work that requires experience, special tools, lots of time, and generous outlays of cash. Complete frame-up restorations run over $25,000 today and are best reserved for genuine classic cars that will be worth $100,000 to $500,000 when finished.

Fig. 5-1. "Henry's New Car Agency" display was organized by members of the Milwaukee Chapter of the Model A Ford Club at the Wally Rank Car Show. Despite the suggestion here, most old cars are not purchased through dealers. Private owners, car shows, flea markets, and auctions are good sources of collector cars.

Fig. 5-2. Unless you have the skills of a professional-level restorer, avoid the purchase of long-term "project" cars. It takes a lot of work, time, and money to put a convertible like this one back on the road.

In nine of ten cases, the best way to start searching for a ragtop is by checking classified ads in a newspaper or magazine (Fig. 5-3). The classifieds in a local paper might list a few ragtops for sale, but be careful. The so-called last convertible syndrome of 1976 hasn't been put into its proper perspective by many nonhobbyists or regular used-car dealers. Don't be surprised if such sellers refer to their cars as "classics" and price them accordingly. Although they are probably using the term incorrectly, no one (including you or me) will be able to convince them otherwise.

A much better route to follow is use of specialized hobby trader publications. *Old Cars Weekly* (Fig. 5-4) is a good example of this breed, but there are others. In almost every issue, the major trader publications will steer you towards hundreds of convertibles for sale. You will probably find them priced somewhat lower than many local cars. Keep in mind that even hobby sellers will set their pricing a little on the high side to allow for bargaining room. Still, I think you'll see a touch of greater realism in the specialized classified ads.

Another advantage of the traders is that they can help you locate cars in several different ways. The first is through direct contact with private owners. For example, a restorable 1932 Dodge convertible (Fig. 5-5) was advertised for sale by such a party. It was a car that, with just normal fixing, would make a very fine hobby machine. But you shouldn't get the impression that every car listed in the traders will be this old or need this much repair.

The offerings will run the entire range of condition classes from "parts cars" to mint-condition show cars, and will cover all the various types and vintages as well. You'll find ads for antiques, classics, special-interest automobiles, milestones, and late-model ragtops. In many cases, the owner will even use the 1-5 condition class codes to describe the shape the car is in. This is yet another benefit of the trader magazines. You'll have a better idea of general condition even when a car is located far from your home. The Dodge shown in Fig. 5-5 looks like a Number 4 car (one in relatively "good" shape).

Fig. 5-3. Tony Hossain is the editor of *Collectible Automobile* newspaper and a convertible collector. Tony regularly checks out the classified auto ads in many publications in search of ragtops for sale at good prices. His favorite sources include local newspapers, hobby trader magazines, and shopper tabloids.

Fig. 5-4. Old Cars Weekly newspaper is one of several trader magazines commercially available to old car hobbyists. Hundreds of ragtops are listed for sale in this periodical each week. (Courtesy Krause Publications)

The trader magazines also publish a regular calendar of upcoming hobby events. Such a list will help you find car shows in your area where there might be some convertibles for sale. Don't assume that every car brought to a show is a show car. Most cars entered will look good at first glance, but those wearing For Sale signs should be inspected carefully to see how much finishing work will be required to make them just about perfect.

A 1948 Chevrolet convertible cabriolet (Fig. 5-6) spotted at a show in New Jersey exemplified this point. It was a nice car showing few signs of wear and had a fresh coat of bright red paint. An inexperienced buyer might easily have rated it Number 1 (current value approximately $14,000).

A closer look showed that it had been "hot-rodded" at one time. A number of nonoriginal features could still be seen. Taking this into consideration, the Chevy actually is classified as a Number 3 (very good) condition car with a current worth of around $5,500. So you can see that

condition has a very strong affect on the prices you should pay.

Old car flea markets (also called swap meets) will also be listed in the calendar of events printed in trader publications. They might be held in conjunction with car shows or separately. Those who sell merchandise at flea markets are called vendors. They often handle both new and used (sometimes well-used) items.

It's not uncommon for a vendor to run across something like a convertible while he's out searching for obsolete parts. He may take the ragtop along to the shows with him. He might even use it as a pickup truck to carry his parts (Fig. 5-7). If you are interested in buying such a car, check out its condition very carefully. Some will be excellent buys while others will require major rehabilitation.

Swap meet vendors spend most of the year traveling quickly from one show to another. This leaves them little time to fix up a car. Their goal is to buy in one town and turn the car over (sell it) quickly. There's nothing wrong with this. It can be to your benefit because cars sold this way are usually priced for a quick sale. Be careful, however, not to buy too quickly. Make a good appraisal of the work that's needed and consider this factor into the 1-5 condition scale rating that you make.

The hobby traders will also include display advertisements for upcoming classic car auctions (Fig. 5-8). Contrary to what many seem to believe, recent auctions have not driven collector car values up. Typical prices bid for cars at these sales are very realistic. Auctions are extremely helpful in pinpointing fair market values. The highest bid on a certain car at auction is tantamount to what it will bring in open market trading.

Several respected old car price guides refer to actual auction results as the basis for their pricing data and value estimates. Auctions represent an accepted and established method to bring buyers and sellers together in the collector car market. Thousands of convertibles are bought and sold at the auctions each year. Ragtops represent a very hot item at such events.

HOW MUCH TO PAY?

Whatever you do, don't automatically assume that convertibles are out of your price range. It's easy to feel this way after reading a few ads for absolutely flawless (Number 1 condition) cars. Though it might seem at first that all ragtops are just perfect and expensive, this simply isn't true. If you're willing to do some degree of fix-up work yourself, a car in the right price range is sure to turn up.

A friend of mine, Dick Fuesz recently purchased *two* ragtops for under $500. He paid only $50 for a 1969 Pontiac Catalina. Sure it needed some work—mostly dent removal—but the car ran like a clock. He had been

Fig. 5-5. A standardized 1-5 Condition Code grading system is popular with car hobbyists. Under the system, this 1932 Dodge convertible would be classified as a Restorable, Number 5 condition car.

Fig. 5-6. Care should be taken when you are considering the value and condition of cars for sale at a car show. This '48 Chevrolet convertible–although basically a good car–has been slightly modified and would rate no higher than Number 3 condition "as is." It will take an expensive restoration to put the car in Class-1 condition. (Mike Carbonella photo)

Fig. 5-7. Flea-market vendors can be a good source of convertibles for sale, but carefully check the condition of the car. This Mercury ragtop has been used as a "pickup truck" and will need a great deal of restoration.

Fig. 5-8. Lists of upcoming classic car auctions are regularly published in hobby trader magazines. Today, auctions seem to be a good place to get nice convertibles like this 1936 Ford Cabriolet being bid on at the Bud Josey Sale, in Tampa, Florida.

searching for a one-year newer model, but couldn't pass up the low price on this car.

Wouldn't you know that a few days later he found a 1970 Pontiac Bonneville convertible and bought it for $350. He then sold the first car for $200, using his fast, "windfall" profit to start buying parts for the fancier one. Of course, the Bonneville needed some rust repair, but nothing Dick couldn't do himself. No, he's not a mechanic or body man! His occupation is farming; the convertible is strictly a hobby machine.

What you should pay for a convertible isn't necessarily the lowest price or the highest, but it should be about the "right" price. The exact figure will depend on different factors; the condition of the car is just the first. Consideration must also be given to things like age, rarity, desirability, comparative cost, difficulty of restoration (including the availability and price of parts), ultimate value when restored, and the manner in which the car is actually being sold.

When you're searching for any collector car, including ragtops, hobby price guides should be used as your initial pricing tool. Many guides will give you a ballpark estimate of what the model is worth in different conditions. In other cases, you'll find high, low, and average prices listed for cars that are assumed to be in "generally good" condition. The exact system used by each publication will always be fully explained in the book's introduction. Read the opening pages before turning to the price chart section.

Keep in mind that such books establish their value ratings as a reflection of the nationwide old-car market. They do not (and indeed cannot) cover specific buying and selling conditions in different parts of the country. Therefore, they should be referred to mainly as a pricing guide and not as the gospel truth etched in stone.

For example, a ragtop listed as a $3,000 item might sell for $2,500 or $3,500 in your town. Don't expect local prices to match up exactly with the nationwide averages. On the other hand, if you find an owner asking $20,000 for a car ballparked at $2,000, it's a pretty good indication that the car is way overpriced.

Even when armed with a good guide to prices, the beginning hobbyist might feel insecure about making his first purchase of a collector car. There's nothing wrong with such a cautious attitude because ballpark estimates and actual asking prices can be quite different things. The numbers jotted down in a book can only gauge what a certain car might bring in the collector's market. This won't always be the same as what that car is worth to you. It might be the same model you drove 20 years ago (in which case you'll be willing to pay a small premium for it).

For beginners, let's assume that you spot a 1949 Cadillac convertible (Fig. 5-9) parked in a local shopping center and it's for sale at $6,000. Take out your pencil and pad and write down the obvious problems along with a quick estimate of fix-up costs.

☐ You'll want to replace those modern, thin white-

Fig. 5-9. The owner of this 1949 Cadillac convertible had it for sale at a good price. It needs some work, but the cost of repairs seemed most reasonable in relation to normal appreciation trends. At the right price, a car such as this would represent a solid investment.

wall tires with authentic looking gangster-style wide whitewalls. The new tires will cost around $383; the old ones can be sold for about $100. Your cost is $283.

☐ The convertible top is stretched out of shape and will need replacement. This will cost $500 or more.

☐ The front hub caps are from a later model Cadillac, but you should be able to trade them for the correct type without cost.

☐ The rocker panel shows some minor rust-out that will cost around $100 to repair.

☐ The rear gravel shield is dented. Figure about $50 for a new one.

Considering all of these points, the Cadillac seems to be in Number 3 condition. Reference to the *Old Cars Price Guide* indicates that this is $500 on the high side of the scale. But this car is a recognized milestone model and is one of just 2150 copies built. The graph method indicates that approximately 86 examples should still be around today. This means that this car is rare and desirable. Considering that no really major parts are needed, it's not a bad buy. The owner hasn't priced it sky high and he doesn't seem to be a real old-car hobbyist. He will probably take a little less than his asking price, but don't push for exactly what the *Old Car Price Guide* shows.

This car will probably appreciate fast enough to offset payment of a premium price today. Loping off or adding on round figures brackets your offer too clearly. An odd figure is usually a better way to go. Try offering $5,625 for the Cadillac. If things work out according to your estimate, for $933 worth of fixs-ups you'll have a Number 2 condition car worth about $7,000. That will set you ahead of the game in the long run.

Foreign convertibles (Fig. 5-10) make nice collectibles, but a Mercedes–Benz cabriolet, for sale at a local truck stop, should be inspected very carefully. This car looks like another Number 3 condition car on first glance. There's no collision damage or bad rust out, but those missing headlights indicate it hasn't been used for awhile. Also, the open top suggests a danger sign. It just might be stuck in the lowered position, meaning that sun or rain has possibly damaged the leather seats. This can weaken the fabric or seam stitching in a way that won't show up until later. Leather interiors cost around $2,000 (or more) to replace.

Why hasn't the car been used? If engine work is needed, that's also a $2,000 to $3,000 job for a Mercedes. If you can't get this car for a Number 4 price, or less, it might be wise to pass. Even though it looks one grade higher, there's too many potentially high repair costs involved to make a quick jump into ownership.

Cars owned by hobbyists that are partially disas-

Fig. 5-10. It costs a little extra to obtain parts and restore imported cars. If there are danger signs you should avoid the purchase of foreign models that might require repairs to the engine or interior. Exotic powerplants and leather interiors are costly restoration items.

52

Fig. 5-11. Although it looks like a wreck, this rare 1953 Buick Skylark convertible seemed like a good buy. Obviously owned by a collector, the Skylark had been disassembled for restoration, but all of the valuable parts were included in the sale. For a handy hobbyist, this car would be an investment. For the novice, it might be no more than a $7,500 pile of rare parts. (Mike Carbonella photo)

sembled (Fig. 5-11) can be difficult to evaluate. This rare 1953 Buick Skylark convertible (one of only 1690 built) looks like a wreck, but it is actually quite a solid automobile that someone has started restoring. In "as is" condition, it's probably worth nearly $7,500! Of course, the fenders have been removed so new ones (which the owner has) can be installed. The missing grille and bumper are at the chrome shop being replated. When all of these valuable parts are attached, this will be a $17,000 vehicle. I doubt if you could tell this if you spotted the Skylark, by itself, in a different location. Figure 5-11 shows other collector cars on either side and the dry, indoor storage conditions.

A car like this is probably a good buy if all the parts are included in the sale and if you can reassemble it yourself. On the other hand, if there are missing components or you never actually worked on a car before, the most practical move would be to look for a more complete vehicle of the same model. Skylark parts are quite expensive to buy, and professional restorers charge between $15 and $30 an hour for their skilled labor. A novice purchasing this car, without parts, would probably make little progress in completing the job. There's little more frustrating than a $7,500 pile of rare parts that will never get put back together.

Exercise particular care when a convertible stored out of doors—even a very rare model—shows a damaged top or rear window. A top in poor condition might allow water to seep inside the interior or convertible top well and cause damage in the body or floor pan. Rust or corroision of this sort is much harder to repair than moderate dents or dings in sheet metal. Rotted metal can also affect the car structurally, making it unsafe to drive as well as unattractive.

Indoor storage of a car is almost always a plus factor when it comes to questions of condition and value. The beautiful, classic 1931 Stutz cabriolet (Fig. 5-12) is clearly an "indoor" car. Even though it has been stored in an old, wooden barn, this Stutz will probably be relatively free of deterioration caused by the elements. This is an especially important point when it comes to appraising prewar automobiles built prior to 1936 or so because wood-frame body construction was used in those days. Once the wood is attacked by moisture, it will begin to rot and must be replaced. This means that the metal body components must be completely removed and new wood framing fashioned; this is a very expensive operation.

Commercial re-wooding kits are available for some of the more popular, mass-produced cars like Model A Fords. These kits make it relatively simple and inex-

Fig. 5-12. Because it's been stored in a secure, wooden barn, this '32 Stutz convertible seems like a fairly good prospect for a quick restoration. Chances are good that the wood body framing is intact and will not have to be completely rebuilt.

pensive to tackle this type of work. When it comes to low-production classics, the job of rebuilding wood framing will, most likely, have to be farmed out to specialists who handcraft new parts. This adds immensely to restoration costs. With the wood framing intact, this Number 3 condition Stutz is valued at around $21,000 by the *Old Car Value Guide Annual* (which classifies it as an "unrestored" car). It would be worth much less—about $4,000—if the indoor storage had not been provided to protect the wood.

Some inexperienced old-car buyers make a big mistake in accepting the premise that a car's condition should be considered as a factor relative to age. Quite frequently, the person wishing to sell a vehicle will remark that it is "in pretty good shape for an antique." Don't accept this type of sales pitch! The older a car is the more you will have to pay to correct any faults. Consequently, you should argue for a break in price on exactly the opposite basis.

Take the 1935 Ford Cabriolet shown in Fig. 5-13 for instance. According to the *Old Cars Price Guide* (spring 1983), the values for this model in each of the five standard condition classes are as follows:

Class 1 = $24,000   Class 4 = $7,000
Class 2 = $16,000   Class 5 = $4,000
Class 3 = $9,000

note the big jump in value between the Class 3 and Class 2 appraisals. The reason for the jump is related to the high cost of restoring a prewar model today. The car shown in Fig. 5-13 needs quite a bit of work that includes removal of dents in the left front fender, replating of the chrome

on the front bumper, new hub caps and running boards (note the incorrect chrome strips used to cover running board damage), tires, and painting.

It is a Class 4 vehicle at best and, because of its age, will cost more to fix. For one thing, original parts will be hard to find for a 48-year old car. Also, labor costs will probably go higher. Although the hourly rate you will have to pay for restoration will be the same as for newer cars, working the old metal will require extra time. Still, the standards that other collectors use to grade such a car will be uniform. Old age does not automatically make a Number 4 car a Number 3!

Another factor to consider when thinking about the purchase of off-condition, prewar car is the brand of automobile you are buying. Some brands are traditionally more popular with collectors. This will affect the amount of technical information and parts you can get as well as the cost of the same. This makes the more popular car in poor condition a better buy. The less popular make can have a higher top condition value due to its rarity and the fact that it cost more to restore.

For example, a 1937 Ford convertible in Class 4 condition (Fig. 5-14) is currently valued at $5,800. A 1938 Hudson Convertible Brougham in the same general shape (Fig. 5-15) is worth around $2,000 less. When both cars are restored to Number 1 condition, the Ford will carry a $16,000 appraised value and the Hudson will have a $16,500 value.

Several factors explain this seemingly illogical situation. First, the huge, Early Ford V-8 Club has, over the years, accumulated a wealth of technical data about

Fig. 5-13. The painted bumper, dented fenders, and battered running boards on this 1935 Ford Cabriolet are reasons to argue for a lower price. In top shape, this model is valued at $24,000, but in the condition shown it is worth less than $9,000.

Fig. 5-14. Prices on prewar convertibles vary with the make of car. Because many hobbyists are interested in Ford products, this Class 4 condition 1937 convertible is worth about $5,800 "as is."

Fig. 5-15. Hudsons are not quite as desirable as Fords, so the going prices for comparable Hudson models in lower-condition classes are more reasonable. This Class 4 condition 1938 Hudson ragtop brings about $2,000 less than a Ford in the same shape. In top condition, the Hudson's value would be just slightly above that of a Ford ragtop of similar age.

Ford models of the 1932–1954 era. This makes it easier (and less expensive) to repair such cars. In addition, there are many commercial suppliers of Ford parts, some of which manufacture authentic reproduction parts. This also eases restoration problems. On the other hand, the Hudson restorer will have to seek out original parts, and there will be extra time involved in doing this. Time means money, of course, so it will probably be more expensive to fix up the Hudson.

Technical advice from the Hudson-Essex-Terraplane Club will help, but there simply isn't as much information available on Hudsons as there is for Fords. Therefore, in anything less than top shape, the easier-to-fix Ford will be worth more to a larger number of collectors.

EXTERIOR INSPECTION TIPS

Assuming that you've settled on a couple of models as cars that you might like to own, there are a number of items you'll want to inspect more closely. Start on the outside of the car and take a close look at the condition of the exterior sheet metal. The first thing to look for is obvious impact damage such as the dented fenders, a bent-up grille, twisted running boards and sloppy fitting hoods (as with the 1935 and 1937 Fords shown in Figs. 5-13 and 5-14).

To most collectors damaged sheet metal repaired with "bondo" or fiberglass fillers is unacceptable. Impact damage on collector cars should be repaired by working the metal back to its original contours by hammer-and-dolly techniques or by replacing the parts with new ones. Where fillers must be used for finishing operations, lead-soldering techniques are preferable. The use of very small amounts of fiberglass filler for final surfacing might pass inspection, but in no case should fiberglass be used to fill in a hole or very deep dent. Repairs accomplished in such a manner are rarely permanent and will lead to additional problems.

If you suspect that a car might have had extensive repairs with fiberglass, you can check out the possibility with a magnet. The magnet will be drawn to metal or to surfaces with just a very light coating of fiberglass filler, but will not be attracted to panels having a heavy layer of fiberglass. This technique will also be useful in determining if fiberglass reproduction parts—such as fenders—have been used for a quick, nonauthentic restoration. You might still want to purchase a car with fiberglass replacement fenders, but it should not be priced as high as one with metal fenders.

In addition to impact damage, check for corroded metal. Extensive rust out in a door sill panel is not uncommon in prewar cars and is very hard—sometimes impossible—to repair by patching methods. In some cases, reproduction parts will be available. They are installed by cutting out the old metal and welding in the new panel.

Corrosion damage to sheet metal is caused by dirt and moisture collecting in parts of the car that are bolted or welded together. The points of attachment create a space between the two parts or a bridgelike shelf between them. These spaces or shelflike areas become a natural resting place for water, road salt, dirt, mud, grease and other accumulations of foreign matter. When these substances interact with the water kicked up from the road (or rain falling from the sky) a corrosive, chemical reaction takes place. Over a given amount of time, the reactive agents will eat through both paint and metal.

Common areas that are prone to such damage include panels surrounding the headlights, rocker panels, junctures where chrome trim and body metal come together, lower fenders behind wheel wells (where the fender braces collect debris), and panels around the rear bumper. The lower part of a door might also exhibit corroision. This is caused when rubber window seals deteriorate, allowing rain to slide down into the door and pool in the bottom for a time. Convertibles are especially prone to this type of body rot because the window glass in a ragtop has less structural support than windows in a closed-body car. Window seals will therefore deteriorate more rapidly and, as the fabric top starts to age, there's a very good chance of rainwater entering the doors. Some convertibles—especially those which were not regularly stored indoors (Fig. 5-16) will exhibit a great amount of body deterioration.

The deterioration of a convertible top—due to age or damage or incorrect fit—will almost always promote corrosion in the car's floor pan. During the restoration of his 1940 Ford convertible, Tony Vacarro found that he had to weld in a complete, new floor pan. The original floor was rotted so badly that, after disassembling the car, it was necessary to temporarily add bracing just to hold the car together after the corroded floor was cut out. The car has now been totally reconstructed and the nonoriginal bracing removed. Luckily, the car owner also owns an auto body shop. You can just imagine how much custom work like this would cost if outside labor was required!

To check the condition of a convertible's floor pan, be sure to lift up the carpets. This might take a little work and annoy the person who's selling the car, but insist on inspecting the floor this way. Unscrew the inner door sill trim plate and carefully lift the carpet.

If you can't see the condition of the floor sheet metal, slide your hand below the carpet and feel around for corrosion. When you are finished, remember (I doubt if the owner would let you forget!) to push the carpet back into place and re-install the door sill plate. If the owner balks at your right to make this kind of inspection, it does not necessarily mean a problem exists, but it certainly gives you reason to wonder. Don't buy until you have further proof—or a written guarantee—that the floor pan isn't rusty.

Fig. 5-16. The dark spots on this light-colored Oldsmobile ragtop indicate some of the common places where rust and corrosion attacks postwar convertibles.

Don't forget that the pan usually extends back into the luggage compartment. Don't be fooled by a trunk that looks immaculate due to the installation of new rugs or mats (Fig. 5-17). Both interior carpeting and replacement trunk coverings are readily available for the majority of collector cars and it's far easier for the owner of a rusty car to install carpeting instead of a new floor. In the case of the Oldsmobile shown in Fig. 5-17 (seen at an auction), both the floor pan and trunk floor were in perfect condition. This doesn't mean the ragtop you're buying will be this good. Check very carefully to ensure those new rugs aren't covering some old rust!

Still on the outside of the car, inspection of the convertible top comes next. This should include a close look at the top riser mechanism and roof bows as well as the fabric itself. You can purchase a mail-order convertible top for an old car for as little as $59.95 from one source, while specialty shops are charging up to $1,200 for a custom-fit rag top today. When first installed, the two tops won't look at all that much different, but you can bet that won't be the case after a couple of months.

Check the top closely. Look for any obvious damage to the fabric such as a rip or a spot showing excessive wear. Check the stitching or glue hold along the seams. Spotting or discoloration of the fabric is a sign that a chemical or foreign substance has attacked the fabric to one degree or another. Fabric along the sides or around the rear window opening (Fig. 5-18) should not be trimmed too closely. There should be an adequate hem around these areas. A top cut too close may tear off due to normal wind buffeting that occurs when the car is driven with the windows lowered.

The snaps and fasteners should be in good condition and the zipper should open and close easily and not be rusted. The shape of the rear window opening should conform to original specifications. A good way to check this, as well as the roof bow contours, is to compare "factory photos" of the same type of car with the real thing. A good top will look just right; it won't be too loose or too tight. The bows should support the fabric without stretching it out of shape.

If possible, check the original factory parts manual

Fig. 5-17. In addition to the floorpan, the metal trunk floor can also be weakened by rust. Ask the owner if you can open the luggage compartment and look or feel under the new trunk mats. In this case, the floor on an Oldsmobile ragtop proved to be in good condition. Don't take things like this for granted.

Fig. 5-18. Check the fit and general appearance of the convertible top. It should look right and feel tight. Also, the shape of the rear-window opening must conform to original factory specifications. You can check this by referring to sales literature or contemporary factory photos.

for the car to see if the top is a correct color. Frequently, the top was color keyed to the exterior body paint. Small considerations of this nature will spell the difference between a Number 1 condition car and lower-grade examples.

Just how good the top must be to warrant an acceptable rating depends upon how you are classing the car as to condition as well as the price you are paying. If you are buying the car with a full restoration in mind, you probably won't worry too much about the originality factors, but remember that an incorrect fitting top promotes other problems such as rust and corrosion. Even though you plan to replace the roof, the damage might already have been done. Your quick but careful checking at this stage will keep you from purchasing a very poor car.

Before you check inside the car and under the hood, it's a good idea to visually inspect the chassis components and a few other parts. A look underneath the vehicle can be very revealing. Things to watch for are corroded gas tanks, broken leaf springs or spring shackles, cracks in the frame (or obvious welding repairs) and the condition and tightness of the exhaust system components.

If the car has been operated within the last hour, the exhaust pipe, muffler, and tailpipe might be too hot to touch. You should carry a wooden stick or insulated gloves to allow for a good inspection of such parts. Give the pipes and muffler a shake with your gloved hand or a poke with your stick. Don't overdo things and create new damage, but a firm, solid poke or shake will tell you if everything is as sound as it should be.

If you are planning to restore the car, don't be too concerned about exhaust damage because parts are

relatively inexpensive and easy to get. Just don't drive home the car with the windows closed if exhaust gasses are leaking. Exhaust fumes can be fatal!

INTERIOR INSPECTION TIPS

Inspection of the interior comes next. Things to look for include the general condition of the interior door panels, inside door hardware, door trim, etc. Convertible interiors are very likely to show some wear and tear because the materials are so open to damage from the elements when top-down driving takes place. A sudden rainstorm might have resulted in moisture getting inside the car at some point. Often, a leaky top will allow the same kind of thing to happen.

On a postwar car with a padded dashboard, there's a very strong possibility of the sun causing the padded materials to shrink, warp, or buckle. Padded dashboard replacement is an almost impossible job unless reproduction parts can be obtained in kit form. Generally, this is the case only with some Chevrolets, Fords and Chrysler 300 letter cars (plus other models where part interchanges with these models occur).

Cars that do not have as large a following within the hobby simply do not warrant tooling-up by repro parts manufacturers. About the only way to find a padded dashboard for most makes is by through locating the same kind of car in a salvage yard.

Beware when you see an aftermarket, lace-on steering wheel cover (Fig. 5-19). It probably means that the wheel's plastic rim has cracked with age. This is especially prevalent on Chrysler products of the late 1950s and early 1960s, such as the popular 300 letter cars. I

Fig. 5-19. A lace-on steering wheel cover of the aftermarket type could indicate cracks in the wheel rim. This should not prevent buying an otherwise good car, but some reduction of price may be called for. Note such problems on a checklist so that you document the problem.

would not totally reject the purchase of an otherwise excellent vehicle because of cracks in the steering wheel, but keep in mind that it costs about $100 to buy such a part—even a used wheel in good condition. This must be taken into consideration in arriving at a fair selling price.

In a Number 1 condition car, the floor mats and carpeting should be in like-new condition. Carpeting kits for almost all old cars are readily available. Quality kits will match the originals exactly in terms of both the type of material and color. Considering the ease of restoring carpeting, a car showing wear cannot be considered in excellent condition. If you are paying the price of a Number 1 car, the carpets or floor coverings should be either perfect originals or top-quality repros. If you are purchasing a lesser-grade vehicle with restoration in mind, the wear on such items should be in conformity with the word description of the applicable condition class.

The amount of wear showing on rubber brake pedal and accelerator pads should, likewise, conform to the milage showing on the car's odometer. This is a good way to determine if a car advertised as a "low-milage"

automobile has actually been around the clock (past the 100,000 mile mark). Because speedometer laws were not in effect prior to the late 1960s, it's not very uncommon to find cars with 120,000 miles of use being sold as 20,000-original-mile vehicles. If the rubber pads are very worn, you can almost always assume that the car has been driven 100,000 miles, plus whatever reading shows on the odometer. On the other hand, a car that has traveled only a few thousand miles will usually have pedal pads that look almost brand new (Fig. 5-20).

When you are checking over the interior of the car, it's a good practice to compare the rear upholstery with that on the front seat and front door panels. In most cases, the front compartment will get more wear than the rear and the driver's compartment usually suffers the most. It's fairly common to find cars in which the front door panels have been replaced. Problems occur when the replacement materials are not strictly original types. Compare the design of the rear panels with those on the front doors. There should be a continuity in the two-toning patterns and materials.

The rear interior components in the 1957 Pontiac convertible shown in Fig. 5-21 seem to be in perfect

60

condition. All of the trim and stitching are intact, the window riser mechanisms work, the welting looks like new, and the window sills showed no wear. The only problem was that some of the parts belonged to a Super Chief two-door hardtop—not a Star Chief convertible!

The person who "fixed-up" this car could not obtain the right materials and located, instead, a good hardtop interior. The result was still a nice interior, but surely not Number 1. A good way to check for such things is to secure original sales brochures from old-car-hobby literature dealers. These booklets will contain artwork or photos illustrating the original upholstery combinations. This particular car originally came with a much fancier two-tone, waffle-pattern, all-vinyl interior.

The final stage of your initial inspection should cover the under-hood compartment. A little research through factory literature and specialized car clubs will be helpful in determining the correct color for an engine, as well as the use of correct engine parts and accesory equipment. For example, the motor in a 1932 Pontiac cabriolet should be painted dark green. This car should have "braided" style electrical wiring and screw-on type spark plug cables. The hose clamps and fittings should be of the old-fashioned "squeeze" type instead of the modern "worm gear" type. On all Number 1 condition cars, the engine compartment should be completely detailed to look exactly like it did the day the car left the factory.

Engine detailing is also important to postwar car collectors. The engine shown in Fig. 5-22 is on a high-performance Chevrolet. The muscular 325-horsepower, 396-cubic-inch Turbo Jet V-8 has chromed engine parts and air cleaner decals. A car in top original shape, or one that has been expertly restored, will have all features appearing as new. To accomplish a good restoration takes a lot of research and work. That is why a Number 1 car warrants top pricing in the collector's market.

BUYING CARS PIECE BY PIECE

Old-car flea markets are organized primarily to sell parts for antique, classic and special-interest cars. It is not unusual, however, to find vendors selling either complete cars or major subassemblies (such as complete bodies or fully restored chassis). Money spent wisely at a flea market can lead to obtaining an older convertible at an attractive price.

Fig. 5-20. Pedal-pad wear is a good way to tell the original mileage on some cars. Factory-script rubber floor mats are an accessory that add to the vehicle's value.

Fig. 5-21. Give the interior a careful inspection. Do the materials used to cover seats and door panels match from front to rear? Make sure the seats on the convertible you're buying did not come out of a two-door hardtop. The two types will interchange as far as size and shape, but authenticity will suffer.

To shop the flea markets, you first have to know where they're being held. The trader publications such as *Old Cars Weekly*, *Hemmings Motor News* and *Cars & Parts* are the best sources of flea market schedules. If you are interested primarily in postwar cars, *Collectible Automobile* magazine should be consulted. Lists of upcoming flea markets appear in the calendar of events in such publications. Larger shows will also be separately announced through display advertising. Many flea market promoters will also run classified ads in the automotive section of local newspapers, to announcing the shows.

Flea markets are generally held in fairgrounds, parks, shopping centers or campuses of local schools. Sometimes a farmer's field will be cleared for a site. Indoor flea markets are starting to gain popularity in urban areas. Space at the indoor shows is limited by the size of the exposition building, but at least weather problems are avoided. In general, the outside shows will have more complete cars for sale and the indoor shows are geared mainly to the merchandising of parts.

The sale of complete cars is secondary to the sale of parts for most flea-market vendors. Therefore, most of the cars for sale will be vehicles that the vendor picked up in his travels while searching for caches of like-new, old parts. Such parts are usually described as New-Old-Stock or NOS parts. This means that they were made years ago, but never attached to a car. After sitting on the car dealer's shelves for many years, they were purchased by the hobby vendor.

Rarely does the parts man have the time to fix or restore such a car. He simply sees it as a quick resale item. If you're mechanically inclined, this is much to your benefit. You can do the fix up and be ahead some bucks in the end.

The main things to think about when buying such a car are the asking price and the condition of the vehicle. In a lot of instances the vendors acquire these cars from wrecking yards while they are gathering good, used parts from junked vehicles. This means that there must have been something wrong with the car when it was originally junked. Don't assume that the problems are major ones simply because the car was probably found this way. Years ago, it was not uncommon for cars to be discarded for old age alone. During the strong economic period in the 1960s, many basically good cars were scrapped in this manner. Of course, such machines have been setting for over 20 years so they will still need a good dose of restoration.

At a recent flea market, there was a solid MGA roadster/convertible for sale (Fig. 5-23). The asking price noted on the windshield was in the right ballpark for this Class 4 vehicle. In most cases, the asking price will be 10 to 20 percent more than the owner actually expects to realize in a final sale. As the buyer, you might have to put up a strenuous argument for knocking the price down that much, but this is all part of the game where flea-market selling takes place. At the knocked-down price, this car would be a good buy for the MG enthusiast able to do his own restoration work. Expect to haggle a bit if you're planning to buy at a flea market. Don't pass on an excellent bargain just to avoid talking prices.

A second thing to look for at flea markets are major parts of an old car. Such parts must be in good condition to help you begin a restoration project. At a flea market in Florida, one stall had a Ford cabriolet body displayed (Fig. 5-24). This body had been re-worked into solid condition and primer-painted to protect the repaired metal from rust. Chances are it had been purchased (as part of a parts deal) from a hobbyist who began resto-

ration and ran out of time, energy, or cash.

To the person who already owns a good Ford chassis, a body like this could represent a real treasure. Suppose you were working on a Ford sedan at home and had already fixed up the engine and running gear, but still faced a lot of body work. A sedan would be worth around $10,000 in fully restored, Number 1 shape, but a cabriolet in comparable condition would be valued at over twice that amount. Therefore, a body like this would add over $10,000 to the finished project! That's certainly something to think about the next time you visit a flea market.

BUYING AT CAR CORRALS

In recent years, the car corral has become a popular method of buying and selling old cars. The term refers to a section of a car show or flea market that is exclusively set aside to display cars for sale. A small fee (approximately $10 to $20) is charged by the show organizers for entering cars in this area. In exchange for his money, the seller is provided a one-car space in an area that will draw potential buyers.

For the seller, the car corral represents a way in which to market his vehicle without paying an auction fee or commission. He also avoids other expenses such as

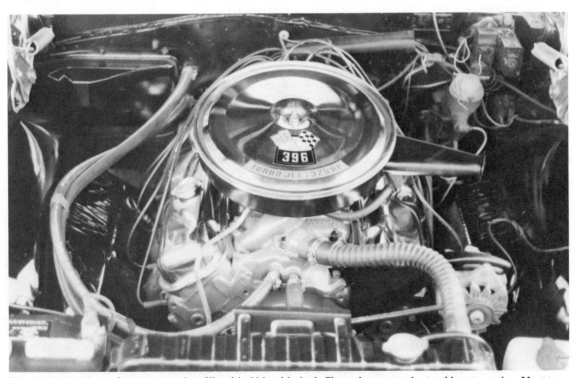

Fig. 5-22. A high-performance engine, like this 396 cubic-inch Chevrolet powerplant, adds extra value. Most true high-performance motors will have a number of chrome-plated parts (such as the air cleaner).

Fig. 5-23. Good buys can be located at a swap meet if you shop very carefully. In most cases, cars found in flea markets are going to need lots of work. They should be priced accordingly.

Fig 5-24. Don't automatically avoid buying cars that are disassembled. Any old car is simply the sum of its parts and many good, partially restored components show up at flea markets from time to time. If the price is right, there's no reason to buy such parts for a long-term restoration project.

traveling to an auction and renting a high-priced motel room in the cities where big auctions are held. He'll still need a place to stay during the show, but because most car corrals are staged in rural areas the local rates will be lower. Savings of this type can run up to $500 to $1,000 in most cases. This allows the seller to keep the price of the car a bit lower than usual.

As a potential buyer, the car corral will generally offer you a fine selection of cars at prices that don't include high travel costs for the seller. The cars on display will usually cover the full range of condition classes.

If you are interested in purchasing a car as a restoration project, you'll find plenty of vehicles from which to pick. For instance, the Number 3 condition Plymouth ragtop shown in Fig. 5-25 was offered in one such sale. This car needed some minor dent work, a new trunk handle, rocker panel moldings, gravel shields, and wide whitewall tires to move up the ladder to Class 2 grade. Still, it was a very solid car and the price was well under the $5,000 listed by the current *Old Cars Price Guide* for this model in such shape.

Car corrals also draw many better cars such as the 1963 Tempest convertible (Fig. 5-26) that showed up at the 1982 Iola Car Show. This car seemed almost perfect in all respects.

In most cases, the owner will attach a note to the windshield advising what times he plans to return to the space. You should carry a notebook to jot down the cars you are interested in and the times that the owners plan to return. If you are interested in more than one car, keep making your rounds, but plan to get back at the designated time.

If only one car has caught your eye, the absence of the owner can be to your advantage. Because there's not a lot of high-pressure selling involved, you might be able to spend several hours closely inspecting the car as it sits. Go through the inspection routine as completely as practical. Start with the basic steps previously outlined in this chapter—except for the under-carpet and under-hood checks. Closely examine the condition of sheet metal, paint, trim, tires, exhaust system, seats, carpets, and steering wheel. Reach under and into the fender wells for signs of recent body work. It should be okay to swing the doors open. Look for variations in paint color between the inner door jambs and exterior panels. This will tell you if the car has been repainted recently.

If the owner has not returned yet and you're not completely knowledgeable about the particular model, you might want to visit the nearby flea market and look for a literature dealer who is carrying sales brochures for this car. Carefully browse through the catalog (with the vendor's permission, of course, tell him you'll buy it if you get the car). Check the illustrations, text, and charts for original colors, upholstery patterns, technical specifications, whitewall tire designs and equipment features. Make notes and return to the car at the designated time.

Fig. 5-25. Car corrals are usually held in conjunction with major flea markets. Car owners rent a selling space for the weekend where hundreds of potential buyers can view what they offer for sale. This Plymouth convertible is one good example.

Fig. 5-26. To contact the owner of a car-corral car, look for notices attached to the windshield indicating when the person will return. It's a good practice to look over the exterior and interior while waiting for the owner to show.

Once you have contacted the owner, ask for permission to check under the hood, inside the trunk (and under the trunk mat), and ask him if you can make the floorpan check (or will he guarantee that it's solid?). The next step is to have him raise the top. See that the mechanism works smoothly and look the fabric over closely.

Starting the car is essential. See if the engine runs smoothly. Look close for any fluid leaks such as oil stains on the valve covers. Listen for unusual noises: clickety valves, a squealing power steering pump, knocks in the engine, etc. Insist on driving the car. You might have to wait until the show has ended to get the car on the street for a test drive. It's better to wait for this opportunity than to jump in and purchase a car you haven't driven. What you'll be looking for in a test drive are the same things outlined in many books written about purchasing used cars. As an enthusiast, you've probably read a number of such books and articles. TAB book No. 2062, *How To Make Your Old Car Run Like New*, by James Flammang, includes an evaluation checklist for test drives. There are no special things to check on convertibles other than correct operation of top mechanisms.

If you don't have a bit of luck reaching the owner of the car (he may not return on time), don't feel you still can't buy the car. Leave a note or business card attached to the dashboard, steering wheel, sun visor or ash tray.

Tell the owner that you would like to inspect the car further, including a test drive. Leave your address and telephone number and request that he get in touch if the car isn't sold. If you are worried about someone else buying the vehicle, just park your body beside the car and wait until the end of the show. This is an especially smart thing to do if you see a dozen other notes and cards inside the car!

One last bit of advice is don't forget to bring your price guides along to the car corral. They will tell you if the asking price is unrealistically high—or better yet, too low.

BUYING AT AUCTIONS

As opposed to private sales and car corrals, the auctioneering field is a high-pressure method of trading collector cars. Classic car auctions evolved during the early 1970s. If you've participated in the old-car hobby for awhile, you'll recall that this was the boom period for interest in old cars. The auctions were a natural outgrowth of this trend, and a sort of carnival-like happenings where buyers and sellers of antique and Classic cars were able to get together. When convertible fever spread just a few years later, almost-new ragtops began showing up at auctions. Therefore, the name classic car auction is a bit misleading. Nevertheless, it is the term that most people use in describing such events.

Some people love auctions and attend almost every one; others hate them. The haters accuse the auctions of being dishonest and of driving old car prices too high for average hobbyists. These claims were both partly true about five years ago. Then the collector car market stabilized a bit. A few auction firms that were floating along on nothing more than momentum came tumbling back to earth. A number of them collapsed or simply folded shop overnight and left hobbyists to absorb the problems bad auctions had created.

The better-run auction firms managed to survive while realizing they had to fight a tarnished image. The result was a number of general improvements in this industry such as same-day-payment plans, more realistic commission rates, flat-rate entry fees, etc.

Since 1978, the companies that were strong enough to survive have done an admirable job. There is still a touch of carnival atmosphere at most auctions, but no longer do they drive old-car pricing up. Auction sales of the 1980s have provided a very clear reflection of fair market values for all types of collector cars.

Well over 100 auctions are held in different cities across the United States each year. There is a sale nearly every weekend in some part of the country. They are useful to buyers and sellers alike because of the fine opportunities provided for the fair trading of collectible cars. Upcoming auctions can be located through the hobby trader publication display ads as well as classi-

fieds in many local newspapers. In addition, *Car Collector & Car Classics* magazine runs an auction schedule near the front of each monthly issue.

As a buyer, the main rule to follow at auctions falls under the old slogan of "buyer beware." This high-pressure method of selling is a strictly commercial enterprise. The auction company reaps its profits by
☐ Selling catalogs.
☐ Charging entry fees to those who want to sell a car.
☐ Collecting spectator admissions.
☐ Selling bidder's numbers to potential buyers.
☐ Charging a commission on each successful sale of a car.

All cars are sold on "as is" condition terms. In some cases, buyers have little real opportunity to carefully inspect a car. There are times when car haulers drive up, unload a car, and the vehicle is driven directly to the auction block. This means a bidder has 10 minutes or less to give it the once-over. Obviously, the seller of such a machine is seeking the impulse buyer.

Some extremely fine cars are brought to auctions, but other auction cars need various degrees of restoration work. While some sales are strictly of the quick, 10-minute, impulse type, most sellers give the buyer some opportunity to make a close inspection of condition. At the midwinter auction held during February, in Atlantic City, New Jersey, the majority of vehicles go on display for at least several hours prior to start of the sale. See Fig. 5-27. A problem, however, is that all inspections must be made under indoor lighting conditions. For

Fig. 5-27. At the giant Atlantic City classic car auction, most of the entries can be looked over before they are put up for bids. In most cases, a test drive will not be possible at auctions (whether they are held indoors or outside).

example, a Cadillac Eldorado at this auction in 1979 looked like a Class 1 car at first glance. The flourescent lighting hid the fact that the chrome trim needed replating. Also, a push on the gas cap door showed the mechanism to be quite rusty. This was still a very nice car, but only a Number 2. The difference in appraised value between the two condition classes is around $6,000. As a buyer, you should spend as much time as possible checking out cars in an auction—especially those sales taking place indoors.

How about mechanical condition? Well, this is one of the most difficult things to gauge at an auction sale. In the majority of cases, you won't be provided with the opportunity to hear a car run or take a test drive prior to its appearance at the auction block. When the car is rolled out for sale, you'll have a couple of minutes to look under the hood and listen to the motor operate. This means you must quickly appraise the car's mechanical condition usually under noisy, crowd conditions with the auctioneer's voice blasting over the microphone. If this is your first collector-car purchase, you should take a friend—with more mechanical experience—with you to the auction.

As the car rolls up to the auctioneer's podium, the ring men working for the auction company will also open the doors and the trunk. You have to accept that an under-the-carpet check is nearly impossible here, but you should be able to quickly reach below the trunk mat to feel for rust or corrosion. Ask one of the ring men to have the driver raise and lower the top. This is usually done as part of the standard auction routine. If it does not happen, you have a good reason to expect possible trouble. Speaking of drivers, the person behind the wheel of a car at auction is usually not the car owner. It won't do much good—and it will be a waste of precious time—to ask him lots of questions.

Sometimes there is a very important difference in the prices of different brands of cars at auctions. Because this business is very commercial and based on lots of promotion and hype, there's a tendency for the mass-market collector cars and high-dollar classics to trade at prices near or above their fair market value. This is partially because many antique car dealers shop at auctions. These people are looking for models with appeal to large markets or prestige buyers; in other words, the kinds of cars that they can turn over rapidly.

Models that have a smaller, special-interest following tend to sell under market. A good example is a 1965 GTO convertible brought to an auction in a Texas city. See Fig. 5-28. To the specialized Pontiac/GTO enthusiast, a car like this is worth over $7,000. But the market for Pontiacs is a small one, and the dealers at this

Fig. 5-28. Some brands and models do not sell as high in auctions as they might in private-owner transactions. You might be able to pickup a great bargain such as this 1965 GTO that got no higher than $3,500 at an auction in Texas.

Fig. 5-29. A knowledge of automotive history is a good thing to bring to an auction. This rare Chrysler Hemi-Charger isn't a very flashy car and didn't draw much attention at one sale. To Chrysler enthusiasts, however, this is probably a more valuable machine than the auction bidding indicated.

auction refused to go higher than the mid-$3,000 range for this GTO ragtop.

This car did not sell that day. Nevertheless there was a good chance that a real Pontiac collector could have picked it up by going just a little bit higher in price than those dealers. The owner wanted to sell it, but not at half price! He probably would still have let it go for far less than its real value. The point is that if you shop for the right brands of cars at an auction you can usually find some really good deals.

How can you know the right cars to look for at bargain prices? The best way is to obtain a copy of two different types of price guides. First, get hold of a book called *C.A.R. Values*. This is an "auction reporter" type publication that keeps an annual record of actual activities in such sales. It lists the type of car, the class 1-5 condition, and the actual highest bid for the particular car. A coding system is used to tell you in what auction the car appeared. West Coast prices run higher than East Coast prices. Also, the book tells the reserve price that owners set for their car. This is what the owner "wanted" and can be much higher than the actual high bid.

Your second step is to purchase a copy of another price guide that gives national ballpark price estimates. In comparing the two listings from the different books, you will usually find that auction prices on certain brands run as high as the national averages. At the same time, you'll detect a trend for some cars (such as GTOs) to fall short of their real values quite consistently. These will be the cars that represent good bargains at auctions.

As a serious buyer, another factor in your favor at auctions is that you might know more about the appeal of specific models than a lot of the other bidders. Auctions tend to attract a great many casual car collectors (people who don't know cars, but are looking to invest in the field). Over the years, this group has included famous artists, baseball players, movie stars, and other such people who tend to concentrate on buying those flashy, glamour cars.

Such buyers won't be much interested in a plain-looking—but historically significant—model, such as a 1951 Chrysler ragtop (Fig. 5-29). Only 950 examples of this model were made during 1951–1952 and they were the first Chryslers to feature the famous Hemi V-8. Surviving examples are highly valued by experienced collectors, but the cars just don't look flashy. Armed with a basic knowledge of automotive history, you will find good buys on this kind of vehicle an many such sales.

At all old car auctions, keep an eye out for cars selling under "no reserve" conditions. This means that the owner has decided to sell the vehicle to the highest bidder whatever the final bid might be. According to author Bob Lichty, writing in the January 1982 issue of *Car Exchange* magazine, "We know a man who was active on the auction circuit buying only the first 3-5 cars (no reserve vehicles) at each sale. After cleaning them up a bit and running them through the next sale, he made a good profit on each."

Most auction run through the first five to ten cars on a no reserve basis to start the sale with lots of action. No reserve sales excite the crowd and get the bidders in a buying mood. They also provide the chance to pickup a bargain car for well below its going market value. It's not uncommon for the buyer of the first car in an auction to offer the same car later in the sale and make a profit on it the very same day! Don't assume that this will work for you. Never buy a car you don't like merely on this speculation. It might fail to sell later on and you will be stuck with it.

GETTING YOUR CAR HOME

Once you have completed the purchase of a convertible, you might have a problem in getting the car home. If you buy the car close to home and the car is in good operating condition, you'll probably decide to drive it. In this case, you should check local motor vehicle department codes and also check your insurance liability. You won't want to move an uninsured, unregistered car over the streets illegally. There's always the possibility of an accident during the transportation period.

Laws about moving unregistered vehicles will vary from one state to another. The authorities in your town can give you the best advice on how to do this. Some states have provisions for temporary registrations. Also, most insurance companies will be glad to issue a short-term policy that allows you to move the car safely and legally.

Some hobbyists rely on tow bars to move cars short distances. It is usually possible to rent these devices from firms that rent cars and trucks. When using a tow bar, it's a good idea to put a sign on the car that reads "Vehicle In Tow." In many cases, such a warning is required by law, as are remote taillight hook-ups and the use of dual, truck-style outside rear view mirrors. In many cases, these accessories will be provided as part of the tow bar rental fees.

The taillight hook-ups can be a problem. Many older cars, built before 1955, will have 6-volt electrical systems. The modern vehicle will generally have 12-volt electrics. For a longer-than-normal tow operation, you might need a device to step down the voltage reaching the taillamps of the old car. Such devices can be obtained through electrical equipment supply houses. For short-distance towing, this won't be a real problem because the old taillamp bulbs will probably handle 12-volt connections.

Tow bars have their limitations and the use of trailers is becoming much more popular with old car hobbyists today. A well-built trailor is, without a doubt, the best and safest way to transport a valuable collector car. Most collectors start with the purchase of an open trailer. A dual-axle unit is the best type to have because

the vehicle will ride with greater stability and less rocking. The trailer should be of sturdy construction and specially designed for the transportation of automobiles. Avoid units that use mobile home axles. These axles are originally 10-feet wide and must be modified for trailer use by cutting them down to 8 feet and rewelding them together. When this is done, the caster-camber and toe-in angles are changed. This often leads to premature tire wear or failure.

The frame of the trailer should be of I-beam or rectangular-tube construction; the latter is the preferable way to go. Thick-wall rectangular tubing is best. Avoid trailers showing the use of extremely thin cross-members. Skimpy crossmembers promote chassis flexing and will not give a stable ride.

Even with the best open trailers, it's a good idea to check the attachment of axles to the frame. While towing in New Mexico one time, I heard a noise, looked in my mirror, and found the almost-new trailer sliding down the road sideways. One of the U-bolts holding an axle on had come undone. Since that day, I have strongly advised all trailer owners to modify their U-bolts by drilling a hole through them and inserting cotter pins! I feel that the only reason I didn't loose my car and trailer was that a Reese hitch was installed. This device, manufactured by Reese of Elkhart, Indiana, is designed to stabilize your load and make trailering much safer.

Other points to look for in a trailer designed for hauling cars are as follows:

☐ Slide-in, self-storing diamond plate loading ramps (about 12-inches wide).

☐ Separate, electronic brakes for each axle.

☐ Sturdily constructed jacking device with dolly wheel.

☐ Heavy-duty safety chains heavily painted to protect against rust.

☐ Adequate provisions for taillamps and side safety reflectors.

☐ Incorporation of a heavy-duty winch for getting unoperable cars on the trailer.

A good, open trailer might cost up to $3,000, but if you're serious about collecting convertibles, you won't want to be without one. With a good trailer, you'll be able to visit car shows, flea markets, car corrals, and auctions anywhere and get the car that you purchase safely back home. You can also use it to rescue restorable cars or parts cars from salvage yards. In addition, you'll find it handy for towing your finished restoration to car shows. I used an open-car trailer for my last household move, and it saved me the cost of renting a moving van.

As the value of older convertibles continues to increase, more and more car collectors are starting to use enclosed car trailers to transport their vehicles. The enclosed type of trailer offers greater protection from flying debris and also prevents wind buffeting from damaging convertible tops. The basic construction of the chassis on such a trailer should conform to the same rules listed for an open unit. The difference comes from the construction used for the trailer body and in some of the features available.

Jim Cular has been involved in the auto restoration business for 18 years and has also restored several antique cars, many of which were national first-prize winners in concours competition.

Cular relies on Dexter, heavy-duty axles for all trailers. Electronic brakes are used on both axles. The trailers ride on 8.55-×-15 six-ply tires mounted on white spoke rims. All units come equipped with jacking devices and dolly wheels, safety chains, diamond plate, slide-in loading ramps. The chassis is constructed of 6-×-2 inch tubing of strong steel. The frame members are 24-inch-types, center-sized to the full width of the frame. All side members are 16-inch, on-center types and are fully gusseted to the chassis.

As for construction of the trailer body itself, the job begins with the building of the floor. It is made from 4-×-8 foot sheets of special, water-proofed Blandex plywood. These are 1 1/4 inches thick and are installed in one continuous piece with no seams. This allows the floor to support the full weight of the vehicle. The underside of the floor is undercoated to keep moisture out.

Cular warns against so-called "glamour floors" used in some general-purpose trailers. These floors are fashioned with strips of wood resembling tongue and groove construction. They look like bowling alleys, but they have numerous seams that permit moisture to get inside the unit. This promotes warpage and leaking. Similar floors coated with poly-varnish finish look even nicer, but they get as slippery as ice when wet with water, grease, or oil. This will cause a car to slide from side-to-side during towing. The use of Blandex plywood eliminates such problems.

Cular also warns against trailers made in a fashion similar to trailer-truck boxes. In constructing trucks, these boxes are shipped in unitized form, with floors attached, but they are shipped to car trailer makers without floors. This can pop out rivets, cause stress cracks, and promote buckling.

Avoid steel construction units constructed by welding a series of stamped steel "hoops" to a chassis and attaching aluminum siding with sheet-metal screws. This siding comes in 4-×-8 foot sheets, leaving seams in the trailer that are then filled with caulking compound. This is the least expensive way to make a trailer, but it is generally considered unacceptable for car-hauling use.

Wood-frame construction—used in the RV industry for many years—is also a poor way to build a car hauler. When the wood breaks or rots, the screws holding the trailer together work loose. This promotes poor alignment of body panels after a few tows.

Probably the best way to build a trailer, according to Cular, begins with bolting the seamless, waterproofed (and undercoated) plywood floor to the frame and cross-members. Next, the 3-×-2 inch framing for rear doors is welded in place, at the rear crossmember, and triangular braces are welded to this frame for additional support. Wood framework for the box is constructed using Number 1 Grade wood treated with a preservative. All joints are glued and triangle-braced with rust-proof fasteners used in attachments. Metal wheel wells are then installed. Next comes the interior paneling; fiberglass insulation is installed to prevent "sweating" inside the trailer.

At this point, the exterior siding is added. Use fiberglass reinforced plywood that won't dent, crack, scratch or stain like aluminum. The siding is made by bonding .040 pebble-grain fiberglass to 1/4-inch plywood.

The roof is constructed of galvanized sheeting with crimped joints. A special epoxy is applied, every 4-feet, to allow for expansion and contraction. Special sealers are used on outer edges and full-length rain gutter moldings are added. This type of roof is usually guaranteed against leakage. In a well-built trailer, double rear doors with cam locks and heavy-duty hinges will be featured. Also, many makers are going to wind-cheating, aerodynamic frontal designs to allow the tow vehicle better gas milage.

A well-made enclosed trailer will cost around $5,250 today and you might want to add options like spare wheels and tires, curb-side entrance doors, brake-a-way switches, electrical hook-ups, rear leveling jacks, and an electric winch (don't forget that Reese hitch). You'll probably hit $6,000 to get the perfect trailer, but if you're serious about collecting convertibles the rig will be a good investment. Well-kept trailers don't depriciate very much in price.

When putting the car in a trailer, the diamond plate ramps will slide out of the storage slots once the fasteners that hold them in place are undone. The hook on the winch is attached to a solid point on the frame of the car—*not* the bumper—and the vehicle is slowly drawn up the ramp. Going slow allows you to make last-minute adjustments of ramp positionings so that the car stays on them. A diamond plate pattern prevents the tires from slipping.

The Ancura-Latex Polyester Rachet Securing System with "E" track and retails for around $175. That's far less than the cost of bodywork that might occur (to car and trailer) if the vehicle slides on rounding a curve or corner. The polyster straps are strong enough to hold the vehicle, but flexible enough to allow some "give" so components are not pulled from the car on a bad pothole. The ratchet mechanism makes tightening operations an easy task.

A side door is an option priced around $350. When towing cars with wide bodies (this includes most postwar cars) this feature is handy. It allows you to get in and out of the vehicle while it is inside the box. With custom-built trailers, the door can be placed in the best position for

Fig. 5-30. For most hobbyists, even the used truck with an hydraulic loading ramp will be overly expensive, and such trucks don't protect the car from the elements. A closed trailer would probably provide a safer ride for this car.

your particular car. The lower the trailer the better the tow car's gas mileage will be.

Some hobbyists have been lucky enough to purchase older trucks equipped with hydraulic lift beds (Fig. 5-30). This is a dandy way to haul a car around, but I'd still prefer an enclosed trailer. The open truck doesn't protect the car from dirt, wind, or stones and, most likely, even a used truck of this type will cost more than a trailer with many accessories and options.

STORING YOUR CONVERTIBLE

Indoor storage for convertibles and most other collector cars is virtually a must. If there's room in your family garage, it should do fine. The main thing you will want to do is preventing moisture from getting inside the car. Strong sunlight can also wreck that new convertible top, causing it to fade or deteriorate. If you live in an apartment or don't have a garage, see if you can rent one. A classified ad in your local paper will usually do the trick.

A roomy garage will also afford a good place for you to work on the car. Steel pole buildings offer a relatively inexpensive way to build a garage. For advice on constructing a pole building for car-hobby use, read *The Best of Old Cars Volume 4*. It contains articles on this subject written by Bill Mason and LeRoi "Tex" Smith. The cost of such a building will be in the $5,000 range (if you already have the property to build on). When completed, your pole building will be an investment as it increases the value of your property.

Neatness is a must in any storage area where a collector car is being kept or restored. Low-cost steel shelving is a very good method of increasing useable space. The shelves can be used to store parts and service manuals.

The peg board approach is another way to solve the problem of storing those extra parts you'll need for restoration. Hooks mounted to a pegboard can hold everything from fan belts to tools and a spare hub cap.

The main thing is having a place to keep the open-body car out of the elements. Moisture is the car hobbyists' biggest enemy; it's the main cause of rust and corrosion.

6. Restoration

Restoration of any automobile is a difficult and complicated job that takes a major investment of time, money, and energy. When it comes to convertibles, special considerations include the repair of the top operating mechanism and installation of fabric convertible tops. Therefore, this chapter is divided into two general parts. The first part covers the common steps required for typical automotive restorations. The second part is geared to the specialized skills and techniques required in the restoration of convertibles. Aside from extra emotional appeal and a fun-driving characteristics, there's a purely practical explanation for the higher prices that convertibles in nice condition draw. They cost more to restore because there is simply lots more work to the job.

The convertible restorer will usually face one or more of the following extra tasks:

☐ Top support mechanism refinishing.
☐ Door panel replacement.
☐ Reupholstery.
☐ Dashboard repair.
☐ Carpet replacement.
☐ Power top system repairs.
☐ Convertible top installation.
☐ Rebuilding of top support structure.

Which of these jobs you will want to tackle depends on the condition that your car is in, the amount of money you want to spend, and the degree of authenticity or show worthiness desired. If you plan to use the car frequently and want to lower and raise the top a bit, it won't pay to strive for absolute perfection. Operation of the top will normally lead to some scratching of the paint on moving parts and will also stretch and wrinkle the fabric roof. Repainting all parts and having a perfect roof aren't very practical aims. On the other hand, if you're shooting for a show-winning car, anything less than perfection simply won't do, but don't plan on driving your show car everyday. Select the restoration work that's most suited to your own collecting goals. This might mean doing all eight steps or only one or two.

In the great majority of cases, a new fabric top will have to be installed. This alone can run above $1,000. The top support structure will usually require work that ranges from refinishing the bows, roof rails, links and hinges, to completely replacing damaged parts. Some restorers have gone as far as rebuilding the entire mechanism; this often requires the custom-making of parts.

When the convertible top is power operated, there will usually be extra procedures to consider. Motors might have to be rebuilt or replaced and the vacuum, hydraulic, electric or hydroelectric systems might have to be rebuilt. There are hundreds of different components in the average convertible top mechanism and that means spending many extra hours in the garage or restoration shop.

Another consideration is that upholstery and interior trim parts on convertibles often suffer greater deterioration than similar items on closed cars. Even in normal service, the convertible interior will be more open to attack by strong sunlight, rain, ice, snow and wind. With even typical deterioration caused by normal use, the fabric top will often begin to stretch, wear, or tear—allowing rain to leak inside the car. With older models, evidence of this will appear as rust, corrosion, water-stained dashboards, buckled door panels, damaged carpeting and unsightly upholstery.

All such factors mean that the restorer has more to deal with in bringing the open-body car back to factory-fresh condition. This explains why some convertibles might be worth less than comparable closed cars in poor condition, while still being more valuable in top shape. See Table 6-1.

As you can see from the 1-5 Condition value figures given in Table 6-1, the 1968 Olds Toronado hardtop is valued higher than all three ragtops in Restorable (No. 5) and Good (No. 4) conditions, higher than just two in Very Good (No. 3) condition and Fine (No. 2) condition, and lower than all three in Excellent (No. 1) shape.

ASSESSING YOUR PURCHASE

The first thing to think about in any restoration is a realistic assessment of the machine that you have purchased. If you have used wisdom in selecting a car, you have already assessed its condition perhaps by rating it on the standard 1-5 condition-class scale. Nevertheless, you will almost certainly find that the car has a few flaws that you've overlooked. Emotion plays a large role in the buying experience and will often prompt the anxious buyer to see the car through rose-colored glasses. When it comes time to consider what has to be fixed, these positive emotions disappear quickly. What seemed to be a touch-up operation in the beginning will often turn out to be a much larger job in reality.

Now that you have the car in your driveway or garage, the time to deal with condition on a face-to-face

basis has arrived. Shed some light on the subject (Fig. 6-1) and give the car a good going over. You will probably find that those rusty runningboards are actually attached to a rusty door sill. Patching the holes with some lead body filler is not going to give you a permanent fix. Before you can repair the damage the right way, you will need new parts for the door sill repair. Then you realize that the new parts will have to be painted, and there's no way that new paint will ever match the faded original finish. So figure on a complete paint job. Of course, the new paint will make your old chrome plating seem inadequate, so that will have to be redone as well. In most cases, you'll end up with a long list of things to do.

Interestingly, the less car you had to begin with the easier you'll spot things to do. If you began with a disassembled car (Fig. 6-2), the problems will show up right away because they'll be easy to see. In other cases, unseen problems might be hidden under a new coat of paint where they'll show up later. If you're shooting for a first-class, show-winning restoration, it's possible that a car that has already been restored to amateur standards might have to be disassembled and done over from the chassis up.

Determining exactly what you want in a car is another part of the assessment. Ultimate value should also be considered here. If the car is a milestone or a classic, the most logical step is to consider nothing less than a full, ground-up restoration. Only then will the work be a true investment. A valuable car restored the cheapest way becomes a cheap car, worth almost nothing to other collectors who are interested in concours competition. They would have to have the job done again—at a cost up to $25,000—to wind up with a top-grade, professional restoration. Experts conclude that it usually takes that much money to move a car from the 95 percent perfect level up to 100 percent on the concours judging scale. That's $5,000 per point! With a classic or milestone, go *all* the way or don't even bother to start.

When it comes to a more common antique auto, a special-interest car or a late-model ragtop with potential

Table 6-1. Value-to-Condition Comparison for Selected 1968 Oldsmobiles.

	5	4	3	2	1
F-85 Cutlass "S" Convertible	$700	1400	2000	2600	4000
Delmont "88" Convertible	$650	1300	1700	2000	3800
Ninety-Eight Convertible	$750	1500	2600	3700	5000
Toronado Hardtop Coupe	$800	1600	2500	2800	3700

Source: Standard Catalog of American Cars 1946–1975

Fig. 6-1. Throw the garage light on and take a close look at the car you bought. You might find the fender that a rusty runningboard is attached to also needs repair.

Fig. 6-2. With a disassembled car, the pluses and minuses are easier to spot. This car has new wood in the doors, but still needs lots of work.

collectibility for the future, it's usually wise to buy the very best car you can possibly get and give it a partial restoration. This entails fixing the car up without doing a total disassembly. In this case, whether you are doing the job yourself, or having it done by professionals, it's a good policy to try to estimate how many hours of work will have to be invested.

Professional shop rates run between $20 to $30 per hour so a week's worth of labor is going to run $800 to $1,200 in this case or cost you about three weeks of your own time to do the same job. When you throw in the price of parts and special services, you can see that even a quick restoration can begin to outstrip the value of many cars. You must try to determine the "break-even" point by balancing the cost of restoration with the fair market value of the car in Number 1 condition.

Of course, you might not be shooting for this high a grade if you plan to use the car for everyday driving. Here you are mainly interested in getting the car to look and run good for a set price, but it's still wise to avoid false economies. For example, I know a hobbyist who has been trying to fix up his 1954 Chevy for several years. The car has a rust spot in one front fender that's been fixed three times by three different body shops. A few years ago he found a brand new front fender at an old car flea market. It was priced $250, which he felt was too high, so he did not buy it. Now he has sunk more than $400 into repairing the fender and it is still not as good as that new one would have been. Meanwhile, the value of the same car with a good fender has already jumped more than $250, which would have offset the cost of the part.

Estimating the cost of a good restoration is part and parcel of assessing your purchase. If you are going to have the car professionally restored, you may want to follow the rule of thumb established by one expert. According to Dr. Ralph Goldman, in a lecture about restoration at Marquette University, in Milwaukee, "Estimate the number of hours the job will take and what you expect to spend getting parts. Take this figure and double it. Now double it again. You then wind up with a good *approximation* of what the work will cost, but only if you plan to have the car finished within the next five years. If the job is going to take longer than that, expect to pay even more due to the ever-rising cost of restoration."

An at-home restoration will run you less in dollars, of course, but will take more in terms of time. Many old-timers who restored their own cars years ago will brag that "the labor was free." In today's more sophisticated world, I think we all feel that our own, personal time definitely has a dollar value. You probably have a very good idea of what your time is worth. It's probably not as high as the $20 to $30 per hour the professional restorer will demand. If it takes you three times as long to get the same work done, the bottom line will work out the same. The general concensus is that a mechanically minded

amateur can handle the same restoration for about one-half the cost (with all the various factors totaled in). This means that a full, ground-up restoration is going to consume from $12,500 to $25,000 worth of your time, energy, and money. This is based on the half the cost of the average professional job in 1983—$25,000 to $50,000. The higher prices would be for classics, with other types of cars moving down scale accordingly.

Another part of assessment that is frequently overlooked is the cost of tools and equipment. The novice who plans his first restoration might approach the job with a tool box full of screw drivers, pliers, and wrenches expecting to turn his beat-up old ragtop into a prize-winning convertible. Chances are that he won't get very far. Restoration work entails many heavy-duty operations that require far more than hand tools. A hydraulic press (Fig. 6-3) might be required to remove axle

Fig. 6-3. A hydraulic press is a good investment if you plan to restore several cars. There are numerous press-fit parts in the automobile's drivetrain and running gear. (Courtesy Johnson Engineering Co.)

bearings, engine components, drive-train parts, and to handle transmission repairs. Other large equipment that might come in handy would include an engine-removal hoist and engine stand (Fig. 6-4).

The prices for such equipment run into the hundreds of dollars and must be considered part of your hobby overhead (the same as renting a garage and heating your own working space). If you plan to restore only one car, buying such equipment might be foolish. You can probably locate a business that rents such devices and keep your costs down. If you will be restoring a number of cars, it's wise to buy. Today there are many tool suppliers servicing the hobby market at swap meets and you'll find attractive prices on tools.

How about the question of working space? This has to enter into the overall assessment. A small, one-car garage is not the place to begin restoring a car. Take it from my experience. If you disassemble a car in a small garage, you're going to have problems getting yourself inside to do the work.

According to James Hovarth, a professional restorer who teaches automotive restoration classes at McPherson College, most jobs require a minimum of a two-car area, and a three-car area is probably more of the average need. You need the first space to store the car, the second to store the parts, and the third to share between yourself and the tools you'll be using. Individual cases will vary. If you rent the heavy equipment and keep the car as a rolling chassis, you'll probably be able to work in the driveway. A large one-car area might do but the comfort factor will be low. On the other hand, a more total restoration (Fig. 6-5) is going to take much more room.

The important thing is to know where you're going before you get there. If you are going the rolling chassis route, plan every step of the job accordingly. If it decides to rain, your schedule will get out of wack, but at least you can roll the car back inside and wait for the sun to come out. The same won't be true if you strip a car completely to the chassis. There's no way to move it until the job is completely done. Likewise, if you take a car completely apart in a too-small garage, you might box yourself into a corner. There will be no place to store the parts and no room to work. That means the job won't get done.

The assessment of the vehicle's condition does not stop when you begin disassembly either. As you start taking body parts off, you might find certain weaknesses that will need either temporary attention or immediate, on-the-spot repairs. When the doors are removed, you might discover a weak floor pan that will threaten the integrity of the vehicle and which, if left unattended, might cause the body to actually cave in.

You can temporarily weld-in support braces (Fig. 6-6) to support the structure of the body until a replacement floor pan is purchased or hand formed. The braces can later be removed when integrity is restored. Still, the

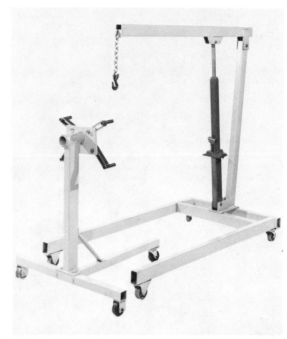

Fig. 6-4. An engine hoist can be rented or purchased outright. Specialized suppliers in the old-car hobby sell such equipment at fair prices. (Courtesy Johnson Engineering Co.)

extra time and materials needed for these stop-gap measures are going to add to total restoration costs.

Disassembly of the engine is likely to turn up other undetected problems requiring repair. This can include such things as a blown head gasket, cracked cylinder heads and engine castings, worn pistons, and hundreds of other hidden ills. There are tests that you can make to spot such weaknesses in operable vehicles such as compression gauge tests, cylinder leak-down tests, and vacuum gauge tests. These tests are covered in most general repair manuals or in the instructions packed in with the test equipment. Nevertheless, many old cars can't be pretested because they aren't running when purchased.

A final assessment, prior to beginning restoration, is the study of parts availability and price. You will be wise to start keeping a restoration logbook and a section of it should be devoted to parts. Make a list of the items that you are going to need to get the job done. The list should have a minimum of three columns:

☐ one for listing parts needed.
☐ the second for listing possible suppliers
☐ the third for keeping an estimate of costs.

If at all possible, buy every part you feel you need before beginning the actual work. This will save you

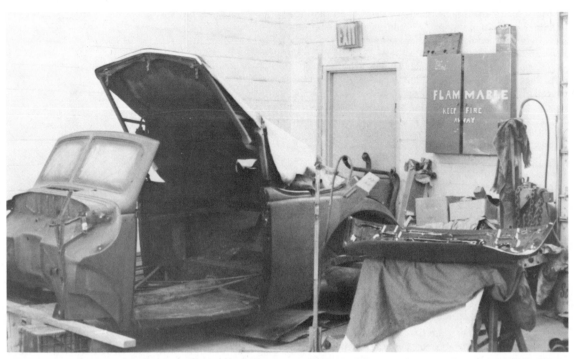

Fig. 6-5. A total, body-off restoration can't be accomplished in a one-car garage. Don't disassemble a car like this in too small a working area. It will hinder your progress and discourage you.

Fig. 6-6. Disassembly is the first step in a major restoration. As the parts come off label them. You might find additional flaws not seen when the car was assembled. Bracing was required to support the body panels on this 1940 Ford ragtop, due to a rusty floor pan. (Courtesy Michael A. Carbonella)

money in the long run and prevent midstream delays. Parts prices tend to jump every couple of months. Having the parts on hand will also keep your momentum going. You won't have to stop restoration to wait for parts shipments.

Don't feel that every part has to be hunted down at an old-car flea market. I know people who have stopped restorations in the middle of the winter to wait until the summertime swap meets begin. Many parts are available for old cars right at auto supply stores in your own town, and others can be found in unusual places such as hardware stores, plumbing supply shops, and upholstery shops.

You have to think about the way that cars were built to understand why many parts—especially mechanical components—are still readily available today. Engineers do not design a car and then ask parts manufacturers to make parts especially for them—at least not in the majority of cases. The parts are usually made to SAE standards and cataloged. Then the engineers use such catalogs to specify the best parts for a particular application. It is true that new standard parts are added to SAE catalogs each year, but few are dropped. The tricky thing is that the applications will frequently change. Your job, as a restorer, becomes finding the parts used in modern applications that were used in different ones years ago. Parts will be packaged differently, but the design won't change.

A good example of this can be found in the rubber cups and pistons in a brake cylinder rebuilding kit. If you visit an auto supply house and ask for a 1938 Oldsmobile brake repair kit, they will probably tell you it's not available today. The modern parts listings won't carry this application. If you look in the Bendix catalogs, you will find these parts listed by their size and design—rather than modern application. And you are likely to find that one modern car uses the same size rubber cups as a '38 Olds and another uses the same size pistons. So you'll have to buy one kit to get the rubber cups and another to get the pistons. The main thing is that you will have the parts you need.

According to Jim Hovarth, whose own restoration work (at Customs by Beaver, a shop in Sturtevant, Wisconsin) is concerned primarily with classic cars made in the 1930s, "I can usually find almost every mechanical part that I need through local auto parts suppliers." Hunting for parts in this manner can be greatly simplified if you become expert in the use of *Hollander Interchange Manuals* (Hollander Publishing Co., P.O. Box 9405, Minneapolis, MN 55440). In addition, many car club newsletters print firsthand experiences that members have when discovering parts interchangeability.

Ball bearings, gaskets, thermostats, brake parts, rubber components, bearings, pistons and rings, universal joints, seals, valves, fastenings, and miscellaneous small hardware are all good examples of parts that have thousands of different applications from the early 1930s right through the current year. In fact, there are several companies that now publish specialized catalogs just for old car restorers. It's getting easier—not harder—to find parts for old cars.

ENGINE REBUILDING

Engine rebuilding is probably one of the primary concerns of most beginning restorers. On one hand, this is a simple job compared to other operations involving body work, painting, interior restoration, and running gear. On the other hand, the problems that will be uncovered inside the engines of older cars can stop the average hobbyist in his tracks. A cracked cylinder block, for example, is something that professional mechanics will not even attempt to fix. It has to be understood that the repair of and old car sometimes requires work that goes beyond accepted practices of the modern auto-service industry. Today, the emphasis is generally placed on throwing away the old parts and replacing them with new ones in order to accomplish a fix. In a restoration, the job becomes one of saving the old parts, rebuilding them, and making them useful again. This is the big difference between fixing up a car and restoring it!

In this book, I do not cover automotive systems basics in great detail because that is the simple part of rebuilding a motor. If you look at the shop manual for a 1953 car and a 1983 car, there's not really a great deal of difference in how to rebuild the motor. Most of the step-by-step procedures will be exactly the same, except for final adjustments and settings. A piston is still a piston, valves are still valves, and the crankshaft still does the same thing it always did. There are plenty of very good how-to-do-it manuals that will outline the way to disassemble a motor, replace the parts, and put it back together again. Before even starting to work on your car, you *must* obtain such a book or, better yet, the manufacturer's shop or service manual for that particular vehicle. You can purchase such a book for your own car at old-car flea markets. It will cost you from $15 to $50 (a bit more for classics) and be well worth the price.

What this book provides is a very quick run-through of the basics, a great many special restoration tips, and solid advice on how to tackle those seemingly impossible jobs such as having a cracked cylinder block repaired. I think that these are the things that restorers want to read instead of a rehash of basics.

Carburetion

A wide variation in carburetor designs will be found among collector cars. Certainly, the one-barrel updraft type on a brass era touring car is going to look and operate differently than a four-barrel downdraft type on a 1960s high-performance ragtop. Yet, there are general principles that apply to all carburetors.

The job of this device is to combine air and fuel, outside the cylinder, in a combustible mixture. Theoretically, the perfect mix is 14.7 parts air for each part gasoline (or thereabouts). Anything from a 7:1 (rich) mixture to an 18:1 (lean) mixture will generally support some degree of combustion. Within these limits the car will run. Most old cars built before antipollution devices were mandatory are set up to run on the rich side.

Carburetors have mixture adjusting screws. They control small needle valves. Carburetors also have a screw adjustment to regulate idle speed because the carburetor is connected to the throttle of the car. A float is built into the carburetor. It is a hollow metal or plastic part that "senses" the level of fuel in the carburetor *bowl* (a fuel storage area). This level is regulated, by the float, through its connection with a valve that lets fuel in.

The main carburetion enemies that old car restorers face are dirt, corrosion, and the effects of old age. A piece of grime in the needle valve can keep it from seating properly (thus upsetting the proper mixture). A rusty throttle linkage can hinder correct speed regulation. Aging can ruin cork gaskets, leather plungers, or result in wear that puts a hole in the float.

A car that runs unevenly or stumbles on acceleration usually has fuel-system or carburetor problems. Restoration entails disassembling the carburetor and cleaning it thoroughly with special chemical cleaners made for this purpose. These solutions remove gummy gasoline residues as well as foreign matter. Linkage lubrication—with silicone or graphite—usually takes care of binding caused by rust. New gaskets, needle valves, and other parts are sold in carburetor repair kits.

These rebuilding kits are available for most old cars. Here again, applications will have to be investigated carefully. I once needed a rebuilding kit for a 1953 Pontiac carburetor and was told it was no longer available. Later I found that the same model carburetor was used on late-model American Motors cars and Jeeps, but with the linkage reversed to the other side of the carb body. When the linkage was redesigned, the number of the kit was changed and the old applications were no longer listed. Nevertheless, all of the parts were still the same, and they fit the 1953 Pontiac carburetor perfectly.

Carburetor repair kits also include special measuring tools and gauges that are used for adjusting parts to their proper positions so that relationships between the parts will be in accordance with factory specifications. Restorer Jim Hovarth recommends saving all of these gauges because they might also be useful in setting other model carburetors. "I never throw those gauges out," says Jim.

Fine adjustments for proper carburetion are outlined in all shop manuals and repair guides. Sometimes the instructions seem very complicated. Nevertheless, even roughly accurate settings will usually get the engine running. Once this is achieved, final adjustments can be made "by ear." The general procedure is to set the idle speed to factory specifications with a tachometer. Then back-off mixture adjustment(s) until the engine starts to "lope" (run unevenly). Next, move the mixture screw back inward (clockwise) until the engine starts to stall. At all times, turn the screw slowly, while counting the number of turns between the two extremes. Move a quarter-turn at a time. The halfway point is what you want. Once it is reached, re-adjust the idle speed to factory settings if necessary. See Fig. 6-7.

Multibarrel carburetors have a mixture setting for each barrel, but the basic procedure doesn't change. You have to reach a balance point; your ears will tell you when the engine sounds the best.

This is a simple discussion of carburetion, but the disassembly, cleaning-rebuild-kit-lubrication-basic-adjusting procedures will serve 90 percent of all difficulties restorers face in this area. TAB book No. 814, *Step-By-Step Guide: Carburetor Tuneup and Overhaul*, offers a more detailed look at the topic in case the preceeding guidelines don't work.

Specialists who deal exclusively with the supply or repair of obsolete carburetors include Jim Alexandro, P.O. Box 144, Maspeth, N.Y. 11378, and Jon Hardgrove (The Carburetor Shop), Rt 1, Box 230-T, Eldon, MO 65026. The latter source stocks over 6000 carburetors for cars, trucks, and tractors from 1900–1983.

Gaskets and Seals

Gaskets and seals in the engine, chassis, exhaust system, or body of an old car often present difficulty for restorers (Fig. 6-8). Aging and general deterioration can ruin parts that are made out of perishable materials like cork, rubber and leather—as well as soft metals. Luckily, it's fairly simple to find many replacement parts of this type. Most are made to SAE specifications that have been in use for years.

The hardest part of these repairs will be disassembly required to reach the area of damage. It sometimes takes hours of take-apart work to replace a damaged seal worth less than fifty cents. You will often have to deal with rusty bolts and use plenty of penetrating oil. Heat might help, too, but be extremely careful using a torch around gas tanks, fuel pumps, carburetors, and oil soaked parts.

Cork gaskets are easiest to deal with and many are readily available from commercial supply houses. You can also buy sheets of cork and fashion your own gaskets by cutting them out with a tool called an arch punch.

You will not usually be able to make compound gaskets such as cylinder head gaskets. They are actually

Fig. 6-7. Fast-idle cam adjustments and other carburetor settings are not usually difficult to make. A simple procedure will usually get the car running and allow making final adjustments "by ear."

sandwiches of copper and cork. If your car is a prewar model, the major gasket manufacturers like McCord or Fel-Pro might have discontinued the part. Don't assume this is true. These companies have special antique-auto catalogs that will tell you for sure. Assuming your gasket is not available, the next step is to check with the hobby suppliers who deal exclusively with gaskets. Examples are Head Gasket Co., 164 S. Park, San Francisco, CA 94107; Gerald Letteri, 132 Old Main St., Rocky Hill, CT 06067, or Andrew Young, Eagle Rock Ave., Roseland, NJ 07068.

Rubber gaskets and other parts can also be made. Some are simple, flat gaskets that you can cut out of rubber sheets yourself. Others such as windshield channel gaskets are molded into more complicated shapes. There are companies that reproduce thousands of rubber parts for old cars. Try Brentwood Co., P.O. Box 761, Brentwood, TN 37027; Metro Molded Parts, 9251 Foley, Minneapolis, MN 55433; Lynn H. Steele, Rt 1, Denver, NC 28037; or Wefco Mfg., 1655 Euclid, Santa Monica, CA 90404.

Seals are generally available today from the same companies that make them for new cars. That means you'll find most of what you need at your local auto parts store. Again, modern applications might be hard to cross-reference with those for old-time cars. Take your old seal along as a sample for the counterman to match. There will be few cases where a match is not possible.

ENGINE VALVE-TRAIN REPAIRS

As with carburetor fix-ups, general engine repairs are covered, in step-by-step manner, in any auto repair manual. There are no special rules for convertibles. A detailed discussion falls beyond the scope of this book. For information beyond just the basics refer to TAB book No. 2062, *How To Make Your Old Car Run Like New.*

Repairs to the valve train are referred to as top engine jobs by restorers. The valves are under the cylinder head in flathead motors, in the cylinder head in overhead valve engines, and half-and-half in so-called F-

Fig. 6-8. Intake manifold sleeve gaskets are one on many parts in an auto engine that might require replacement. Reaching the problem area takes lots of work, but parts are usually inexpensive and available.

head powerplants. The valves work as doors to the hollow cylinder chamber (the place in which combustion takes place). Intake valves allow the fuel air mixture to enter the chamber. Exhaust valves allow burnt gases to escape the chamber—after combustion. Both kinds of valves seal the chamber tightly, during the engine's combustion stroke and power stroke. A leak-proof seal is essential.

Leaky valves are caused by dirt or wear or, sometimes, by misadjustment. Moderate wear can be compensated for by re-grinding the original valves to a smooth, leak-proof finish. Valves that are worn excessively or have been re-ground many times will have to be replaced. The same is true of other worn (or broken) valve-train parts such as springs, valve guides, etc.

Top-end engine repairs are usually within the abilities of shade-tree restorers who are equipped with the necessary tools. This includes a special clamping device that can compress the heavy valve springs, allowing the valves to be removed. Once the valves are out of the engine block or cylinder head (Fig. 6-9), the guides and valve seats must be restored to a smooth finish. The valves themselves must also be re-ground or replaced. Most valves for old cars are readily available and hundreds of interchanges are possible. For example, a

friend of mine restored a 1923 Durant and discovered the valves were of the same size and design as those used in 1956 Pontiac V-8s. The Pontiac valves were easy to get.

It is possible to re-surface valves, valve guides, and valve seats by hand. The valves can be re-ground using a hand tool that works much like an egg beater. The seats and guides are smoothed with a coarse compound. Tightness of the seal between the seats and valves is then checked with a powder like substance called Prussian Blue. The parts are covered with Prussian Blue and the valve is placed into the seat and rotated. The substance will disappear if the surfaces mate correctly, but will cling to low spots worn into either surface. This is not the best way to attempt a valve job, but it might be the only way for the home restorer to work on a car of L-head (valve-in-block) design. Years ago, automotive machine shops would travel to your garage to grind the valves and seats, but today this is rarely the case. Popular acceptance of overhead valve engines led to discontinuance of such service. If it were still available, I would hate to think what the cost would be.

If the valves and seats on your L-head/F-head motor can't be done by this method, the alternative is to get either the entire car—or the engine—to the machine shop

Fig. 6-9. Once the valves are out of the engine, the valve guides and valve seats must be resurfaced, usually by a professional machine shop. A powdery substance called Prussian Blue is applied to the valve. The valve is then set into the seat and rotated. Low spots in seat will cause the blue powder to cling.

or to purchase the necessary re-grinding equipment yourself.

On cars with overhead valve engines, life gets a little simpler. The cylinder heads can be detached from the motor and taken to a machine shop where the re-grinding equipment is available. In this case, the shop disassembles the valve train and does all the work. Prices range from $50 to $100 per head in most places. The finished results will surpass the do-it-yourself method and result in a smooth-running car.

Final valve adjustments should be made in accordance to a shop manual or repair guide covering your engine. Such books are available for cars dating back to the 1930s in reprint form. For older cars, you'll have to search out old books at flea markets.

Bottom-End Repairs

Bottom-end engine repairs can be accomplished by most old car hobbyists, but in this case machine work cannot be done at home unless special (and expensive) equipment is available. The majority of restorers take their car into a professional shop to have the machining done.

The parts that will be dealt with most commonly here include the connecting rods, the con-rod bearings, the crankshaft, and the pistons and rings. These are the items that work together to move the piston into the cylinder chamber in order to compress the fuel air mixture. When the compressed mixture explodes, the resultant forces are transferred into a rotary motion that spins the crankshaft. This spinning moves through the transmission and driveshaft to the rear wheels (in conventional, rear-wheel-drive models).

The major problem with these parts is excessive wear or breakage caused by improper lubrication or pushing the engine beyond its design limits. Such conditions will lead to excessive oil consumption in the majority of cases. Broken parts might even stop the engine from running or—worse yet—send a connecting rod flying loose with force great enough to push it through the cast-iron walls of the block.

Worn connecting rod bearings (Fig. 6-10) show up in many old cars. These bearings have an upper and lower

Fig. 6-10. Bearing shells fit into the "big end" of the connecting rods: one on top of the crankshaft journal, the other on the bottom. Connecting rod cap holds them in place. This bearing shows wear—appearing as a score line running along the center of circumference on the inside—and will have to be replaced.

configuration. They fit around the crankshaft, inside the lower end of the connecting rod. After many thousands of miles of normal use, con-rod bearings will need replacement. The same problem can occur much earlier when lubrication problems exist. Connecting rod bearings for old cars are not extremely hard to find. Your shop manual will explain how to use a material called Plasti-Gauge to determine what size bearings you need. They come in standard and oversized variations. If even the oversized types will not properly "shim" the connecting rod around the crank shaft, the crank will have to be built up through a process known as rebabbiting. This is a special job that can't be done at home.

To determine if rebabbiting is necessary, you can take measurements of crankshaft diameter with a micrometer (Fig. 6-11). This will tell you if there's enough metal left on the crank to use a standard or available oversized bearing. The crankshaft journals must also be checked for 100 percent smoothness and for possible out-of-round conditions. If such problems exist, it will be a waste of time and money to install new bearing shells because they will quickly wear again. If such conditions exist with your crankshaft, it will have to be removed and machined.

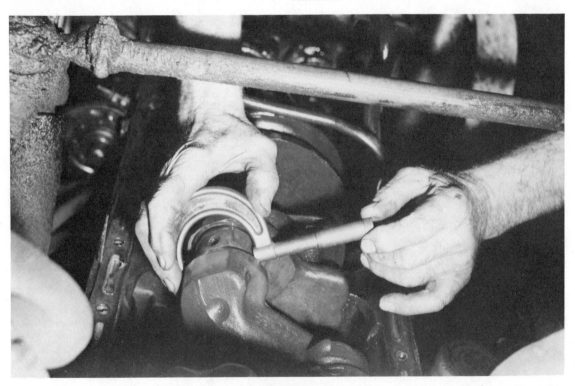

Fig. 6-11. Check the crankshaft journals for smooth finish. To determine if re-babbiting (building up of metal) is necessary, a micrometer is used. Check measurements against shop-manual or repair-guide specifications. Wear within serviceable limits is repaired through use of over sized bearings.

Pistons must also be checked for out-of-roundness (Fig. 6-12) and a micrometer is used again. Egg-shaped pistons, or those that exhibit excessive wear, must always be replaced. The same is true of a broken piston. There are several old-car parts suppliers that remanufacture obsolete pistons. Getting these parts should be no problem.

Pistons are removed from the engine through the bottom of the cylinder bore. This requires removal of the oil pan, the connecting rod cap, the con-rod bearings, and the connecting rod itself. In Figs. 6-12 and 6-14, you can see how the connecting rod fits into the piston at its hollow bottom. A pin runs horizontally through the piston to holding the two components together. It is kept in place by lock rings countersunk into the hole in the side. Removal of the piston and con rod (as a unit) must be done from under the block because the piston usually creates a ridge at the top of the bore that prevents removal from above.

Part of the job of piston replacement is reconditioning of the cylinder bore, including cutting of this ridge from the top. The bore must be checked for out-of-round condition (Fig. 6-13) with an instrument called a dial gauge. This device can usually be rented, but is a good tool to own if you plan several restorations. There are many uses for the dial gauge other than checking for egg-shaped cylinder bores. Reconditioning of cylinders with minimal wear can be done with a boring tool. This is normally accomplished at the machine shop or repair facility.

A bored-out cylinder will increase the displacement of an engine and give extra horsepower. There are limits to how large a cylinder can be bored out before the walls get too thin or a water jacket in the block is hit. A cylinder bored within serviceable limits will require oversized (larger-diameter) pistons and/or rings. The machine shop should know the maximum overbore limits for your motor.

In repairing modern cars, a cylinder that cannot be made round again within the limits of overbore will generally mean that the block must be replaced. There are some exceptions to this with aluminum-block motors (for example, early Chevy Vega engines) that can have repair sleeves installed. With antique cars, it's not uncommon to hear that an engine has been resleeved. It's not easy to find replacement blocks for a Jewett, Durant, or other obsolete brand of car. This kind of work will almost always have to be farmed out unless you happen to be a machinist.

Pistons are equipped with hardened-steel piston rings that serve to make a tight seal against the cylinder wall and keep lubricating oil from entering the combustion chamber above the piston. When an engine is said to be burning oil it indicates these rings are worn to the point where oil gets by them. The rings must then be

Fig. 6-12. Pistons should be checked with a large micrometer for size and out-of-roundness. Pistons that are broken, egg-shaped, or excessively worn must be replaced. (Courtesy *Old Cars Weekly*)

replaced. Some pistons have two rings; other pistons (Fig. 6-14) have three. Parts availability here is very good. You should have little difficulty locating rings for your old car.

Specific instructions on how to replace piston rings, pistons, connecting rods, and bearings in your engine will be outlined in the shop manual or general repair guides. The following list gives some of the sources of parts and services that will help you with your restoration of a vintage model.

Engine Parts

Egge Machine Co., 8403 Allport Ave., Santa Fe Springs, CA 90670; Jahns Quality Pistons, P.O. Box 31369, Los Angeles, CA 90031; Bobco, P.O. Box 212, Urbana, OH 43078; Antique Auto Parts, 449 W Main, Waterbury, CT 06702; Auto Parts & Services, 1201-09 4th St., Port Huron, MI 48060; Parts of the Past, P.O. Box 602, Waukesha, WI 53187; Vintage Parts House, 93 Whippany Rd., Morristown, NJ 07960.

Fig. 6-13. The condition of the cylinder bores is checked with an instrument called a dial gauge. Bores showing minimal wear or slight out-of-roundness can be enlarged with a boring bar at the machine shop and fitted with over sized pistons and rings. This will give more horsepower as cylinder displacement measurements will increase.

Fig. 6-14. The connecting rod fits into the bottom of the piston and is held in place by snap-rings at the side. Grooves at the top of the piston hold the piston rings that seal gases and oils in the motor.

Rebabbiting Service

Bob's Automotive Machine, 38 Maridon Lane, Commack, NY 11725; Knight Engineering, 743 Western Ave., Gloucester, MA 01930; Jim Ash, Route 1 Box 172, Ixonia, WI 53036; Terril Machine, Rt 2 Box 61, DeLeon, TX 76444.

Cracked Head or Block Repairs

The Engine Shop, 111 Hershfield, Pompton Lakes, NJ 07442; Reynold's 2632 East 13 Pl., Tulsa, OK 74104. Thul Engine & Equipment Co., P.O. Box 446, Plainfield, NJ 07060.

Exhaust System Parts

Jim Fortin, 95 Weston St., Brockton, MA 02401; Soloman's, 544 East Main, East Orwell, OH 44034.

Camshaft Regrinding

Jack Bunton, N11315 Anna J Drive, Spokane, WA 99218; Crane Cams, Inc., P.O. Box 160, Hallendale, FL 33009.

Crankshaft Regrinding

Rods and Babbitt Machine Works, 712 135th St., New York, NY 10454.

Note: Whenever writing to any hobby-related business, it's a sound policy to include a self-addressed, stamped envelope. Many of these services are part-time, small businesses that respond only to inquiries containing an SASE.

ELECTRICAL SYSTEM REPAIRS

Electrical system problems that the restorer will face fall into three main categories:

☐ Starting and generating system.

☐ Ignition system.

☐ Wiring harness including connections to lighting and accesories.

The fine points of the three systems would require much more room than we have here for explaining complete testing and repair procedures. These procedures do not vary greatly between old cars and modern types with conventional, breaker-point iginition systems. Therefore, almost any shop or repair manual can be referred to for step-by-step fix-ups. TAB book No. 748, *The Complete Auto Electric Handbook*, is an excellent source for this information.

As far as the starting and generating system, the malfunctioning of major components, such as the starter or generator, will usually call for the rebuilding or replacement of the failed part. With relatively late-model convertibles, it should be possible to locate new parts at your local auto supply shop or at the automotive flea markets. With older cars, the parts will usually have to be rebuilt. In nine-out-of-ten cases, the restorer will have this professionally done at shops that specialize. His main job will be removing the part and transporting it to the auto electric shop. With parts such as starter drives (Bendix), solenoids, and relays, new parts will have to be searched out. Sedmark Auto Electric Co., 5028 Creek Rd., Andover, OH 44003 is a firm that caters to electrical parts needs of antique, classic and special-interest car owners. If you can't find the parts you need locally, try them.

Ignition system rejuvenation generally falls into the tune-up category. The parts you will need include such things as new spark plugs, breaker points, rotors, and distributor parts. You should not have great problems locating the components that you'll need unless you're restoring a V-16 Cadillac or Duesenberg, etc. Even in these cases, specialized hobby suppliers will sometimes be able to help. The price of the parts is very high. For example, an ignition coil for a V-16 Cadillac is a rare part. According to Jim Hovarth, the majority of such cars are restored by a slight modification in which a newer, more readily available type of coil is installed *inside* the old housing. This gives an authentic look, without sacrificing dependable operation, but Hovarth notes that the old coil housings—even those that are completely shot—cost over $200 at flea markets!

Spark plugs will be the easiest type of part to locate. All of the major manufacturers (AC, Champion, Robert Bosch, etc.,) print catalogs designed for restorers. They list the modern spark-plug applications for hobby cars. When it comes to obtaining other kinds of ignition parts, there are numerous hobby vendors who sell them by mail order. They include Auto Parts & Service, 1201-09 Fourth St., Port Huron, MI 48060; David Ficken, Box 11, Babylon, NY 11702; Robert Futterman, 722 Carswell, Holly Hill, FL 32017; and Ronco Co., 463 Norristown Rd., Blue Bell, PA 19422.

With many old cars undergoing restoration, wiring problems will surface. Old age will fray the wiring on collector cars and cause a number of problems ranging from inoperable headlights and horns to malfunctioning instruments, electric windows, electric seats, and windshield wipers, etc. In any ground-up restoration, it is a good practice to plan on installing a brand new wiring harness. These harnesses are readily available for most collector interest models and can be installed by the home restorer. Major suppliers include: Egge Machine Company, 8403 Allport, Santa Fe Springs, CA 90670; Harnesses Unlimited, P.O. Box 435, Wanye, PA 19087; Narragansett Reproductions, Woodville Rd, Wood River Junction, RI 02894; The Wire King, P.O. Box 222, N. Olmstead, OH 44070; and Y 'N' Z Yesterdays Parts, 1615 W. Fern Dr., Redlands, CA 92373.

Note: A firm might be the exclusive supplier of

harnesses for specific models. When searching for the wiring you need, write (with an SASE) requesting their literature.

One last area of electrical restoration is the battery. Some old cars take batteries that are obsolete in design or voltage characteristics. Because you can't repair a worn-out battery, a new one will have to be found. If you plan on restoring the car authentically, the only sources of obsolete batteries will be specialized hobby suppliers, including: Keystone Battery, 35 Holton St., Winchester, MA 01890 or A & M Enterprises, 3448 Moon Ridge, Cincinnati, OH 45211.

Don't overlook the fact that some batteries obsoleted by the automotive industry (6-volt types for example) are still used in tractors, fork lifts, and other additional industrial applications.

Other than listing sources of hard-to-find parts, there is not much else to know about special tips for electrical work. Your shop manual or reprinted editions of older repair guides will completely cover the hands-on work and list all the final adjustments and settings necessary. Electrical restoration is a very basic—but important—part of fixing up old cars.

BRAKE REPAIRS

The specific jobs you'll have to tackle on older convertibles follow the basics that apply to almost every car. Convertibles built between 1927 and 1935 (later on Fords) might have mechanically activated brakes that use cables, toggles, and levers to do the same work that the hydraulic system does on a newer car. To fix the old mechanical braking systems, you will have to locate the original shop manual or a contemporary general repair guide. Such books, for these years, are not yet available in reprinted form. Nevertheless, books on the Ford braking systems are numerous and can be referred to for repairs on other makes if no other manual is found.

Finding brake parts can present difficulties. Parts for rebuilding hydraulic system components can be obtained by referring to the Bendix parts catalog to work out interchanges with similar modern parts. With brake system hardware such as brake drums, wheel cylinders, and master cylinders, getting the parts can be a major difficulty.

Until very recently, the flea market was the only way to go. Nowadays, however, you can at least have the wheel cylinders and master cylinders restored (Fig. 6-15) by a re-sleeving process in which stainless steel liners are imbedded in the old cylinder bore to restore it to original size (diameter). This will make the cylinders even better than new because the stainless steel will wear very little compared to the original cast-iron materials.

If you do a complete brake system tear-down during your restoration, be sure to use compressed air to completely clean-out the old system. Then replace the use

of conventional brake fluid with the new, space-age silicone brake fluids. Make sure this fluid is an approved DOT Grade 5 type (non-hydroscopic) that will not absorb moisture. Use of silicone brake fluid will keep your system from deteriorating later on.

A number of car hobby vendors handle brake system parts, or silicone brake fluids and do re-sleeving of cylinder bores.

Brake Parts

Jim Carpenter, 1102 Gambrell Rd., Greenwood, MO 64034; The Carriage House, 410 Darby, Havertown, PA 19083; Edwards Bros., Lake Hiawatha, NJ 07034; and A. Petrik, 10436 Crockett, Sun Valley, CA 91352.

Stainless Steel Rebuilding

White Post Restorations, White Post, VA 22663; (for Corvettes with disc brakes) Stainless Steel Brakes, 11470 Main Rd., Clarence, NY 14031; Vette Brakes, 3150 23rd Ave. N., St. Petersburg, FL 33713.

Silicone Brake Fluid

Ernie Toth, 8153 Cloveridge, Chagrin Falls, OH 44022; Street Specialty Products, 843 Bliem Rd., Pottstown, PA 19464.

Power Brake Rebuilding

Dale George, Co., 1350 W. Sheridan, Oklahoma City, OK 73106.

CHASSIS AND SUSPENSION RESTORATION

When it comes to restoring the chassis and suspension components, most restorers find that it's best to locate and install new parts themselves than to have a professional shop set caster, camber, and other wheel-alignment adjustments. Exact procedures on installing parts can be found in the shop manual or repair guide that applies to your model. The availability of parts will vary in direct relationship to the age and rarity of the car.

The manufacturers of high-quality, front-end parts generally stock the components for a long time; this can range up to 30 years for more popular models. With older and rarer cars, you will have to turn to the specialty suppliers. When I first got involved in restoring old cars, during the early 1970s, it was very hard to locate obsolete engine mounts, tie-rod ends, king pins, steering knuckles, etc. Lately it seems that the supply of such parts (Fig. 6-16) has increased. This is because several vendors have started to deal exclusively in this area.

This kind of specialization is of great benefit to the restorer. When the needed parts are widely scattered among hundreds of vendors, it takes a lot of tracking

Fig. 6-15. Worn bores in brake master cylinders and wheel cylinders can be restored to original size by the insertion of stainless steel insert liners. This operation is done by White Post Restorations in White Post, Virginia. Other companies service Corvette disc brakes the same way. After a complete brake system teardown, use DOT 5 silicone fluid.

down to get them. Some small dealers will even have the parts that you need, but not know enough about identifying them to make them easily available. When one vendor starts accumulating all parts of a certain type, the supply then becomes centralized, identifying parts becomes easier and more accurate, and you'll know exactly where to turn to for a certain item.

This is exactly what has happened in the case of chassis and front end components. If you require such parts, try contacting the following sources first: L & S Antique Auto Parts, 645 S. Crawford, Detroit, MI 48209; Bob Urbane, 6634 W. Bryn Mawr, Chicago, IL 60631; or Robert Midland, Box B, Hawley, PA 18428.

BODYWORK

When it comes to doing body repair work on a convertible, only the highest-quality processes and techniques should be employed. Remember, you are undertaking restoration of a machine that is already considered or will be considered a valuable collectible. They are not going to make cars like yours again! That means that the finished job should be able to meet show quality standards and withstand the test of time. Temporary fix ups with slap-on fiberglass body fillers should not even be considered for 90 percent of the jobs you'll face.

PAINT REMOVAL

Restoring the body of a collector car usually begins with stripping off all of the old paint. Spot repairs on small areas should be restricted to very minor damage such as parking lot dings. Even then it will be very difficult to exactly match old paint. You probably won't have a show car if you use spot repairs and the value of the vehicle will be reduced as well.

Mervin "Beaver" Colver is a nationally known restoration specialist who restores classic Duesenbergs, Lincolns, Packards and Cadillacs in his Sturtevant, Wisconsin shop: Customs by Beaver. He warns that paint stripping on collector cars should never be done with a sandblaster except where mechanical components are concerned.

For body work, stick to chemical strippers and use them with respect and care. Always wear a full-length shop coat, suitable gloves and protective head gear with a full face shield. The gloves should be long enough to extend well into the sleeves of the shop coat and a turtleneck shirt is also a good idea. Leave no areas of bare skin exposed to attack by spilled chemicals. Why not use a sandblaster? Beaver advises, "Blasting will warp body surfaces and also compact the pores in the metal in which the paint must pool to achieve good adherence." Colver

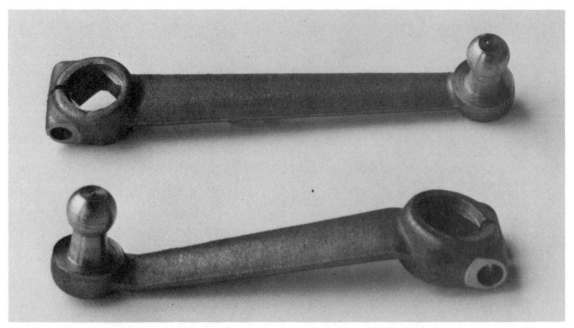

Fig 6-16. Front-end parts cannot be restored; they have to be replaced with new or reproduction parts that are sometimes hard to get. The newer your car the better the supply of such components.

prefers DuPont's No. 52-660S paint stripper for his work. Comparable products are also available from other automotive paint manufacturing companies such as Ditzler and Martin-Senour.

When the body of the car is completely stripped of old finish, it's likely you'll see any and all of the problems. This might include earlier bodywork that has to be redone. This is very typical in the case of prewar cars that might have had an amateur restoration many years ago. With models of the postwar era, unsophisticated fiberglass body fillers might have been applied for previous repairs before the cars became collectible.

Sometimes stripping will expose rusty spots that were hidden below a fresh coat of paint, perhaps indicating the car was "restored" rather quickly just to sell it. You might also find that what you noticed as minor corrosion actually extends much deeper than first assumed. Even areas that are just beginning to corrode will have to be attended to by cutting out the problem completely. If this is not done, the deterioration will be ongoing.

Paint removal on collector cars should never be attempted by the so-called dip-tank method where the entire body is immersed in a large vat filled with caustics. According to experts presenting a restoration seminar at Marquette University, the dip-tank methods are now being used by professional sports-racing car builders to lighten the weight of their racing cars. It

seems these processes actually remove some degree of body metal when the car is immersed in the caustic solution. This might not be crucial with later-model ragtops, but with prewar or early postwar models, a great potential for problems exists. In addition, the very porous type of metal used in these cars can retain some of the chemical that will later ruin a restoration.

A rather new paint stripping technique is Oki-Blast. It is a patented, dry-strip process that uses special minerals (in place of regular silicone blasting sand) to take off paint. The minerals are applied with fine-tuned pressure equipment that, the company claims, can be adjusted to remove the blue printing on a cigarette without damaging the rolling paper. Write Oki-Blast, 501 South 14th St., Richmond, VA 23224 for details and literature if it sounds interesting.

DENTS AND DINGS

With paint removed from the car, you'll first notice the dents and dings that need immediate attention. To repair such problems, your main task is to reform the metal panels back to nearly original contours. The work should always begin by removing all traces of incorrect repairs made earlier. This means cutting out amateur patches and chiseling away any bondo. Then you will be smart to invest some money—as much as your hobby budget will stand—in a set of high-quality metalworking tools and essential supplies. This includes a selection of different files and a hacksaw with carbide blades (Figure 6-17).

Two carbide blades, mounted with the teeth facing in opposite directions, will ease rough cutting work and prevent the blades from snagging and breaking. Single blades are always used for finer work. A complete list of basic tools and supplies might include the following.

Basic Equipment and Tools

☐ Low- and high-crown bumping spoons; pry spoon; offset spoon and rough service spoon.
☐ Set of pry rods.
☐ Slide hammer with screw tip (dent-puller).
☐ Caulking iron tools.
☐ Bumping hammer and dolly blocks.
☐ Wooden file holder; rasp holder, and sandpaper block or holder.
☐ Heavy-duty electric disc sander.
☐ Wire brush tool (or drill attachment).
☐ Propane torch or oxyacetylene welding equipment.
☐ Safety goggles and insulated gloves.

Highly Recommended Optional Equipment

☐ Nibbling tool.
☐ Bead roller.
☐ Shrinking and expanding tool.
☐ Panel flangers.
☐ Stainless steel restoration kit.

Basic Supplies

☐ Refined tallow.
☐ Tinning fluid.
☐ Solder flux.
☐ Lead sticks.
☐ Solder Paddles.

The basic theory of dent and ding removal is that the impact (collision) that causes body damage displaces the metal and this results in dents, bends, stretching and, sometimes, tears or broken welds. The character of the damage is caused by the direction and the force of the impact. Theoretically, repair can be accomplished by inducing like forces, of equal strength in the *reverse* direction. In real life, the direction/force of the original impact can only be approximated. The forces of a car hitting a car or a door swinging into a front fender will not be exactly duplicated by bodyworking tools. Nevertheless, the closer the approximation the more completely the damage will be undone. Using his special tools, a good body man can pull, re-bend, or shrink the panel back to a form very close to its original shape. This can then be refined by use of fillers.

The tools are used to create a close-to-equal-and-opposite force. For example, employing a hammer-and-dolly procedure or dent puller re-shapes the dent or bends. Heating shrinks the metal (without warping it, if applied carefully). These tools will not repair tears or broken welds, but will bring the original seams back into a position where they can be solder filled or re-welded.

Such sheet-metal repairs are not specialized for

Fig. 6-17. A good selection of files and a hacksaw with carbide blades are some of the tools you'll need for starting body work.

convertible restorations so step-by-step methods of using the tools lays beyond our primary subject. Two fine books available to hobbyists come to mind for further reference. They are: TAB book No. 949, *Do-It-Yourself Auto Body Repair & Painting* by Charles Self, and *Automobile Sheetmetal Repair*, 2nd edition, by Robert L. Sargent (Cilton Book Co., Radnor, PA)

The Eastwood Company has gone as far as sending representatives to Europe to find tools—used by craftsman there—that long ago went out of use in America. I mention this because years ago, when I first became involved in the hobby, special body tools and supplies for doing metal-filling were nearly impossible to buy. Through the efforts of these firms, the hobbyist now has the means to accomplish first-class sheet-metal repairs in his home garage. Among companies that can be of help to you in this regard are The Eastwood Co., 15 Waterloo Ave, Box 524-T, Berwyn, PA 19312; Lou's Automotive, 189 Union Ave., Paterson, NJ 07502; William Lowbuck Tools, Inc., 417 S. California Ave., Narco, CA 91760; Hoosier Distibuting, 3009 W. Sample St., South Bend, IN 46619.

SURFACING AND RUST REPAIR

After the panel-straightening problems on your convertible have been dealt with, you will face additional tasks having to do with resurfacing the body prior to painting. By resurfacing, I mean fixing those tears and broken welds as well as repairing damage caused by rust, scale, and corrosion.

In resurfacing metal, the aim is to finish the job you started when the damaged panels were returned to near-original form. This includes installing sheet-metal patches (the right way) and filling seams, breaks, tears and depressions with quality body fillers (preferably lead solder types). There is much debate on the topic of resin fillers (plastic or fiberglass) versus the lead solder type. Beaver Colver reports that the modern plastic fillers are very good for surface repairs when used correctly. They should not, however, be used to repair stress points such as joints and seams where the body undergoes some degree of normal flexing. Plastic fillers applied here will crack when the body moves. The lead fillers, on the other hand, will "give" a little during flexations—enough to prevent cracking.

Rust and corrosion is caused by condensation and moisture collecting in seams where several body panels are welded together. They are usually inner panels, normally hidden from view, but the corrosion will ultimately extend to outer surfaces if left unchecked. See Fig. 6-18. The easiest way to effect a repair is to purchase reproduction panels (Fig. 6-19) from specialized hobby vendors. These are usually limited in availability to more

popular types of cars (although the supply is constantly growing). If you cannot find reproduction panels for your model, or if the specific panel you require hasn't been reproduced, the only course of action is to fashion your own sheet-metal patch (Fig. 6-20).

Beaver Colver recommends using relatively soft metal for patches. It's not necessary—in the case of prewar models—to find a metal that has exactly the same poracity as the original. Actually it might be almost impossible due to improvements in metallurgy. Nevertheless, the patch should be of the same gauge as the body metal.

Before applying the patch, cut out all of the affected areas no matter how slight the corrosion. Metal that is just beginning to corrode will continue to deteriorate, if it is not repaired. The new metal can be rough cut with shears or tin-snips (Fig. 6-20) to a size slightly larger than the damaged region. Next, scribe alignment marks on both the original panel and the patch (Fig. 6-21) and make a final trim, if necessary.

Attaching the metal should be done with a butt-welding technique (Fig. 6-22)—never braze the parts together or try spot welding. Spot welds allow condensation to form; later this causes the lead filler to bubble. Gas (acetelyne) welding equipment is preferred to the electric (arc) type for better control of heat. Hammer welding techniques should be used to keep the metal from buckling due to excessive heat application. Always wear safety goggles when you're welding.

When lead solder is used for filling, the basic process begins with cleaning the metal by mechanical means (usually wire brushing). Next the metal is coated with melted solder. This is called tinning and includes application of the flux (normally a liquid in auto body work) that does the job of chemical cleaning. This is put on with a paint brush or rag (Fig. 6-23) after warming the surface.

More heat is applied until the surface is hot enough to melt the bar of solder when it is touched to the metal (Fig. 6-24). Wipe the melted solder with a rag. A solder fill is thus built up to even gaps left by seams and attachment points. Your torch can be used to slightly reflow the filler (Fig. 6-25) for final forming. Filing and shaping (Fig. 6-26) is done with hand tools and electric grinders. Final finishing is to a smooth surface and usually accomplished through use of fine-grit sandpaper. If electric sanding is used, take great care to avoid overbite. Solder is quite soft and won't withstand heavy-duty sanding with a high-speed tool.

I highly recommend the use of lead body filler on 90 percent of all collector-car bodywork. The first car I restored was my wife's 1954 Chevrolet 210 sedan. It's not a very valuable car (thank goodness!), but it has a lot of nostalgia appeal to us. We decided to go with plastic body fillers for a simple and logical reason. A man who bumped into our car was the owner of a body shop that

Fig. 6-18. Corrosion usually starts on inner panels where two pieces of metal are welded or bolted together. Rust will eventually be extended to the outer surface of the body. The rusted panels must be completely cut out even if corrosion is only very minor.

repaired only fiberglass-bodied Corvettes. He offered to fix the car and we agreed to let him even though fiberglass was to be used. It wasn't a very good move. Less than 10 years later, the car has to be redone, and it's going to cost a bunch more than the Chevy is worth to anyone but us. So much for major repairs with resin fillers!

On the other hand, it is perfectly acceptable to use light applications of high-quality plastic fillers *over* lead-repaired panels, prior to final finishing (paint). With the lead solder doing the structural repair, the smooth-finish properties of the plastic can enhance the final repair. The light coat of resin filler should be surfaced using a rasp (Fig. 6-27) for rough work and fine-grit sandpaper (mounted to a wooden block or holding device) for final smoothing. A very light coat like this will not usually crack if the body flexes a bit.

To become expert at sheet-metal repairs is going to take a little more reading and a lot more hands-on experience than I have presented here. It is usually wise to practice dent and ding repairs, welding, paint stripping, patching, and final resurfacing techniques on pieces of scrap metal or an old, junked car. You might

even want to sign up for evening adult classes at a local high school to get the basics down completely before restoration commences. The bodywork must be nearly perfect before applying paint.

PAINT BASICS

One of the most exciting steps in the restoration of your convertible will be painting the car. This isn't the final stage of the job, but it does mark the point where the fruits of your efforts start to show. At this stage, you have already stripped the body to bare metal and repaired impact damage and corrosion. Metal patches have been welded into place with seams and depressions in the sheet metal brought to a smooth, flush surface.

The first thing you must do, prior to applying the paint, is to remove as much bright metal trim and bolt-on accessories as possible. Depending upon the extent to which the car was disassembled, you will be painting the major part of the body as a single unit or adding paint to different components separately.

With a prewar car, it is best to remove the hood,

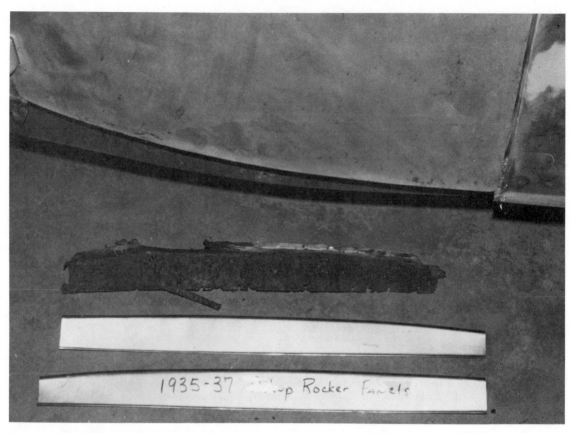

Fig. 6-19. After the corroded panel is cut out it must be replaced. Reproduction panels, if available for your model, are the best and easiest way to go. These rocker panels fit 1935–1937 Fords.

Fig. 6-20. If reproduction panels are not available for your model, or for the particular area that needs repair, homemade patch panels can be cut out with metal snips. Start with a large piece of metal of the same gauge as the body metal when making rough cuts. It must later be trimmed closer to the size of damaged area.

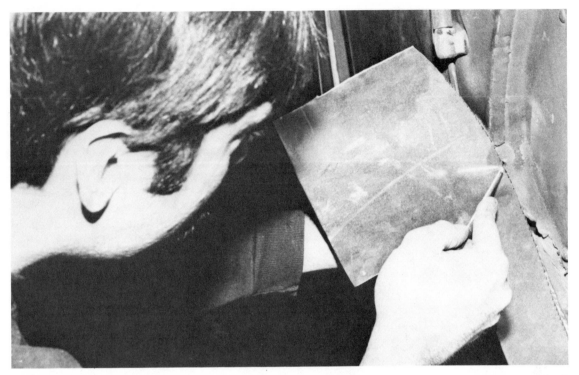

Fig. 6-21. Use a scribe to mark both the patch and attachment point on body. Then trim the piece closer to the final required size according to your scribe marks. Move slowly and carefully; shape the piece of patch metal through trial and error.

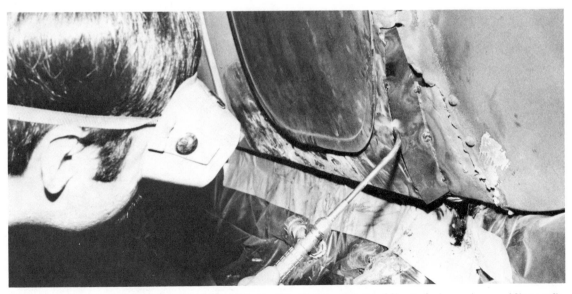

Fig. 6-22. Sheet-metal patches are attached with butt welds. Do not use spot welding techniques. A gas welding outfit is preferable to the electric arc type. Always wear safety goggles and gloves when making welds.

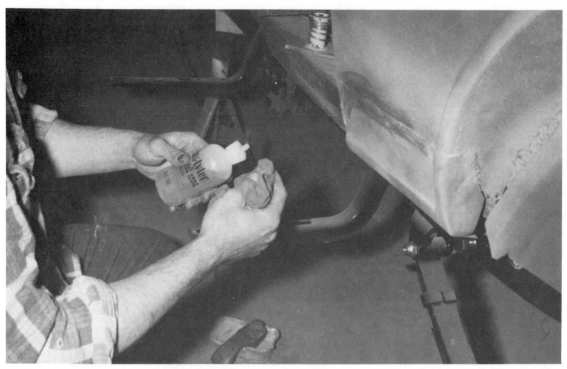

Fig. 6-23. A flux must be applied to chemically clean the surface to be filled with lead solder. Liquid fluxes are usually employed in auto body work. Apply with a rag or brush. After heating, wipe all traces of burnt flux away with a clean, cotton cloth.

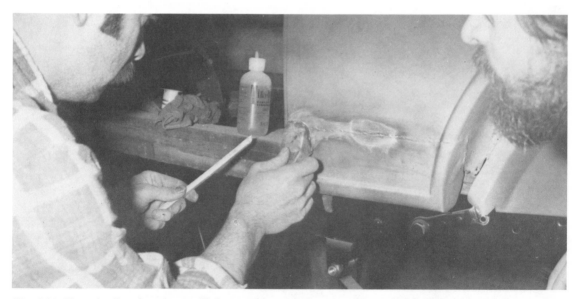

Fig. 6-24. Heat the fluxed surface until the metal becomes hot enough to melt the solder when the bar is placed against it. Do not try to fill the whole depression or seam with one application of solder. A gradual buildup is required.

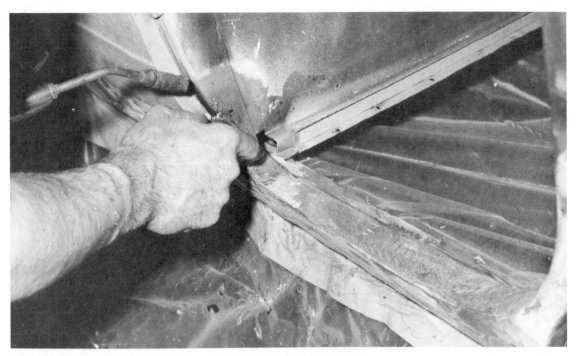

Fig. 6-25. Don't worry about high spots. Solder can be re-flowed for final surfacing by heating with the torch. Care must be used in applying heat. Too much heat will buckle the metal panels.

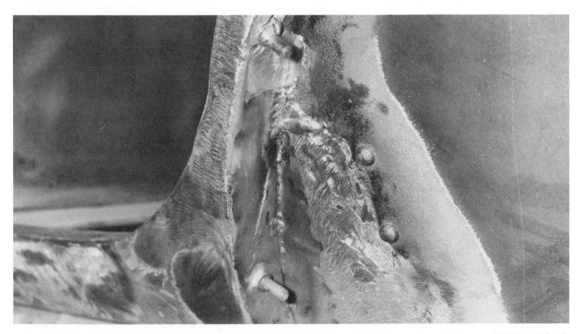

Fig. 6-26. Rough finishing operations are done with files. An electric grinder can be used. Be careful! The solder is soft and will not give much resistence to grinding. Avoid removing too much solder with an overbite of power tools.

Fig. 6-27. A light coat of plastic (resin) filler, used over lead-solder repairs that are structurally sound, can help create a very smooth surface. Use a rasp like this for rough finishing; use wood block-mounted, fine-grit sandpaper for final smoothing.

fenders, and doors and refinish each of these panels separately. This will make it easier to get the paint onto all of the surfaces. With a postwar car, the front end sheet metal (hood and fenders) can be removed without great difficulty, but fenders and doors are usually left in place. In both cases, headlights, taillamps, radio antennas, door handles—anything you don't want painted—should be removed. Use twist-wire tags to label the parts and any electrical connections. This will help you re-install the parts correctly. If any of these parts need re-chroming, now is the perfect time to ship them off to your favorite plating shop.

Before the paint is added, you will have to spray the body with a primer to prepare the surface and give the paint good adherence. Before doing this, wash the car with water and treat it with a wax and tar-removing solution. Next, use newspaper and masking tape to protect the windshield, window glass, and any nonremovable trim items from overspray of paint. Automotive body primer comes in different colors; it should be chosen according to the finish color you've selected. For example, a red primer would be best if the car is to be painted maroon, a dark grey primer works good under

black paint, and a light-grey primer is preferable on cars being painted white. Ask the counterman at the paint store about the best primer to use if you are unsure.

Before priming, you must scuff up the bare metal. Scuff marks increase the surface area being painted and give the paint better adhesion. On old cars it is best to use course, 80-grit sandpaper for this step. Take extra care around trim moldings and grooves in the body because it is relatively hard to get good adherence in these areas. The car must be treated with a metal prep solution. If slight surface rust is present, use #3 steel wool along with the metal prep. Clean the prep solution completely off the car.

To provide a longer lasting paint job on an old convertible, use a synthetic primer-sealer before applying primer to the surface. Do not apply the primer-sealer too heavily (especially in corners or around moldings).

Next, apply the primer—working from top to bottom. Primer should be applied with a high-quality spray gun and air-compressor outfit. The sprayer should be able to maintain 30 pounds of pressure per square inch. For safety purposes, you should not paint a car unless you wear a respirator mask that prevents breathing the paint fumes. Most spray guns are sold with instruction sheets or booklets that outline good techniques. Practice on scraps of sheet metal or junked cars before painting your car.

Do not change your technique in midstream. This is very important. Years ago, before cars were painted via automatic spray equipment or electrolytic dip-tank methods, auto manufactures selected their assembly line paint personel very carefully. Because each side of the car coming down an assembly line was sprayed by a different person (Fig. 6-28), the companies tried to match worker's techniques. If this wasn't done, each side of the car would look a little different even though the type of paint and color was the same. It's important to perfect your own techniques and use them uniformly.

After you have sprayed the primer on the car, wait until it dries. Then sand with fine-grit (#320) paper and blow the residue away with your air compressor. A second primer coat will have to be applied, allowed to dry, and re-sanded with even finer-grit paper (#400). When the car shows a nice primer coating, it will be time to begin applying color coats. The basic technique that you used for priming will be employed again. You can plan on doing several coats of paint (with light sanding or rubbing out between each one).

Beaver Colver advises that the number of coats required for a show-quality paint job today is less than used years ago due to imporovements in paint technology. "The idea of thirty coats of hand-rubbed lacquer is out," Colver said at a Marquette University seminar.

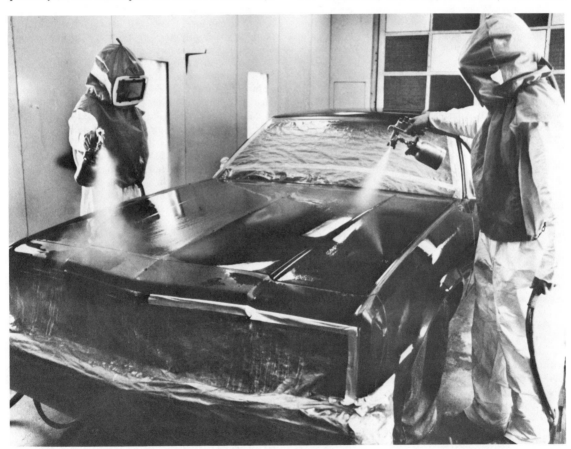

Fig. 6-28. Your own spray technique should be developed carefully by practicing on scrap metal or a junk car. Work from top to bottom using an even stroking applied in a horizontal pattern. Begin at one end of a panel and move quickly across to the other end with even pressure on the trigger. Release pressure on the trigger toward the end of the stroke, but continue past the seam or end. Press the trigger again and move quickly back across the panel—slightly lower, in the opposite direction. Work to bottom of panel in this manner. If two people are spraying, the spray-gun operating techniques should be nearly the same or each side of the car will take on a different look. Always wear a respirator, or better yet, full safety gear; modern synthetic paints can be lethal if inhaled.

Beaver adds that these "new" paints give excellent, original-looking finishes and provide exceptionally long-lasting durability. There's no need to demand the "old-fashioned" formulas for judging purposes. Just be careful to get a good color match to old paint chips.

Most manufactures design their product lines as a complete refinishing system. That means that all of their products—tar remover, prep-sol, primer-surfacer, primer and paint—are formulated to work together. According to Beaver Colver, it pays to use the same brand of paint products for all jobs and all surfaces. "There's enough problem between choosing different enamels and lacquers," notes Beaver, "Why use different brands of each?"

On top of this, I would suggest using a system with which other restorers have had good luck. There are rare cases where new products haven't worked out for restorers. For example, instances in which the latest paint begins to "lift" after just a few months. To avoid this, stick to the products other hobbyists have used successfully. When you see a good-looking paint job at a car show, ask the owner what system he used and how well it has held up over a long period of time. Then go with the proven system. You'll be better assured of the results you will get.

When you have finished painting the main portion of the body, it will be time to move on to the re-finishing of those special parts that came off in the disassembly, plus the painting of items such as wheels, chassis parts, the undercarriage and the motor. In addition, you might want to pinstripe the body, if such trimming was done originally. All of this is usually referred to as "detailing" the car.

Each of these jobs can require special skills and materials. For example, glossy black enamel is commonly used to paint such areas as the underside of a hood, the radiator, the chassis, inner fender panels, and radiator support crossmembers. Great care must be taken to apply this paint smoothly to give an original look.

An alternative to this is the use of a finish called "Poxy Coat" that is marketed by C-Way Supply, P.O. Box 127, Green Bay, WI 54305. This paint is one-part component consisting of epoxy ester and phenolic resins that dries to a very hard, shiny finish while remaining flexible. It can even be applied with a brush, but gives a true, factory-look appearance to the inner sheet metal and chassis parts.

The restoration of wood spoke wheels, used on 1930s models, is another specialty operation. Rough sanding will "dent" wood and make paint scratch or peel easily. Fine sandpapering will give a better surface. Only extremely light coats of primer and paint should be used on wooden wheels. Heavier build-ups of paint will promote cracking of the finish. After wheels are painted, tires should be put on from the back side to prevent damaging the finish.

Wire spoke wheels that were used on many cars built in the 1920s and 1930s should be treated differently. Here a heavy coat of synthetic primer is applied with no surfacer. Then paint should be applied in heavy coats; move as quickly as possible. It is best to do this job in a single day.

Pinstriping should be done by an expert in this art. This will be relatively expensive, but it will add much to the value of the restoration. Never wax the car's new paint before having it striped. You can, however, apply a course rubbing compound to the area to be trimmed. This will help the stripe stay on. The best idea is to have the striper put on two coats. To ensure the authenticty of striping, refer to brochures or factory photographs of similar cars. Write letters to marque experts if the sales brochures and factory photos do not show correct designs. You can loose points or a "Best of Show" award if the car is incorrectly striped. This would include a wrong color as well as incorrect design.

Another difficult step in detailing 1930s to early 1950s models can be refinishing the simulated wood-grained dashboard appearance. This takes a great deal of careful effort using an antiquing kit such as those available for use on furniture. You must know the exact color and type of graining that was used on your model. Be especially careful with 1940s convertibles because many manufacturers used wood-grained-look dashboards in closed cars, but painted dashboards in convertibles. The best way to authenticate the grain design for your car is to check original sales literature or locate the same type of car at a show. Make sure the same design was used on ragtops!

The car should be completely reassembled, detailed, and road tested before you even consider restoration of the interior (upholstery) and the installation of a new convertible top. You might have to make final mechanical adjustments or body panel alignments after road testing the car. You will not want to be sitting on new upholstery with dirty shop coats or tools in your pockets. Actually, it might be best to put off interior restoration for a few months while the car is driven with the old seats in place because you will have to let the door alignments and window adjustments "settle" for awhile. They usually have to be re-done after several hundred miles of use.

Interior restoration is usually accomplished in one of two ways. Where upholstery kits are available, hobbyists might want to attempt this difficult job themselves. If a kit is not offered for your car, it's probably best to farm out upholstery restoration to the professional shop. Other than convertible top and boot installation, interior restoration lies beyond the scope of this book. Two books on auto interior work are: TAB book No. 2102, *Car Interior Restoration, 3rd Edition* by Terry Boyce; and TAB book No. 1213, *The Coach Trimmer's Art* by Lynton Francis Sherrington.

When purchasing the paint, buy a large enough

quantity to have some leftover for future touch-up work. This will ensure that you achieve an exact match if small repairs to the paint job are needed. To preserve the leftover paint for the longest period of time, transfer the remainder to a smaller container. For example, the paint left in a 1-gallon can should be placed into a half-gallon. The shelf life of the paint will be extended by decreasing the amount of air remaining in the container and the amount of paint exposed to that air.

REFINISHING A TOP SUPPORT MECHANISM

This section comes under the category of minor restoration and won't be of interest to everyone. But when show cars are judged against each other for authenticity, the repainting of the interior top mechanism can be a crucial point.

In normal service, the parts in this mechanism (bows, rails, links, hinges, etc.,) move to raise and lower the fabric top (Fig. 6-29). As they pivot against each other while the top is going up or down, they can become scratched. This removes paint and exposes metal surfaces to rust. To have a true Number-1-condition car,

these parts must be repainted. The color should be the same as the original.

The first part of the job is to identify the original color. With relatively modern cars, this is not difficult. Look for traces of original paint that's still intact and try to match the color. On many such cars, the correct color will be either shiny (gloss) or flat black.

On older cars, it may be more difficult to pinpoint the original color. Of course the older the vehicle the better the chance that paint will be missing. In extreme cases, the only "finish" on the mechanism might be an orange coat of rust. Faced with this situation, there are several things you can do to determine the original color.

The easiest is to find a similar car at a car show, but don't take authenticity for granted. Upon spotting cars like yours, find out if they are low-milage (unrestored) originals or an excellent restoration. Seek out the owner or restorer and ask questions. They will tell you if you're looking at the original, factory-applied finish or a correct substitute. Ask for documentation or a source of proof such as original sales catalog illustrations, factory literature, or original color photos.

Car club "Technical Editors" can often supply the same type of information. For example, members of the

Fig. 6-29. A portion of the roof riser mechanism can be seen in this photo of a Chrysler interior. Authentic refinishing of the components will add to your restoration.

Chrysler 300 Club, Inc. have compiled "judging data sheets" for this marque. They reveal, for instance, that the bows on the 1961 Chrysler 300G's convertible top (Fig. 6-30) were originally painted tan. This information came from study of the factory specifications.

With other brands of cars, service or sales literature may be as big a help. It will always take some personal research on your part to dig-up such materials, but a show-quality restoration will be the result.

To re-finish the parts, the old paint has to be stripped off. If the fabric top is missing or due for replacement, this should be easy. You can remove the paint by chemical means (paint strippers—always wear gloves and goggles) or mechanical means (sander, grinder, wire brush, sandpaper). Be careful to remove only paint—not metal.

If the fabric top is going to be used again, don't employ a chemical stripper. It might get on the fabric and eat that top away. Instead, rely on careful sanding. Shoot for spot repairs. use the sandpaper to feather into the bare spot and apply your paint using a thin, soft brush. Try to use a type of paint that, when applied by brush, still dries very smooth.

When the top is off the car or when the entire top structure is removed, you can spray the paint on without worrying about overspray. Apply the finish carefully. Use only very light applications to avoid running or pooling of the paint.

Some of the space age finishes available today will do a super job. C-Way Supply's poxy coat is a two-part system combining epoxy ester and phenolic resins. It gives an armour-hard finish that goes on smoothly with a brush. Likewise, the new polyurethane enamels will spray on and give a very scratch resistent finish.

Never use any paint on bare metal. The parts should first be washed and treated with a prep-sol. The spot to be painted should also be roughed up with sandpapers and coated with a primer-surfacer before top coats are applied. This is true in the cases of both spot finishing or a complete respray.

When finished, remember no paint is immune to careless treatment. It might be a good idea to protect the

Fig. 6-30. Car club tech advisers can provide lots of helpful information such as the correct color to paint convertible top bows for a 1961 Chrysler 300.

Fig. 6-31. Replacement of door panels is a common job faced by hobbyists who restore convertibles.

surface of moving parts with old shop rags whenever the top is to be raised or lowered (also where top mechanism parts touch body sheet metal). This might seem like a pain in the neck, but the alternative is refinishing these areas regularly—an even more tedious prospect.

REPLACING DOOR PANELS

The interior door panels on many older convertibles (Fig. 6-31) will require replacement because moisture can cause these panels to buckle. Old age can have a similar effect. If the panels were ever removed for broken window glass replacement, there's a good chance they have been incorrectly reinstalled. Normal wear and tear or inadvertant damage such as cigarette burns are other problems.

A door panel is usually nothing more than a heavy piece of cardboard upholstered with fabric, vinyl, leather, or carpeting to complement the car's interior trim. On some modern cars, molded plastic panels are used, but this is rarely seen on ragtops. Vinyl-covered cardboard panels are most common.

To replace a door panel, you will have to remove the old one, make a new one out of cardboard, and cover the new panel with the old trim or new trim or a combination of the both. Preferably, the trim materials will be an exact match for originals. If this is impossible, a near match has to be devised. For most popular convertibles of

the 1960s and 1970s, door panel replacement kits are now available.

To remove the old door panel, start by removing everything that holds it in place. This includes the door handles, window riser handles (or power window controls), armrest, bright metal moldings, clips, and self-threading trim screws. You can use either an Allen wrench, screw driver, or special flat-bladed tool to remove the door handles. These flat-bladed tools—which are inexpensive and readily available—are designed for removal of retaining clips on specific brands of cars. You can buy them at any auto-parts supply store.

The perimeter of the panel is also held on by clips that mate with slots in the door structure. They can be "popped-out" of the slots with a screwdriver or flat-bladed tool. Label every part removed. This should include the original trim materials (if at all reuseable). If the lower trim is shot but the upper trim is perfect, save the upper panels. It's easier to find replacement materials for a single section of trim rather than the entire panel.

Remove all clips from the back of the old panel. Then, with a razor blade, cut through the original overlapping trim approximately 1/2 inch from the edge—along the entire outer perimeter of the panel. Pull the original material off the panel carefully. Different trim sections, such as carpeted lower panels, might come off separately.

Use the old panel as a template for your new one. It

should be fashioned out of cardboard of the same type and weight. Kits might already include a replacement panel or you can shape your own panel using a coping saw, razor blade, or an artist's matte-cutting tool. All openings in the original panel should be transferred to the new one.

You must now trim this new panel with the upholstery materials you have saved, purchased, or found. Vinyl and carpeted panels will be the easiest to match or closely approximate. It might be impossible to find fabrics or anodized trim that looks just like the original materials. If this is the case, try to pick materials that at least conform to the correct colors and overall design character.

Most trim suppliers will provide samples of the materials they sell for around $1 plus a self-addressed stamped envelope. It's often possible to locate some trim pieces in a wrecking yard. In many cases, original trim and hardware will be reuseable. It won't pay to reuse any items that don't look "almost new."

Once you've located the materials that you'll be using, the job of trimming begins. First, repair any torn foam areas if there is foam backing under the panel. Now, place the new "skin" over the cardboard panel. With a pliers type of stapler or staple gun, staple the panel on the top and bottom approximately 6 inches from the front. Keep all staples as close to the outer edge of the panel as possible.

Next, move to the backside of the panel—stretching the skin tightly over the old panel. Staple around the entire rear curvature. Staple the rest of the panel top and bottom with the staples placed about an inch apart. At the front of the panel, apply contact cement to the back of the new skin at the point it overlaps the perimeter. This area should be approximately 1 inch wide and run from top to bottom and back as far as the new skin overlap runs. Allow sufficient drying time and fold the new skin over the edge of the panel backing.

If the original door panels on the car were of a two-tone trim combination or had lower carpeted panels, you will have to re-skin separate sections and add the necessary carpeting. This requires a little more time to ensure proper seam alignment and to staple on the necessary carpeting. Other things that might have to be added are beading and piping; this can be obtained from trim suppliers.

On some cars, pleated vinyl sections are used. These pleats will have to be made by stitching the panel skin with a heavy-duty sewing machine using the proper color thread and correct stitching pattern.

Once your skin covering has been completed, the next step is to re-install the newly skinned panel on the door of the car. Line up the spring clips with the corresponding holes in the door panel and tap them into place with a rubber mallet. Then re-attach all fasteners, bright metal trim parts, and armrests, etc.

REUPHOLSTERY

With 90 percent of all amateur convertible restorations being done today, reupholstery work will be handled by farming the work out to a professional trim shop at prices from $2,000-up or by owner-installation of an upholstery kit (Fig. 6-32) designed for a particular year, make, and model car.

Reupholstery kits for almost all popular ragtops are available starting well under $1,000. These kits are easy to install. They make it possible for you to completely redo an interior in just one afternoon. Dozens of different kits are being advertised in hobby magazines as well as car club newsletters. They are also sold at the major old-car parts flea markets.

For about $1 and a self-addressed stamped envelope, many companies will send you upholstery material sample swatches and literature on their product lines. About 80 percent of all postwar and many prewar ragtops can be reupholstered through use of a kit.

To install a typical kit, the seats must come out first. Each auto seat consists of a cushion (the part you sit on) and seat back (the part you rest your back against). The rear seat cushion can usually be pulled loose from its attaching sockets in the floor with a good, strong yank. Lift it out of the car. A few screws will normally hold the rear seat back in place. When the screws are removed, the seat back also comes right out.

In most cases, the front cushion and seat back will be either a single unit type or two separate units, semi-permanently attached. With bucket seats there will be two individual cushions and two seat backs. You will have to remove floor carpets and any floor pan plug buttons. Next, take out all seat track retaining nuts. Remove the seat track retaining studs (usually accomplished from below the floorpan). Remove the seat assembly, or individual bucket seats, and place them on a clean work surface. Remove any screws used to fasten the track assembly to the seat cushion and remove this assembly completely. Now, stretch out in the seatless interior and take a short nap. Afterall, restoration work can be tiring.

When fully rested, start with the rear cushion. Remove the hog rings (Fig. 6-33) from around the perimeter of the seat bottom and carefully strip the old upholstery off. Inspect the seat pad (Fig. 6-34) and, if used, the spring assembly. Seats on modern collector cars can be rebuilt by simply adding new foam rubber padding. On older models, broken or sagging spring assemblies wires have to be replaced or repaired.

Visit your favorite wrecking yard to get springs of a similar type. In this case, the used parts don't have to be anywhere near perfect as long as some good coils are salvagable. Avoid completely rusted coils because they tend to loose much of their spring.

If you are lucky enough to find an assembly in "very

Fig. 6-32. An interior kit like this one can be a big help to the amateur restorer. Kits are available for many cars.

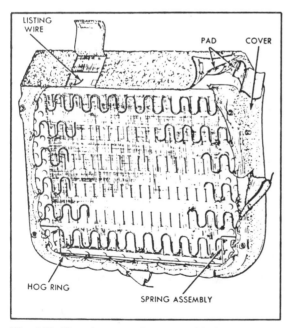

Fig. 6-33. Hog rings must be removed before stripping seat cushions of old upholstery.

good" condition, install it as is. Otherwise, splice the remaining good coils into the old assembly to replace broken ones. Pad and cushion the seat with new stuffing. Use extra foam padding in very weak spots, but be careful not to overstuff the seat. With the high-quality foam backings available today, it doesn't pay to stick to original straw-and-cotton padding. Car show judges don't have X-ray vision!

A listing wire will be used around the perimeter of the seat bottom to shape the contour. Use the wire from the original or wrecking-yard seats on the final product. Position the new seat surfacing material over the frame and re-padded spring assembly. Pull it taught, without stretching, and use new hog rings to hold it in place. Reinstall the cushion inside the car.

The rear seat back should be covered in the same general manner. The main differences are the detachment and reattachment procedures. The screws that fasten the seat back in place can be threaded through tabs at the top or at the top and bottom. If the tabs are at bottom only, there will be retaining hooks near the upper attachment point.

Generally, the rear cushion should be removed/installed prior to doing the same with the seat back. With many cars, rear seat removal is a real adventure because of the unusual things you'll find under old car seats.

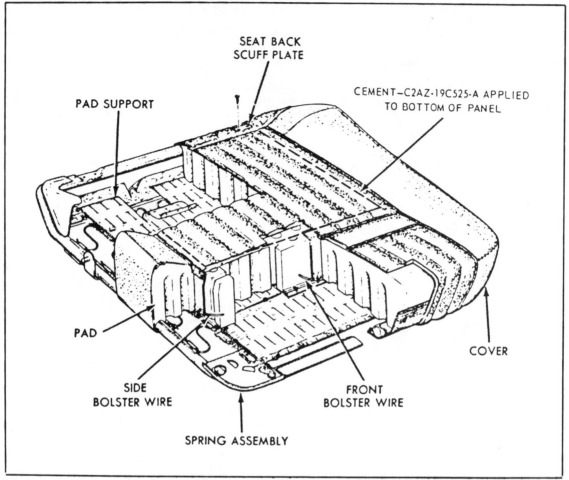

SEAT BACK
SCUFF PLATE

PAD SUPPORT

CEMENT—C2AZ-19C525-A APPLIED
TO BOTTOM OF PANEL

PAD

COVER

SIDE
BOLSTER WIRE

FRONT
BOLSTER WIRE

SPRING ASSEMBLY

Fig. 6-34. Inspect the slat-cushion pad. Cushions can be rebuilt by adding new foam-rubber padding or spring assemblies.

Anything might show up from broken ball point pens to crescent wrenches and a variety of unmentionables.

In addition to being slightly harder to remove, front seats take more work to recover. Sometimes the cushions and backs do not even come readily apart and it will be best not to disassemble them. This means removing and replacing the trim by the tug-and-push-and-pull method. You will have to squeeze the coverings between the two parts, pull the material through, and still try to avoid creases and wrinkles. It's not easy. A delicate touch and steady-as-she-goes technique must be mastered. Just go slow and smooth.

If the cushion and back can be separated, it means careful disassembly of all hinging hardware, brackets, trim parts, etc. Label the pieces and sketch yourself a re-assembly diagram. All shims and spacers, rubber bumpers, lock washers, and fasteners should go back in their original location.

If separable, the two parts of the seat can be recovered more easily and expertly. General procedures are the same as for the rear seat except that the rear surface of the front seat back also must be covered. Hog ring attachments are made *below* the front seat for cushions and backs. There might be a robe cord, ash recepticle, or cigarette lighter built into the rear surface of a front seat back. These items are held in place by selfthreading screws or by force fit into a depression, and they often help secure the covers in place. They must be removed and replaced through the proper openings in the cover. There are usually overlapping edges designed for retention purposes. Don't try to cut corners by stuffing the cover material under the edges without removing such parts.

The front seat goes back into the car by reversing the removal procedures. Attach the seat track assembly to seat bottom. Place the seat in the car. Place nuts/washers on the studs and draw them tight. Install the floor pan plug buttons (if used). Replace the carpeting. For cars with power seats, procedures will vary and should be checked by referring to a body service manual for your specific year, make, car line, and model.

Buy only the highest-quality reupholstery kits. Beware of cheap imitations available from discount houses and suppliers that service the general auto market. Companies that specialize in jut one brand of car (or models built by one corporation—because kits for General Motors, Ford, Chrysler cars, etc., tend to be similar) are preferred. Also look out for "generic" kits where one pattern design is claimed to fit 20 types of cars.

Years ago, this type of broad coverage was the only way kits could be marketed commercially so available kits were made to fit "typical" seat dimensions. Now the value of old cars has climbed enough to allow greater specialization. This means higher prices, of course, but this can also be a sign of quality. Remember that the $600 reupholstery kit will raise the value of your car and it is still under half as costly as visiting the professional trim shop. On the other hand, if you're not confident of your ability to install a kit properly, don't spend $600 and blow the job.

Another problem is owning a car for which no kit is currently available. There are three alternatives. First, find a good, original interior in a "parts car," wrecking yard, auto flea market, or ancient dealership's spare parts bin. Some car dealers never throw out anything and others toss out old parts as soon as they become obsolete. The "toss-out-for-credit" philosophy is relatively modern. Always check with that local car dealer who's been in business many years. He might have just what you need and an unbelievably low price.

Alternative number two is to make your own reupholstery kit. I advise doing this only when original covers can be removed *completely* intact. When this is the case, it's sometimes possible to use the old covers as a pattern, but only if you find that they haven't been stretched out of shape. Even the slightest degree of distortion will leave you with a faulty pattern. This can be a big problem with some materials. With genuine leather seats, your cost for seat surfacing materials alone will be around $1,500. If the pattern is off, you will have expensive nonfitting seat covers.

Another problem with making your own covers is finding the right fabrics, vinyls, or leathers. The color, texture, and grain must be just like—or very similar to—originals. Color matching is the least crucial factor because it's possible to dye any material. Still, it is something to think about. I would not recommend making your own seat coverings unless authentic materials are known to be available and an experienced pattern cutter is willing to help on a strictly hobby basis. It makes more sense to go with a reputable trim shop if everything isn't just right.

The third alternative is simply waiting until someone comes out with a kit for your car. This is a personal judgement. For example, one of my cars is a 1954 Chevrolet. Just a few years ago, a kit for this car wasn't available, but kits for older and newer Chevys were available. I decided to wait, and this has paid off because a new kit has just been released for this model. If your car is a low-production model, don't hold your breath waiting for a kit. The wrecking yard would be a better alternative because demand for a kit would be low.

In general, demand will be based on car values. It costs suppliers a pretty penny to manufacture and market new interior kits and there must be enough restorations in progress to warrant the production costs. Restorations will only occur, on a mass scale, when a car costs less to restore than it is worth when done. With the convertibles, this is the common case so the supply of interior kits is growing steadily.

DASHBOARD REPAIR

The interior of your convertible can't be considered fully restored unless the dashboard looks just like new. Work involved here can include partial disassembly and cleaning, complete refinishing, or spot repair of damaged dash panel padding.

Because the convertible interior is open to the elements more than that of the closed car, there is usually a higher degree of weathering on all dashboard surfaces. Common problems will include general dirtiness, cloudy, clear-plastic dial faces, and damaged or heavily tarnished bright metal trim.

Instruments usually come out of the dashboard separately or in clusters. They are held in place by several bolts or screws. When removing gauges, remember that they can easily be damaged because they are very delicate devices. Handle with care. Clean each instrument or cluster individually; use pipe cleaners or Q-Tips to remove stubborn dust that builds up around edges. The clear plastic or glass lenses can usually be cleaned with a household glass cleaner.

The best time to refinish a dashboard is when the instruments are removed. Pinpoint original colors by referring to paint charts, paint chips, car-club technical bulletins or show cars that are completely original or correctly restored. Remove all trim and mask off surrounding areas with newspaper held in place by masking tape. Carefully spray the paint over the entire panel. Move your spray gun horizontally, end to end. At the end of each stroke, let off the trigger.

On many cars of the late 1930s to late 1940s, the convertible dashboard will have simulated wood grain trim. This can be refinished by using a furniture antiquing kit or (better yet) special wood graining kits that hobby upholstery suppliers sell. These kits rely on a two-part process. A latex base coat is applied to create the grain pattern and a stain of the proper color is used for final refinish operations.

Padded dashboards (Fig. 6-35) present a more difficult challenge due to limited parts availability. The easiest fix is to re-pad the original with new foam, followed by gluing the cover back in place. New bonding agents have helped many hobbyists through this job, but if the cover is badly buckled or stretched, replacement parts will have to be found.

The main sources of replacement dashboard covers are old-car wrecking yards. In general, coupes and sedans of the same type will use the same dashboard cover as convertibles. Also, the closed cars' interiors will usually be in better shape. Trim suppliers are beginning to market kits for repairing padded dashboards for popular cars like Mustangs, mid-1960s Chevrolets, Chrysler 300s, etc. If you can locate a kit for your car, it is definately the right way to go.

CARPETS

Replacement carpeting for old cars is readily available via hobby trim suppliers. For some years, makes, and models, a precut molded carpet kit can be purchased. These kits provide an exact fit and come in original colors and designs. The primary installation work will consist of removal of the seat cushions (or bolsters) and the inner rocker panel/door trim. Once the carpet has been put in place, these parts can be reinstalled with the new carpeting underneath. The fasteners that hold the seats and trim in place will also secure the edges of your carpeting when all components have been re-installed.

If you can't find a molded carpet kit for your car, you

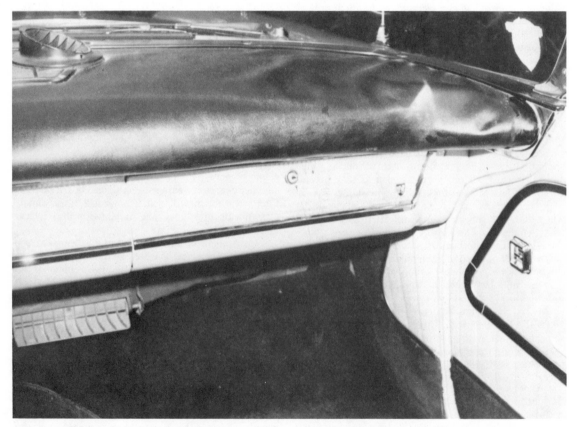

Fig. 6-35. Deterioration of padded dashboards is common. Kits are available for some cars but used parts have to suffice in most cases.

will have to purchase suitable raw materials and do some of your own cutting and sewing. Find carpeting, that has the correct texture and color, through dealers who advertise in hobby magazines or through those who exhibit at the various flea markets.

If possible, the carpet should be cut to shape using the old carpets (or floor mats) as your pattern. If the car has no carpets, you will have to make your own paper patterns by the trial-and-error system. Lay the paper on the floor pan of the car and trim the edges until you have a pattern that will give a nice fit. Remember to allow for sufficient overlap under the seats and rocker trim plates. Always use a top-quality padded mat under new carpets.

Because the carpet won't be molded to fit over the transmission hump, a proper fit in this area will have to be obtained by cutting and piecing together several different sections. In the majority of cases, this is how the original carpets were shaped. All that's required is to cut the new sections along the same pattern. Then stitch or have them stitched together on a heavy-duty sewing machine.

Two other problems you might face are cutting out openings (for gear shift levers, bright light buttons, etc.,) and binding the perimeter of the carpets at the borders and seams. Holes should be cut out with a tool like an arch punch or a heavy-duty razor cutter. Crisscross two diagonal slits, fit the carpet over the protrubence, and then cut the opening around the protruding part. The slits can be sewn back together if they are very large.

Binding material must be used along the exposed edges of carpets to prevent fraying and to give the correct appearance. Binding strips or tape can be purchased from hobby trim suppliers. It can be taped, glued, or stitched in place. It's a good idea to use two to three stitches for a more permanent job.

TOP-LIFT ASSEMBLY (MANUAL)

Some convertibles have manually operated tops. Manual lift assemblies usually incorporate a dual-action, heavy-duty spring that helps compensate for the weight of the folding-top mechanism when the top is at full-up or full-folded positions. When the top is in the up position, the spring is under compression; when it is in the folded or stacked position, the spring is under tension.

If you find problems with a manually operated top, the lift assembly will have to be removed to install replacement parts. Never attempt removal when the spring is under compression or tension!

Begin by removing the rear-seat cushion and back. Fold the top compartment side trim panel to relieve compression/tension. Have a helper support the top if both assemblies have to be replaced.

Remove inner and outer bolts securing the top assembly to the male hinge and remove the assembly from the car body. Install new parts and replace the lift assembly by reversing the preceding procedures.

TOP-LIFT ASSEMBLY (POWER)

The first convertible to feature a power-operated top mechanism was the '39 Plymouth ragtop. On most prewar cars, power tops were operated by hydraulic pressure generated by a motor run by vacuum lines from the engine. After the war, vacuum-hydraulic systems were replaced with hydroelectric types. The typical system consists of a 6-volt or 12-volt reversible motor, a rotor-type pump, dual hydraulic lift cylinders, and upper and lower hydraulic hose systems. In most cases, motors are installed in the body directly behind the rear seat.

If the top fails to operate, the first thing to check is the electrics—beginning at the control switch. This is accomplished by disconnecting the terminal block from the rear of the switch. A simple test light can be used to determine if current is reaching and passing through the switch. One lead is connected to the feed terminal and the other is grounded to the body, making a circuit. Should the light fail to shine, the switch is not working.

If the switch is okay, there might be a short between it and the motor. This possibility can also be checked with a test light connected between switch and motor (in place of the regular leads). If the lead wire(s) prove(s) defective, a new one can be spliced into the harness to provide complete circuitry.

The test light can also be used, in a similar fashion, to check out the motor itself. If the tester indicates that the motor is burned out, it should be replaced.

Hydraulic problems can frequently be traced to a low fluid level in the reservoir, pressure leaks in the hydraulic lines, or low pump pressure. In some cases, the hydraulic lines might be kinked or there might be dirt in the system. Visual inspection procedures will often pinpoint the location of a leak because leaking fluid will leave a telltale spot or stain. A simple pressure gauge can be used to check pressure in the hydraulic pump. A loss of pressure can be caused by internal leakage past seals or O-rings.

The pump must be removed from its mounting, with the lines disconnected. Place a plug into one of the ports (openings) and connect the pressure gauge to the other. In the typical case, readings at the two ports (checked separately) should be in the range of 340 to 380 psi. If the pressure is not within these limits, have the pump repaired or replace it.

To remove the pump, place the top in the fully raised mode, disconnect the positive battery cable (negative on negative-ground cars), shield the rear seat area with a protective cover, remove the wiring harness and clips, disconnect motor leads, apply rubber lube to the pump attaching the grommets and remove them, place absorbant rags under line connections, vent the pump reservoir by removing filler plug with screw driver, disconnect lines, cap open fittings, and take the pump out of the car. Great care should be taken to prevent the hydraulic (brake) fluid from getting on painted parts because it can easily damage most finishes.

After installing a new pump, reconnecting all lines and electrical connections, the system should be ready to go again. Proper maintenance is the key to preventing future problems. At least twice each year, the top lift cylinder rods in the pump should be cleaned and lubricated. This is accomplished by raising the top fully, wiping the exposed portions of the rods with a brake-fluid-dampened cloth, and applying (with a second, clean cloth) a light film of brake fluid to lubricate.

CONVERTIBLE TOP INSTALLATION

Installing a convertible top is a complicated procedure requiring a great deal of skill, patience, and work. Though not an easy job for the average convertible owner, the installation of a custom-fit convertible top kit is well within the capabilities of most amateur restorers who do work on their own cars.

The important thing is to select a high-quality kit sold by a reputable supplier. Whereas trim shops are now charging well over $500 (and as high as $1,000) for top installation, suitable kits for owner installation can be purchased in the $100-to-$200 range. Kits come with full installation instructions that will vary from one model to another. Mustang Sales & Parts, 1249 East Holt Ave., Pomona, CA 91767, produces a line of top-quality convertible top kits for Ford Mustangs.

TOP SUPPORT STRUCTURES

Luckily, very few amateur convertible restorers face the job of completely rebuilding convertible top structures. Nevertheless, this might be necessary in those situations where the car is in very poor condition, but is valuable enough to still warrant a restoration.

In these cases, the only thing for the hobbyist to do is to search high and low for the required parts. In many instances, locating a similar car in a wrecking yard will provide needed parts. Flea markets are another possible source. By finding a complete replacement, or swapping parts between the two, it is usually possible—with some effort—to repair the damaged top structure.

7. Selling a Convertible

Now that you're done with the job of restoring your convertible, your next step is deciding what to do with the car. Basically your options are to keep it or sell it. Whichever way you go, there are several things to consider.

If you are keeping the car, do you want to use it every day or reserve it for show-car purposes? How much work is it going to take to keep it properly maintained? What kind of insurance should you get for it? Should you license the ragtop the same way you license your regular family sedan?

If you decide to sell or trade the car there are other factors to consider. How do you set your price and how to get your price. What is the proper way to compose an advertisement for a collector car? Where should you place your ads? Should you consider selling your car privately? Is it better to enter the convertible in a classic car auction?

KEEP OR SELL

My experience indicates that about one-half of all restorers will hold onto their ragtops for a good many years. The other half will give at least some thought to selling their vehicles. If you purchased the car for fun, as a status symbol, as part of an ego trip, or to take advantage of long-term appreciation, you will probably want to keep it a long time. If you purchased it because you enjoy the job of restoring a car or because you wanted a short-term investment, it's likely you'll want to sell it as quickly as possible.

One thing is for certain. At this point you have made two major investments in your convertible. First, you have put out good money to obtain the car. Second, you have spent time, money, and effort to restore it. Car enthusiasts would say you've got "x" number of dollars

"in the car." The trick is to get "x-plus" satisfaction or dollars out of it.

STANDING PAT

If you decide to hold onto your ragtop, the first thing to think about is how you want to use the car. Some people will drive their collector cars all of the time. Others will use their cars regularly, but not on an everyday basis. A third group will operate the car only for hobby-related purposes such as car shows, tours, amateur racing, and rallying and for driving to and from club events (such as meetings, picnics, and parades). There is also a fourth group that restore their cars only for show. About the only driving they do is when the car is put on or removed from a trailer.

Right from the beginning, you should plan your restoration to correspond to the way in which the car will be used. If you are going to drive it frequently, there is going to be some degree of wear and tear because of the amount of use. Therefore, you might be wise to stop the work when it is in Number 3 (Very Good) or Number 2 (Fine) Condition. I usually think of a Number 3 car as being what you see in the second row of a used car lot. In other words, it's quite a nice looking car that runs fairly well. The Number 2 car is comparable to those on the front row of the same lot. It is suitable for entering in a car show, but it is rarely of the quality needed to capture a Concours d'Elegance trophy in a strictly judged show.

By contrast, the Number 1 condition car is perfection. It will be in perfect condition inside, outside, and under the hood. The engine will be extremely clean and painted in original colors with all original decals and chrome-plated parts. Obviously, the first time you drive a car like this a few miles, it is no longer a Number 1 car!

The Number 1 ragtop is for people who want a status symbol or an ego trip. They will put the car in shows to win trophies. And they will constantly be involved with making the smallest improvements so that their Number 1 car will be just that much better than all others in the same class.

There is nothing wrong with restoring a car to Number 1 condition and using it strictly for show. If nobody went that far, the rest of us would have nothing to dream about. It's just that you have to realize that keeping a collector car for such purposes is geared to the limited-use category and the rest of what I have to say here is for owners of Number 2 or Number 3 condition cars.

If you fall into these catagories, you will be using the car in your pursuit of hobby fun. This means that you're going to have to put some degree of maintenance into it. The old car that's used on a regular or semiregular basis won't stay in good condition by itself. Like any automobile, it will require oil changes, new spark plugs, lubrication, etc., on a regular basis. How often you will have to think about servicing the car depends on how old it is. Generally, the older the vehicle the more service is required.

The best way to find out how much servicing your particular model needs is to obtain an owners manual and a shop (or factory service) manual. Such items can be purchased through dealers who specialize in selling factory literature for older models. Such manuals will tell you how frequently your car requires certain services and what lubricants, parts, and procedures should be considered at specific mileage intervals. Keep in mind that the factory recommendations applied to the car when it was new. Now that it is older, it would be a good idea to change the oil or add new grease a little more frequently. Consider the factory recommendations as minimum guidelines and adjust your maintenance procedures forward a bit.

The normal recommendation on many 1950s cars was to change oil after every 2000 miles of use. This advice was intended for cars that were relatively new and used quite regularly. Over the years, your car might have experienced some degree of piston-ring wear. Perhaps it's not enough to warrant complete engine rebuilding, but enough to produce more than normal oil burning. In such a case, it may be wise to change oil every 1000 miles. This is especially true if the car undergoes long periods of storage because moisture can then build-up in the crankcase, diluting the oil and making it a less effective lubricant.

Whatever you do, don't allow service intervals to extend beyond the points recommended in factory literature. Keep in mind that the car, because of its age, is probably appreciating in value. Consequently, it pays to spend a few extra dollars on more frequent oil changes. Don't ruin the car by being "pennywise and pound foolish."

Every collector car that you plan to use should be adequately insured. In most cases, the best way to obtain insurance will be through companies that provide special coverage for antique, classic and special-interest cars. These firms are run by people who understand the collector-car hobby, and they have special policies geared exactly to your needs. In addition, their rates are usually quite reasonable, and they usually cover liability and collision as well as protection for spare parts.

Most car insurance policies have coverage and rates based on the manner in which the car will be used and the amount of miles you estimate for annual use. Some policies—the least expensive—are set up for limited-use vehicles only. In other words, you will be required to sign a statement indicating the vehicle will be used primarily for car shows, parades, tours, and club events. A specific amount of pleasure-driving use is allowed (usually 500 to 1000 miles per year). In addition, driving the car to work or in races and other competitive events is prohibited. For the great majority of collectors, these conditions aren't a problem.

In recent years, special policies for late-model collector cars have been created. These policies are based on a car's stated value and they extend the mileage limitations so that collectors who drive more frequently can still get reasonably priced insurance that provides full coverage for a special-interest-type car. In addition, there are also customized policies for show cars, Corvettes, vintage race cars, and other special cases.

When you are ready to put your car on the road, write to several companies and see how their policies stack up against each other. Compare the coverage, rates, and limitations and then pick the policy that best fills your needs. Never operate the vehicle—even between your home and a restoration shop—without some type of insurance. You will be taking a great risk if you do.

The procedures and regulations for licensing collector cars vary from one state to another. In almost all states, it is possible to secure special historic, antique, hobbyist, or collector license plates (Fig. 7-1). Generally, your car must be a certain number of years old to qualify. Also, you will probably be required to sign another statement indicating limited use of the vehicle. To determine exactly what conditions govern the issuance of special tags in your state, contact your local motor vehicle department or your local law enforcement branch. They will be able to fill you in on the details. Never take any old car out on the street without license plates or without complete knowledge of laws governing temporary transport immediately after purchasing a car.

In general, the newer your convertible is the harder it will be to secure special insurance and license plates for it. In many cases, a 20-to-25-year-old guideline is used by licensing bureaus. Some more progressive states and insurance companies will recognize even newer cars as collector's items as long as you are willing to meet the limited-use conditions. It is to your advantage to investigate the specific possibilities by contacting the insurance carriers and state authorities yourself. If you belong to a car club, other members should be able to give additional advice. Some clubs have advisors who are experts in these areas.

If you are holding onto your convertible strictly as an investment, you are probably doing yourself a disservice. This is one of the worst reasons for keeping, rather than selling, a collector car. It may sound strange at first, but think of the problems involved in the retention process. First, there's the fact that your restoration is not going to hold up forever no matter how much or how little you use the vehicle. If you drive the car, it is going to pickup paint chips from flying stones, environmental residue, and some amount of wear and tear. If you keep the car in storage, there will be problems with dust, moisture, and rodents, etc. In addition, it will cost money to store the car (renting a garage) or you will have to use space that could otherwise be put to a more profitable use.

Insurance, licensing, and periodic maintenance are other cost factors. On top of all this, it's possible that the car could loose value over the long run. Who knows . . . in five or ten years, car collecting might drop in popularity, thereby dropping the market values for some or all old cars. In addition, there are better investments than automobiles. Coins, stamps, baseball cards, old records, comic books, and even stocks, bonds, and money market certificates will all give equal or better returns on investments—with a lot less trouble involved.

A much sounder reason to invest in collector cars is because you like automobiles. A good reason to specialize in ragtops is because you've developed convertible fever. This is a common affliction suffered by thousands of people who just can't live without ragtops parked in their garages. Two friends of mine came down with slightly different strains of this malady, and discussing their

Fig. 7-1. A "QQ" license plate is used to identify collector cars in New Jersey. Each state has it's own special licensing system for antiques or specialty cars. This is a 1949 Buick.

cases will explain why some owners should never sell their convertibles.

Case Number 1. Gil D. owned a 1957 Pontiac Star Chief convertible that he restored, drove regularly, and began taking to shows. Then it was stolen. Over the next five years, he looked high and low for a replacement—with no luck. He was able to purchase a 1957 Star Chief Sports Coupe, which he restored and sold toward a 1957 Custom Safari station wagon. Even though the Safari was a valuable milestone car, it wasn't a ragtop and it did not satisfy his automotive cravings.

Finally, Gil found another 1957 Pontiac Star Chief ragtop. Naturally, he restored the car and started having fun again. It's kept under lock and key when not in use. It's the one cure for his convertible fever.

Case Number 2. Dick F. never had his car stolen. He sold it. About 20 years ago, he owned a 1960 Pontiac Catalina convertible. Then it was just his everyday car, and he used it for going to the store, getting to work, and for Saturday night dates. He courted his wife-to-be in the car and, in short, grew up with it. The car grew old and was traded in on something more practical for a family man. But no other car that Dick ever owned could ever replace his Catalina ragtop. Dick had contracted convertible fever.

The affliction got so bad that Dick finally realized he *had* to find another Pontiac convertible. First he bought a "ratty" 1969 model, and then a 1970 ragtop in better condition. Finally, he realized that nothing but another 1960 Catalina convertible would really do the trick. So recently, after a year of searching (including some costly dead-end trips to look at some beat-up machines), he found the right car and bought it. This time he swears there's no chance the car will be sold!

This type of love for a ragtop is the best reason I can give you for keeping your restored ragtop. Of course, you have to decide if you are susceptible to Convertible Fever. Not everybody is, but if you're a victim the best move that you can make is to hold onto that car. Never mind what it might be worth to anyone else. It's value to you is in the priceless category and there's no way that you'll be happy without it.

Sure, some people will recommend keeping a convertible as an investment. Others will say it's a good ego trip. There are those that believe all ragtops are extremely rare and valuable (not true) and others who view them as a status symbol. Nevertheless, the only real reason for keeping the car you've restored is because you love it. If this isn't the case, sell it as quick as you can.

With most convertibles, the quick sale (after a fresh restoration) will net you more than you've got invested in the car and you won't have to worry about maintenance, storage, insurance, and license plates. If you're happy with the way things worked out, use your profit to buy yourself an even better investment car, a more ego-building model.

If you love the car, keep it for as long as your passion stays hot. Put up with those costs and other problems as part of your hobby involvement. If you don't, you are likely to come down with convertible fever.

TRADING UP

In old car lingo, the term trading up can be applied to an actual trade (transfer of ownership without exchange of money) or to the sale (for money) of a vehicle. The important thing to grasp is not the means of purchase (barter or cash), but the concept that a car of particular value is being swapped for one of greater value. This is a very common method for the collector to use in creating a collection of particularly outstanding vehicles.

Through the process of trading up, the collector will be using his knowledge of the market, in combination with his restoration skills, to develop a collection that he probably could not afford to put together otherwise.

For example, one enthusiast might have a taste for authentic classic cars that normally sell in the $50,000 range. At the same time, his income limitations might prevent him from purchasing such cars out right. Yet, he knows that there are other cars that he can afford to purchase, restore, and sell for a reasonable profit. He might be able to locate a fairly nice Mustang convertible for $3,000, restore it to Number 1 condition and, finally, sell it for $10,000. Let's assume that he has $6,000 invested in the car. He has realized a $4,000 profit that can be applied to another car worth a little more. This car is then restored and resold for its market value, providing the collector some additional profit. If he continues to follow this process—making several wise purchases and sales—he will eventually be able to purchase the classic he wanted in the first place. In short, he has traded up to the car that he really wants.

Some people are very skilled traders and have successfully used such methods to build themselves excellent collections. The main factors they rely on for their success are knowledge of market trends and the ability to spot basically good cars that other people own, but do not know how to restore. Moving up market like this also demands the ability to spot new trends in the car-collecting field. In other words, if you can buy a certain model just before interest in it starts to grow, by the time the car is finished being restored it might double or triple in value.

At the current time, convertibles seem to be coming on strong as good prospects for trading up. While the ragtop market boomed during the late 1970s, there was a flattening-out period during the early 1980s. This was probably related to the fact that so many convertibles became available that they no longer seemed very special—temporarily. Now the convertible market is building again. With all-new ragtops being sold at prices from $10,000 to $20,000, the prices for older ones has started to spiral back upward again.

In actual figures, a model such as the 1975 Chevrolet

Caprice Classic convertible was selling for $4,000 to $6,000 in the period immediately after 1975. Around 1980, the prices for such a car dropped to the $2,500 to $3,500 range. Recently, this has climbed back up to the $4,500 to $6,500 bracket. If the trend continues, the value for this model will increase even more over the next few years. Collectors aware of this trend are now buying late-model ragtops again. Many are using these cars as a means of trading up to even more valuable models in the near future.

DETERMINED TO SELL?

While some hobbyists will hold onto their convertibles for a long time and others will use them for trading stock, there are other people who are simply determined to sell their cars right now. Many of these people enjoy the restoration end of the hobby rather than the ownership end. They restore many cars, and often sell them for just modest profits so they can obtain yet another restoration project.

Now that you've finished restoring your car, perhaps you're determined to sell it. If you fall into this group, there are several things that you have to consider prior to making the sale. You must know how to set a price. You must also know how to get your price. In addition, you have to know about the various places where you can market the vehicle.

SETTING YOUR PRICE

When you are selling a collector car, the various price guides to old-car values (Fig. 7-2) can be consulted for an idea of what the vehicle is worth. There are two important things to remember when using such publications to establish a selling price. The first point is to make sure that the listings are current. Market prices tend to fluctuate a great deal from year to year. If you consult a listing that is more than six months old, you might be hurting yourself. This time factor is very important to the seller because he will be trying to get as much as possible for the car. Only the latest issue of a price guide should be used. In most cases, collector cars tend to average a 10 percent annual appreciation rate. If you are using an outdated edition, you might loose several hundred dollars by refusing to spend a few bucks for the most current guide. With convertibles, the appreciation rate is generally above average so an even greater variation might be seen.

The second point to remember is that the editors who compile such price guides are trying to establish average figures, rather than values that are extremely high or low. The normal method for doing this is to disregard the peaks and valleys and to pinpoint the normal trend. As a seller, you should strive to obtain the peak (highest) price you can get for your car. If you are willing to settle for just an average price, you are not going to have much

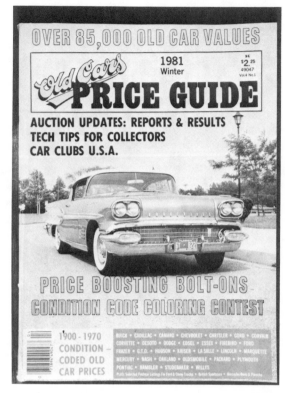

Fig. 7-2. Various price guides can be used to help set the prices for restored ragtops. Always use the most current issue due to the time lapse between compiling data and getting it into print. (Courtesy *Old Cars Price Guide*)

luck realizing a profit on the vehicles that you worked hard to find, buy, and restore.

I would recommend setting your price about 10 to 15 percent higher than that listed in a reputable price guide. This will bring you closer to the high side of the price bracket for your model and, in addition, will allow you a degree of bargaining room.

Another research source that is highly recommended as a guide for pricing a postwar ragtop for sale is the *Standard Catalog of American Cars 1946-1975* (Fig. 7-3). This book combines listings of current market values with technical, historical, and production data. It will tell you how many cars like yours were made, what equipment was standard and optional for the car, and it will help you determine if there is anything extra special about it.

Newsletters, bulletins, and magazines published by car clubs (Fig. 7-4) are another excellent source of pricing information. Most of these publications carry a section devoted to advertising cars for sale by club members. Usually, the prices in these club organs are a

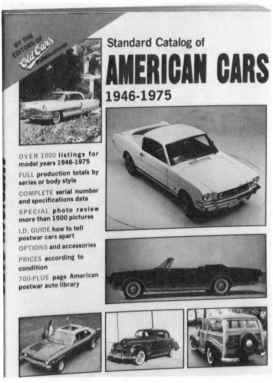

OVER 1000 listings for
model years 1946-1975

FULL production totals by
series or body style

COMPLETE serial number
and specifications data

SPECIAL photo review
more than 1500 pictures

I.D. GUIDE how to tell
postwar cars apart

OPTIONS and accessories

PRICES according to
condition

700-PLUS page American
postwar auto library

Fig. 7-3. The *Standard Catalog of American Cars
1946–1975* combines pricing charts with technical and
historical information that applies to postwar American
built models. (Courtesy Krause Publications)

a model. It's sometimes important to determine if a
dealer or private individual is selling the car. Prices
asked by dealers will be slightly above the going market
value.

GETTING YOUR PRICE

Once you have set the price that you want for your
restored convertible, the next step is to get that price or
at least one in the same neighborhood. To a great extent,
the price will depend upon the make and model of the car,
it's relative popularity, and its appearance. By and large,
these are factors that are out of your hands. You have
restored a certain type of car, but you can't change what
it is, it's level of appeal, or the way that it looks. You can,
however, present it to potential buyers in its best light.

If you are selling a car at your home, have the car
washed, waxed, and ready to go for a test drive (Fig. 7-6).
Place it on level ground and make sure the surroundings
look clean and neat. Keep that garage door closed and
make sure that the lawn is mowed. Buyers who come to
look will associate the appearance of your property with

THE PACKARD CORMORANT

Fig. 7-4. Club magazines, such as *The Packard
Cormorant,* carry classified ads of cars for sale. They can
be used to get an idea of asking prices. Club members
usually stay in more moderate price ranges than
advertisers in commercial magazines.

bit more realistic than those that appear in the more
commercial magazines.

The ads in club magazines are usually free to
members of the club. Consequently, the advertisers avoid
adding a premium to their asking prices just to cover the
cost of an ad (which is sometimes done with a paid ad).
Secondly, the club members realize that they are advertising to people who are experts in a particular make or
type of car. Setting the price too high is a sure way to turn
off potential buyers who know what the market is for
their favorite brand. Thirdly, there exists a high degree
of loyalty to other club members, and this tends to keep
pricing within reasonable bounds. It's not uncommon to
see ads that state "This car is being advertised in
commercial magazines at a slightly higher price," or
something to the same effect.

Another method that you can use to establish a
selling price is to look for cars like yours on sale at a car
show. There will usually be a sign on or near the car
stating the asking price (Fig. 7-5). In most cases, this will
be a little on the high side of the spectrum, but it will
provide a general idea of what people are asking for such

Fig. 7-5. Cars for sale appear in antique, classic, and special-interest automobile shows. These prices, if realistic, will be the most current ones.

the quality of the car. If your property looks like it is well cared for, this impression will automatically extend to the vehicle.

If you are planning to take the vehicle to a car show to sell it, it's a good idea to make it look like something really special. Park it away from other show cars and use some rope or plastic chain to create a crowd barrier. This will do at least two things. First, it gives the impression that the car is out of the ordinary. Second, it will protect the finish from being scratched or tarnished by sticky fingers. There's no better way to draw crowd interest than attempting to isolate a car in a show (Fig. 7-7).

It's surprising how many people take restored cars to a show to sell them, but then overlook small details that can make or break the success of a sale. I have seen cars for sale with flat tires, dirty whitewalls, incorrect radio antennas, two different headlight lenses, etc. Small items like these can be easily corrected without spending very much money. If they are overlooked, there's a good chance the buyer will think there are even more things wrong that he can't readily see. Why miss a big sale by failing to correct minor details?

The color of a car will have a great affect on its attractiveness to buyers. A red car will usually sell much faster—and higher—than a similar model done in a less flashy color. This is an important factor to consider at the beginning of your restoration. Authenticity should be your first consideration when picking a color for a car. If the vehicle has a specific data plate code that calls for a certain color, by all means paint it that shade. Where a choice was offered, it's to your advantage to pick the most exciting color possible. On convertibles, the color red has a degree of extra appeal to a buyer.

Don't be shy about promoting the features of a car or the fact that it is for sale. Place a large "For Sale" sign on the windshield, along with a card giving details a buyer will find interesting. Open the hood and show off that restored engine and engine compartment. If the car has a special type of convertible top, arrange things to show off this feature. Anything special about the model becomes a selling point in the collector-car marketplace.

HOW AN AUCTION WORKS

The classic car auction business is a relatively new way to sell a car. The first such sales were held in the 1960s when several private and museum collections were liquidated. Then the English auction house Sotheby Parke Bennett—well known in the world of art and collectibles—held several auctions. In the early 1970s, the Kruse Classic Auction Company, of Auburn, Indiana began to specialize in this field. In a short time, this firm was organizing dozens of such events each year.

Fig. 7-6. When selling a car, consider the setting in which you place it. Buyer's will be swayed by well-manicured lawns and nicely kept homes as a reflection of the care that the car has received.

In the mid-1970s, Kruse was having great success selling classic, antique, and special-interest cars. Then Detroit stopped making ragtops and the convertible became the hottest thing in the auction market. There was a tremendous boom in activity and new auctioneering firms were formed.

Around 1977, problems set in that ranged from companies going out of business to the bombing of one auction-company executives' car. A large amount of money (after being checked aboard an airplane) was stolen from the Kruse firm. There were problems involving car titles and ownership papers. Some owners who had signed their cars over to other parties were not paid for them. The auction companies served as the middleman between buyers and sellers, but had not refined their business practices to prevent such mistakes. In some instances, this led to companies loosing their licenses and in other cases the firms simply disappeared overnight.

Several companies—such as Hudson & Marshall, Sotheby Parke Bennett, Von Reece and Christies—had no troubles, but it was still clear that reforms in this industry would have to be made for the good companies to survive. Quick action took the form of more rigid control of paperwork, same-day payment plans for sell-ers, flat-fee charges, more attractive commission scales, and a general improvement in conditions. The Kruse company merged with Thorp Financial Services (a division of International Telephone & Telegraph) to regain its former stability.

The auction sales business is still a high-pressure system, but it is a basically honest one today. The auction companies usually work through the sponsorship of a local museum, dealer, or hobby/businessman to share the high operating expenses. This local agent organizes, promotes, advertises, and produces the event. The role of the auctioneers and their staffs is to handle the bids, announce the features of the car, and to try and create a meeting of minds between buyers and sellers.

Each auction company has developed its own system for running a sale, and each tends to have its own character. While the following guidelines won't apply in every case, they will outline the basic rules of the game. If you want to buy or sell a convertible at an auction, you should contact the companies directly to get their specific rules. All of them advertise heavily in the three major hobby periodicals, *Old Cars Weekly*, *Cars & Parts* and *Hemmings Motor News*, as well as in smaller magazines and, sometimes, local newspapers.

Those who are interested in buying a car have to

secure a bidder's number or card. To obtain this, the prospective purchaser must show the auction company that he has the means to pay for cars that he wants to buy. Usually, this means cash, a cashier's check or a personal check accompanied by an irrevocable letter of credit from the buyer's bank. Sometimes a deposit will also be required as proof of intent to pay for a purchase.

The auction company sometimes earns part of its income by charging the buyer a commission on the selling price of the car. If the commission is 10 percent and the buyer places the highest acceptable bid, he will have to pay the price that he bid, plus 10 percent. Commission charges work on a sliding scale. For example, they might run 10 percent on cars selling up to a certain figure (say $100,000) and then drop to 8 percent on amounts above that level. It is the buyer's responsibility to check the practices of the firm he is dealing with. Some have much better scales than others.

The buyer who registers properly, supplying all necessary proof of his personal financial health, will be given a front-row seat at the sale. Rear seating will be for the general public and might require the payment of a general admission charge. At other sales, spectators are allowed to observe the proceedings for free (from the rear seats).

The auction firms sometimes sell catalogs that list the features of the cars. In addition, they usually provide sheets by which records of the sale can be jotted down. Such sheets will list most cars consigned to a sale. There may be open slots for last-minute entries.

A good auction company will know many of the buyers and their tastes in collector cars. They will know the man who wants a Mustang convertible and the lady who owns a dealership specializing in Lincoln-Continental cabriolets. They will recognize the wealthy dentist who likes Corvette ragtops. "C'mon Doc, you know this is the car for you," they will tease.

The auctioneer calls the bids. "I have $30,000 on this car," he'll announce, "Do I hear $35,000 for a beautiful, one-of-a-kind automobile." Dancing around the car and in front of the most likely buyers will be several gents—usually dressed in Tuxedos—waving their arms and running back and forth between the auctioneer and the buyers. They are the ring men. What they're doing is carrying offers up to the auctioneer or trying to work the crowd for the next highest bid. As they move about rapidly, they will open the hood, doors, and trunk of the car or ask the driver (who is not always the car owner) to raise and lower the convertible roof. They are trying to promote the sale of the vehicle during the few minutes when it is driven "across the block" to be sold. It's a strictly high-energy situation.

So much for the buying part of the game. Let's assume you now are trying to sell your ragtop at the same sale. As we noted, some auction firms charge a commission to buyers, but many do not. They see their role as one of working for the seller, and that is where the commission is charged. Even before he pays a commission, the seller must pay an entry fee and supply proof that he has a lien-free title for the vehicle. The entry or consignment fee will usually run $50 to $200. This must be paid whether or not the car is sold. The commission is

Fig. 7-7. When attempting to sell a car at a show, do all that you can to make it seem special. This can include roping it off and using signs to describe it's features.

calculated on a sliding scale. The commission is only paid when the auction firm has secured a bid high enough to encourage the actual sale of a car.

In some cases, the buyer agrees to accept the highest bid for the car. This is an open-bidding situation and the rules of the game require that the car changes hands for this price—even if it is very low. At one auction, I watched as a man paid $200 to enter an original-condition Edsel (Number 4 condition), and then had to accept the high bid of $150 for the car.

No, you don't have to lose money in an auction. When you consign your car, you can set a reserve price that is the minimum you'll accept for the vehicle. Because no-reserve cars sell easier and faster, it costs the seller less to consign without setting a reserve. The entry fees and commissions on cars with reserve prices are higher. This is because the auction company has to work harder to get that established reserve price. With no-reserve deals, the seller is sticking his neck out. On cars with reserve prices, he is paying more for keeping his neck protected.

If the seller sets a reserve of $3,000, but then wants to sell to a man who bids $2,900, the seller can drop his reserve. "The reserve is off . . . this car's for sale," the auctioneer will announce. This will sometimes regenerate the competitive spirit in two potential buyers and bring the bids over the reserve anyway. In other cases, the car will simply sell for slightly less than the original reserve. This is something probably allowed for by the seller when the original reserve price was set.

Generally, as a seller, you are putting trust in the fact that the auction company has brought buyers to a certain sale and knows how to get them interested in your car. Prior to the point where the car comes across the block, you should provide the auctioneers with all information about the car's special features. This will be ammunition for making a proper presentation of your vehicle.

YOUR ROLE AS A SELLER

As a seller, there are certain things you should think about if you hope to get top dollar for your car. Investigate the different auction companies. Check their rates, but also try to find how successful they've been in selling cars at previous sales. The companies with the best reputations usually charge the highest entry fees and commissions because they have the best track record of working for seller satisfaction.

Find out who is sponsoring the sale locally and where it is going to be held. Some auctions are held outdoors under large tents. Others unfold at indoor arenas such as hotels, convention centers, exposition buildings, and coliseums. There is no rule as to whether indoor or outdoor sale sites work better, but if you see a sale advertised as being held outdoors in Alaska during the winter there's probably something fishy. No reputable firm is going to do something like that. On the other

hand, a sale scheduled for Tampa, Florida in midwinter seems more logical. There are several major antique car events staged in Florida during this time and they draw well-to-do collectors in droves. This means that some of these people will probably attend such an auction.

Some individual auctioneers have earned envious reputations for their ability to get high prices for cars. Dean Kruse is one such person and probably one of the most colorful real personalities in the business. Like a top-notch sales rep, Kruse is known for his ability to close a good deal. The auctioneers working for all companies mentioned here are those best-recognized in the specialized classic car field. At many smaller sales, the auctioneer will be someone equally as qualified at selling all types of antiques within a certain area. Always go with either the nationally known specialist or the familar local expert, but beware of Colonel Klink from Transylvania who suddenly pops up with a sale in Illinois. Your chances of selling a car at his auction might not be that good.

As a seller, it's also your responsibility to get the car to a sale and have it looking good and running smoothly. That ring man can't do a good job promoting your vehicle to interested buyers if he steps on the running board and it starts to cave in.

The car should be clean and sharp. Spend the weeks before an auction detailing the vehicle with touch-up paint and polish. If necessary, have it tuned-up or tune it yourself. Last, but not least, make sure there's plenty of gas in the tank (unless prohibited at indoor sales). If the fuel runs out, it might wind up being pushed across the block in front of some uninterested buyers. If you are driving the car yourself, its movement across the block should go smoothly. If you are also a bidder, the driving might be done by an auction company employee hired for this purpose. Make sure they know about the fine points of its operation so that it doesn't stall when it's in the spotlight.

After putting a great deal of thought into selecting a good auction and well-respected auction firm, listen to their advice. Chances are you have set your desired reserve price according to one of the price guides or prices that you've seen advertised in magazines. Maybe it's just a little too high for the current market conditions. I've seen sellers place $10,000 reserves on $500 cars! Also, many owners tend to overrate the condition of their vehicle. They think of their Number 3 car as a Number 1 and set their reserves accordingly. Yet, the experienced buyer knows he is going to have to completely tear down the car to move up two notches in condition. He won't buy unless you allow for at least part of the expense.

The auctioneers and ring men who know their job might beckon you up to the front of the crowd and tell you, "Look, I think you have set your reserve too high. We have a bid of $15,000 and you want $20,000. There's a dentist willing to pay $17,500, and that's really about what this type of car is going for right now. Six months ago, when that price guide was printed, the prices were a little stronger, but they're down a bit now and will probably slide some more next year. I'd recommend selling for $17,500 . . . taking your original reserve off."

Chances are that the ring man's advice is solid. Listen to what he has to say with an open mind. If you're already convinced he's an expert, there's probably good reason to follow his advice. He attends auctions in different parts of the country each week and knows the market. He's also used to making quick, but sound decisions. In most cases, what he says will be as reliable as the recommendations of a banker, stock broker, or real estate agent. Don't follow blindly, but hear him out and concentrate your thoughts on exactly what he is saying. Don't let preconceived notions get in the way.

WHY NOT INVEST IN ANOTHER RAGTOP?

If you are now hooked on being a convertible owner and have sold a restored car for a profit, it's probably wise to take part of the gain you've realized and invest it in another car. Always do this by upgrading. If you invested $10,000 in the car and you sold it for $16,000, put around $13,000 into the next ragtop. This will allow you to move upscale in terms of model or classification. Perhaps, the first car was a more common postwar convertible that you bought for $6,000 and spent $4,000 restoring. Your work earned you a $6,000 profit. Now it's time to get a less common car.

The cost of restoring a more specialized vehicle won't be much higher than the cost of restoring the common one. Admittedly, parts for the rarer car might be a bit more expensive, but the time and labor factors will be about the same. So, let's say that the rarer car will run $5,000 in restoration expense. That means it can be a model with an $8,000 price tag—perhaps a recognized milestone car.

After you have put your $5,000 restoration into the milestone car, you'll have $13,000 invested. The vehicle probably will be worth $25,000. If you sell this one, your profit climbs to $12,000 (on the milestone), plus you still have $3,000 in the bank (from the first sale). Now you can bank $6,000 (half of your profit) and purchase a mid-condition-range classic that might cost $6,000 to restore to Number 1 shape. If you spend $19,000 on the car and $6,000 on the restoration, there's a total of $25,000 invested, but the open-body classic is probably worth at least $50,000. Because restoration costs are nearly constant for all types of cars, you can keep moving upscale by being a smart buyer.

There are limits to this type of thing. As the dollar value rises, you'll find the cars getting rarer and more exclusive. Finally, you'll reach a point where parts prices rise suddenly and significantly. Thereafter, the cost of restoration will grow so high that your profit margin isn't as great.

This is the apex of the collector's market, and it's better left to certain people who have the parts or specialization necessary to restore grand classics and make it pay. Specialists will be able to find the buyers at the tip of the market, but you will have a major problem doing the same. While waiting for a buyer, you could have hundreds of thousands of dollars tied up in a vehicle, possibly with interest payments eating away your investment.

PART 3
Rarities and Trends

THIS SECTION IS DEVOTED TO A CLOSE LOOK AT THE HISTORY AND NATURE OF THE CONVERTIBLE. IT IS THROUGH A DEEPER understanding and appreciation of convertible styles that your skills as a collector will be honed.

To become a collector of convertibles—as opposed to simply owning a ragtop or buying such a model as an investment—it is necessary to know about automobiles and about automotive history. If you know cars, love cars, and understand cars, you will be an expert collector.

I believe that the way to reach this level of expertise is to immerse yourself in the history of the cars you collect. Read everything you can about the glorious automobiles of the past, and do so with an open mind. Don't limit your knowledge to a certain brand or a certain era. It is wise to specialize to a degree, but don't develop tunnel vision. Your main purpose in creating a worthwhile collection of any type of cars is to obtain those models that will appreciate in value and grow in desirability. The cars that you choose should rate as universal favorites. In other words, those models recognized by the majority of collectors as something-special automobiles.

The person who merely comes to own a convertible will focus on only the model he owns. The investor will attempt to study the market trends and base any purchases strictly on rapid value appreciation. The true collector will be able to select the best cars through his knowledge, love, and appreciation of the machines. This is the only, absolutely foolproof way to recognize the best cars to have in a collection!

8. They Were All Ragtops Once

The great majority of cars built prior to 1925 were ragtops, but these cars are not normally thought of as convertibles by collectors. This can cause initial confusion because it is not uncommon to read general-interest articles and books in which runabouts, roadsters, touring cars, and other such body styles are referred to as convertibles. The problem is that it's not very easy to come up with a clear-cut distinction that separates generic terms such as *ragtop* or *open-body car* from the more specific term *convertible*.

It's virtually impossible to define the term convertible to the complete satisfaction of everyone. Even automotive experts, historians, collectors, and hobbyists get into long-drawn arguments over what the word convertible means. The meaning of the word has changed slightly in the last 30-odd years. The reasons for the changes are related to styling changes in automobiles such as the 1957–1959 Ford retractable hardtop (with a top that kind of "flapped," but sure didn't fold) or the Corvettes, Thunderbirds and other sporty cars that came with optional, removable hardtops. Even the slightly broader definition that allows for these styling changes does not spell out the differences between roadster and a true convertible coupe.

To most collectors, a convertible has certain additional distinctions that aren't found on runabouts, roadsters, and touring cars. They include features such as roll-up windows and fixed-position windshields. The automotive buff holds a much stricter definition of the term convertible that is generally more in line with the way that the Society of Automotive Engineers (SAE) standardized it for auto manufacturing purposes.

Sometimes this creates additional difficulties because not all manufacturers played by SAE rules. When Chevrolet introduced the Corvette in 1953, it was classified a roadster-convertible. Even in a very strict sense, this designation seems confusing because it simply doesn't jibe with the standard industry terminology.

What is the common usage in this field? If you ask an experienced collector to point out the convertibles at an old-car show, he will probably select those models that have a folding, retractable or removable top, a fixed-position windshield, and roll-up side door windows.

This doesn't mean, however, that the history of convertibles began in the 1927–1928 period. The term itself appeared one year prior to standardization. The convertible is still part of the larger, generic group that can best be classified as ragtops. The history of ragtop cars begins at a time prior to the turn of the century.

The automobile, or "motor buggy" evolved from the carriage-building trade. The Society of Automotive Historians recognizes the steam-powered Cugnot as the first automobile. For practical purposes, the automobile industry in America got into gear in the late 1880s.

At this point, the manufacture of motorized vehicles was primarily a cottage industry. Hundreds of inventors were building one-off motor buggies in backyards and

Fig. 8-1. The automobile evolved from the horseless carriage and had open-top styling similar to horse-drawn buggies.

Fig. 8-2. The folding top on this 1905 rope-drive Holsman was a $50 option.

small blacksmith shops. These creations resembled the familiar horsedrawn carriages of the day (Fig. 8-1) except that the horse was out of the picture.

The motors used in these automobiles were 1-cylinder or 2-cylinder types and, in most cases, power was transmitted to the rear wheels by straps and pulleys, chains and sprockets, or even simple, rope-drive systems like that used on the 1905 Holsman "high-wheeler" (Fig 8-2). Nearly all of these horseless carriages were open-body vehicles; some came with optional folding tops similar to those seen on wagons. Made of leather or leatherette, the tops added $50 to $75 to the price of the car.

CLOSED CARS VERSUS RAGTOPS

In 1908, the ragtop (Fig. 8-3) was still the predominant body style in the auto industry. Closed cars were available in many lines by 1905, but primarily as custom-built offerings. Mass-production techniques were not employed for building closed cars; this made such models quite expensive to own.

In the early Teens the typical price for an open roadster (Fig. 8-4) was in the $800 to $900 range. Touring cars sold at just over $1,000. By contrast, coupes

Fig. 8-3. A team-powered 1908 Stanley touring car looks less like a wagon and more like an automobile. The folding top was an accessory. (Michael A. Carbonella photo)

Fig. 8-4. Most early cars were "ragtops," but did not have roll-up windows associated with later convertibles. This is a 1914 Abbott-Detroit roadster. (Courtesy Henry Ford Museum)

had a minimum price of around $1,500 and might run as high as twice that figure. Sedans and limousines, selling from $3,000 to $5,000, were out of the reach of most auto buyers. The pricing of the different body styles was one big reason for the vast popularity of open cars.

The manner in which early cars were used also played a role in determining body style trends of the day. Automobiles were thought of primarily as toys for adults. They were rarely used for everyday transportation. Instead they were used for taking Sunday tours into the countryside. If the weather was bad, the car stayed in the garage. For such purposes, open-body cars were sufficient and, most likely, preferable. Taking a ride was like an adventure, and a little wind in the face simply heightened the thrill.

This situation and these price relationships stayed basically the same through the World War I period. When the war ended, there was a sudden spurt of interest in buying closed cars. The change of taste reflected a major transition of the automobile's role in society. Before World War I, the major use of cars was pleasure driving. After the war buyers wanted cars that could be used on a year-round basis, in every type of weather. This type of service could only be provided by close-bodied models.

The more expensive closed cars were extremely expensive, custom-bodied models. But the splurge of postwar buying showed the manufacturers that there was an untapped market for affordable coupes and sedans. The main problem was that these cars were out of the average buyer's reach (except during the period immediately after the war ended).

It didn't take long for Detroit to realize that the prices for closed cars could be reduced by switching these models from specialty items to regular production cars. As long as a sizeable market existed, the coupes and sedans could be built in larger numbers, on regular assembly lines, at a great saving in cost. Efficiencies realized through high-volume production could bring manufacturing costs down.

As the prices on close-bodied cars began to drop, the ragtop's domination of the market diminished. The pattern from 1919 through 1927 is shown in Table 8-1. Once the move to closed cars began, it wasn't limited only to less expensive models. Even buyers of high-priced brands began to change over to closed bodies. This is reflected in Table 8-2. The production percentages for closed cars in each price class from 1919 to 1926 are shown.

It wasn't price alone that was doing the ragtop in. More and more buyers of all types of cars were starting to appreciate the advantages of driving in solidly built, weathertight cars that offered greater safety, comfort, and convenience.

From 1923 on, ragtop models such as roadsters and touring cars started to get more sporty and stylish in an effort to maintain at least some degree of buyer interest.

Common design changes included lowered hood lines, low-cut doors, extra nickle plating, more rakish slants to the windshield, and sleeker-looking rear deck contours (Fig. 8-5). In essence, the open cars were starting to assume the old role of the coupes and sedans (that is, the role of a specialty model). The fancier variations were often cataloged as "sports" models. This did not, however, stem the trend toward more sales of closed cars.

Ford Motor Company was the leading producer of open-bodied styles in this era, and with good reason. In 1928, the company introduced its peppy new Model A. Seven different body styles were made available, including a two-passenger roadster priced at $385, a rumble-seat roadster that sold for $420, and a five-passenger phaeton with a $395 price tag. For the money, these cars were an outstanding bargain. They came with many extra-cost accessories that could be ordered to "fancy" them up (Fig. 8-6).

The Model A roadsters and phaetons helped Ford Motor Company dominate what was left of the open-bodied car market. The company's strength in this field was further enhanced by the addition of deluxe trim versions and a convertible (cabriolet) by 1930. Nevertheless, in the same period the number of closed cars in the Ford Model A line went from four (in 1928) to ten. In 1931, a convertible sedan was added to the line. This was a clear indication that Ford needed even more roll-up window convertibles to keep up with the changing body style preferences of buyers.

As a last ditch effort to salvage the market for roadsters and touring cars, other manufacturers began to follow Ford's lead in offering sportier, more stylish versions of these body styles. Pontiac, for example, added a roadster that had special-appearance features designed to catch the buyers' eyes (Fig. 8-7). The body on this model was built by the W.F. Stewart Company of Jackson, Michigan. It featured a special two-beaded molding treatment having ornate scrollwork at the leading edge and enclosing a bright color contrast panel. Body finish was available in two distinctive color combinations. The first was Atoka Cream with Mohawk Brown window reveals, Ontonagon Maroon moldings, and Warrior Red striping. The second was Sachem Blue with Mohawk Brown and Tacoma Cream trim.

In spite of the extra-sporty styling and eye-catching paint jobs seen from about 1929 on, the market for roadsters and touring cars continued to decline at a rapid pace. None of the special features could turn the sales trends around. In the battle of closed cars versus ragtops the coupes, sedans and other closed styles were proving to be the big winners.

CLASSIC-ERA CONVERTIBLES

The convertibles that are most appealing and desirable to collectors are those that qualify as classic cars. What constitutes an authentic classic? As is true with the word

Table 8-1. Percentage Production of Closed Cars by Price Class.

Year	Percent of Open Cars	Percent of Closed Cars
1919	90	10
1920	84	16
1021	78	22
1922	70	30
1923	66	34
1924	57	43
1925	44	56
1926	36	74
1927	15	85

convertible, there are several different ways in which the designation classic car can be used today.

Classic car has often been incorrectly used to label any vehicle more than 10 years old or any car that seems to be collectable before it reaches antique auto status. An antique auto is generally considered to be one that is at least 25 years old. This led to mislabeling such automobile as 1950 Nash Rambler convertibles and 1966 Ford four-door sedans as classics.

The main problem here is that owners are trying to classify their cars according to age. Because they realize that the vehicle is not an antique, they use the word classic as an alternative label. Classic car—in its prime sense—implies that a vehicle is one of the highest quality, without regard to age. It is wrong to use the designation to classify a car based solely on how old it is.

Certain periods of automotive history have been recognized as classic eras. This does not mean that all cars built during these years were classics, but it does imply that the highest-quality cars of the period have certain, common, identifiable characteristics that elevate them to the first or highest rank.

In the old-car hobby, the determination of classic eras has been made by several different car clubs that, because of either their size or prestige, have become arbiters of the issue. This has created some degree of

controversy because the various clubs have different philosophies or goals. For example, some are conservative in making their classifications; a car listed as a classic by one organization might not be accepted by another. Likewise, some clubs restrict their classifications solely to 1925-1948 luxury models. Others cover only a few, specific post World War II models.

Any car regarded as a classic by any club gains in value because of this special recognition. The two different types of classics are those cars long considered authentic classic cars and modern classics (or milestone cars).

Three of the older, more established hobby organizations are the Classic Car Club of America (CCCA), the Veteran Motor Car Club of America (VMCCA), and the Antique Automobile Club of America (AACA).

In general, the convertibles accepted as classics by these clubs are prewar models (and a handful of limited-production postwar cars) with extremely high collector values in the $40,000 to $600,000 range. By one standard or another, these cars were picked as the most superlative motor vehicles built during the "Golden Age of Motoring," which means the period of 1925-1949, during which custom coachbuilding on special factory-supplied chassis was available to prestige car buyers.

Of the three clubs the CCCA is generally considered

Table 8-2. Production Percentages.

Year	Under $1,000	$1,000-$2,000	$2,000-$3,000	Over $3,000
1919	0.90	08.0	24.0	30.5
1920	19.1	12.0	22.0	22.3
1921	21.5	18.4	36.8	44.3
1922	24.1	39.3	79.8	78.0
1923	32.5	35.8	83.0	90.6
1924	32.1	71.2	77.5	90.5
1925	54.2	80.3	87.0	89.6
1926	72.5	90.1	89.9	79.9

Fig. 8-5. In the early 1920s, the popularity of open cars was dropping. To keep sales as strong as possible, more sporty features became standard equipment. This is a 1923 Oakland sport roadster. (Courtesy Crestline Publishing)

Fig. 8-6. Model A Ford line offered low-priced open cars with many sporty features. This is a Model A phaeton.

Fig. 8-7. To boost open car sales in the late 1920s, attractive color schemes were offered on roadsters and touring cars such as this 1929 Pontiac. (Courtesy Crestline Publishing)

to have the strictest qualifications for rating a car as a classic. The CCCA has created a list of classic cars based on certain concrete factors that include original factory price, production total, equipment features, powertrain features, engine displacement, and a few other points.

By CCCA standards, a classic car is a 1925-1948 model with an extremely high original price, low production total, equipment features comparable to those found on the highest quality cars of the period, an especially powerful drivetrain arrangement, and a large displacement engine. Selections for the CCCA list are made by the club's Classification Committee. There is some flexibility in that cars not normally included on the list can qualify as classics according to individual owner application (if the vehicle meets many of the criteria).

This does not mean that a standard production car—say a 1934 Ford convertible—will be accepted; such vehicles don't meet the criteria. Nevertheless, an unusual 1934 Ford with a Brewster body and special "heart-front" styling would be recognized because it's a special, custom-built vehicle. These Brewster-bodied Fords are now regularly included on the CCCA list.

The rules that the VMCCA and AACA use to qualify a classic car are considered a bit more liberal, but they are also designed to recognize the same general type of factors and features as well as the same basic years.

In this book, the convertibles of the authentic classic era are those models recognized by either the CCCA, VMCCA, or AACA. To a large degree, they are cars that have a number of common attributes that make them highly valuable and desirable to collectors.

To earn approval as a classic, a car must have certain identifiable attributes, qualities, or features that set it apart from the run-of-the-mill automobile. The most obvious classic characteristic is size. This is generally expressed in terms of wheelbase or overall length. In addition, large-sized cars are usually higher, heavier, and equipped with larger-sized tires than the average car of the same period.

For example, the 1929 Cadillac Model 341-B Club Cabriolet in the Fleetwood custom body line (Fig. 8-8) is a classic car. This model rides on a long 140-inch wheelbase and weighs in at 4850 pounds. Large, 32×6.75 tires mounted on artillery-type spoke wheels

Fig. 8-8. Two traits of authentic classics are custom-built bodies and large size. This 1929 Cadillac Model 341-B Club Cabriolet has a huge 140-inch wheelbase and Fleetwood custom body.

were standard equipment. These statistics compare to a 107-inch wheelbase, 2470 pound weight, and 20-×-4.50 tires on a 1929 Chevrolet Cabriolet. You can see that the Classic Cadillac was much heftier than the nonclassic Chevrolet.

To the people who bought these luxury cars, size was considered a measure of stature and prestige. A big car represented a picture of personal achievement and success. It was a quality that luxury-class buyers were willing to pay $2,000 to $3,000 extra to have in their automobiles. Today, a Cadillac like this would be worth around $50,000 to collectors. A 1929 Chevrolet convertible, in top condition, is valued at about one-third as much.

Special styling features are another characteristic of true classic cars. Some of the first real convertibles were available only as coachbuilt models. These cars appeared as limited-edition automobiles for several years (before the automakers began offering similar styling on their regular production cars).

Prior to the late 1920s, styling was not even considered an important factor in the design of factory-built models. Most nonclassic cars—and even some classics—looked a lot like tall, square boxes on wheels. The LaSalle of this era was one of the first American cars to actually be styled to suit different buyer's tastes. Produced by General Motors' Cadillac Division beginning in 1927, the first LaSalles were designed under the direction of Harley Earl, who created the company's new Art and

Colour Section. This is part of the reason that early LaSalles are considered classic cars. For example, the beautiful lines of the 1931 LaSalle Model 345A convertible coupe (Fig. 8-9) gave it an appearance that was far more pleasing to the eye than that of its lower-priced contemporaries.

Most classic LaSalles have special factory bodies that were created in the Fleetwood studios, but built on Cadillac assembly lines. They are also slightly smaller than Cadillacs and other true coachbuilt models. For instance, the 1931 convertible had a 134-inch wheelbase, 4425 pound shipping weight, and 19-×-6.50 tires. Because they were trimmer and somewhat less exclusive than the bigger prestige cars, a LaSalle convertible of this vintage would bring about $60,000. This compares to around $90,000 for a V-8 Cadillac of the same year and body type. This makes LaSalles an attractive buy on the low end of today's classic car market. It also means that there is a lot of room for appreciation.

Most cars that are considered classics today were originally sold to buyers who "loaded" them with plenty of extra-cost accessories. Typical equipment on a 1931 Cadillac Model 355 convertible coupe (Fig. 8-10) included chrome-plated headlamps, a "flying godess" hood mascot, plated landau irons, wire spoked wheels, side-mounted spare tires (with strap-on rearview mirrors), bumpers, dual horns, dual taillamps, and rear-mounted touring trunk. If that sounds like a lot, just consider that this was the lowest-priced Cadillac Series with V-8 power and a $2,995 price tag for the convertible. The company also offered a V-12 convertible at $4,045 and a V-16 edition at $6,900. They were comparably or better equipped.

Accessories for classic cars are very desirable today and that means high prices. For example, one of those touring trunks alone will bring $600 to $1000 at the old-car flea markets.

Large displacement, multicylinder engines are another characteristic of authentic early classics. There are very few such models that don't have at least eight cylinders below their hoods. Some even have 12- or 16-cylinder powerplants. In 1933, the Packard Motor Car Company offered three 8-cylinder lines and a pair of 12-cylinder series (Fig. 8-11).

How highly powerful engines are regarded by collectors today is clearly reflected in prices listed for Number-1 condition 1933 Cadillac convertibles in the *Old Cars Price Guide* (Summer 1983 edition). A V-8 model would be worth about $46,000, a V-12 would bring approximately $70,000 and the V-16 would bring some $95,000. Part of the price variation is related to rarity as Cadillac, in that year, built 2096 eights, 952 V-12s and just 125 V-16s in all body styles.

Duesenberg is another of the Classic marques that reflects all of the qualities we've mentioned so far, though none more important than rarity. Nearly every "Duesie" is a one-off creation that represents the ultimate in automotive craftsmanship. Prices for Duesenbergs begin at around $200,000 and have hit nearly three times that figure for the choicest examples! How rare are Duesenbergs? According to Ken Purdy's 1949 book *Kings of the Road* a total of 650 examples of all types were built between 1921 and 1937. Collectors today place the 1983 survival count at approximately 400 cars.

Distinctive factory styling is one of the attributes embodied in later Auburns and a factor which helped them achieve recognition as classics. A 1936 Auburn Model 852 cabriolet (Fig. 8-12) reflects a most handsome-looking automobile with a character all of its own. These cars were also quite powerful, too. Under the hood was a 113-horsepower Model "GG" Lycoming straight-8 engine with 280 cubic inches of piston displacement that could speed them close to 100 miles-per-hour.

Many open classics of the later 1930s and 1940s are good buys today because of the affordability factor. This was a period where the traditional market for big, luxury cars with coachbuilt bodies was waning. The reason of course was the economic devastation of the Great Depression. To salvage some degree of business in the high-priced field, the automakers began introducing models that were every bit as handsome and technically advanced as the custom body cars, but not quite as exclusive.

The 1936 Packard Series 1401 Coupe Roadster was a good illustration of this kind of machine. Don't be fooled

Fig. 8-9. The classic 1931 LaSalle Model 345A Convertible was a styling innovation. This car was found in a junkyard and restored. (Michael A. Carbonella photo)

Fig. 8-10. Classic car values are affected by optional equipment like a flying lady hood mascot, side-mounted spares, and rear-mounted touring trunk on 1931 Cadillac 355 Convertible (Michael A. Carbonella photo)

Fig. 8-11. Packard offered 8-cylinder and 12-cylinder models for 1933. The bigger the engine, the higher the value in most cases. (Michael A. Carbonella photo)

Fig. 8-12. Auburn convertibles featured distinctive styling and an easily identified grille design. Supercharged versions have pipes extending from the hood, but this is a nonsupercharged 1936 Model 852.

by the model name—it was a true convertible with a weather tight roof and fixed windshield. With a little budget stretching, the contemporary buyer with modest income and taste for fine cars could afford to go the $2,730 necessary to purchase this type of Packard. That money gave him a semicustom design, a straight eight engine, and a substantial 134-inch wheelbase automobile.

Today, cars like this are considered classics the average collector can purchase without climbing into the six-figure bracket. For about $40,000, examples in Number-1 condition will be found in the hobby market. The potential for appreciation is excellent. Unlike the big classics, that are now priced too high for the great majority of hobbyists, the smaller classics seem to have almost unlimited room for value growth.

Classic Car status is not limited to American-built cars. Many of the most desirable models are of foreign manufacture. In the case of Rolls–Royce, both foreign built versions and those made in Springfield, Massachusetts (during the mid-1920s) are full classics. Under CCCA guidelines, postwar Rolls–Royce models are accepted as classics per individual owner application. The VMCCA and AACA recognize all products of Rolls–Royce as classics. With any foreign convertible, the best practice is to consult the classification lists of the different clubs.

There are relatively few postwar brands and models that classify as full classic cars. Among this select group are very few open-bodied types. The majority of postwar classics seem to be limousines and large sedans with factory-built semicustom bodies. Lincoln–Continental is a notable exception for marques of domestic manufacture. All Lincoln–Continentals built from 1940-1948 are accorded classic car status by the three clubs that formulate the lists. The original style of 1940-1941 (Fig. 8-13) and the later style of 1946-1948 featured rather distinctive styling and were powered by a 12-cylinder motor.

For many years, it was considered acceptable, in the hobby, to change the motors in these Lincoln–Continentals without affecting their classic status. The Lincoln V-12 had a few characteristic mechanical problems that made it seem unreliable. Conversions to Mercury, Oldsmobile or Cadillac V-8s were quite common and, usually, did not hurt the value of the cars or their performance in concours judging. Today, however, it is considered good practice to restore these cars with the original V-12 in order to achieve a show quality product. Due to improvements in service procedures and the availability of high-quality replacement parts, the V-12s can now be rebuilt easier and better than was possible 20 to 30 years ago.

The early Lincoln–Continental with a nonoriginal engine today is worth considerably less than a complete car with the correct powerplant. Keep this in mind when considering the purchase of such a model. If the car is V-8 powered, you should be able to get it at a real bargain price and change back to V-12 power without greatly

135

Fig. 8-13. Lincoln–Continental is one of relatively few postwar and prewar classics. This is a 1941 Cabriolet. (Michael A. Carbonella photo)

affecting the total restoration costs. Many hobbyists who do their own mechanical work have taken advantage of this situation to obtain their first classic at a reasonable cost.

When restored to original specifications, these continental convertibles are valued in the $25,000-to-$30,000 range for examples in top condition. Also, they are considered very desirable models to own because of their sleek and rich-looking styling that represents an innovative approach to automobile design during the immediate prewar and postwar period.

Contrasted to the Lincoln–Continental—which represented a progressive approach to styling in the 1940–1948 era—other brands like Packard are popular with classic car collectors because they retained a "classic" appearance during the same period. For example, the 1940 Super Eight convertible coupe (Fig. 8-14) had frontal styling that evolved directly from the 1934 models. Undoubtedly, the fender and rear body lines were modestly updated to reflect streamlining here and there, but in the overall sense Packard followed a conservative styling pattern (on most models) through the start of World War II, with just a slight modernization thereafter, through 1948.

One exception to Packard's traditionalism was the Darrin designed models available in both the 1801 (Standard Eight) and 1808 (Custom Super Eight) Series' for 1940 and the 1096-1907-2006 (Custom Super Special) Series' for 1941–1942. Using the same hood and radiator grille, the Packard–Darrin Convertible Victoria (Fig. 8-15) sported modified front fenders, cutdown upper door sills, special top styling, more rounded lines, and came without running boards. These cars are considered full classics. Owner application might be required in the case of the 1940 Standard Eight version. The name of the model comes from the name of the designer, Howard "Dutch" Darrin, who had formerly operated a custom coachbuilding firm, in Paris, France, with Thomas Hibbard (Hibbard & Darrin).

FOUR-DOOR CONVERTIBLES

The four-door convertible body style evolved from the touring car and phaeton, but never achieved the same level of popularity among contemporary buyers. Four-door convertibles were always built in much smaller quantities and surviving examples are rarities today.

136

Fig. 8-14. The Super-Eight Packard convertible coupe of 1940 features more streamlining. This is probably a factory-bodied job. (Michael A. Carbonella photo)

Fig. 8-15. The 1941 Packard Darrin convertible had special styling features like cut-down doors. (Michael A. Carbonella photo)

Like the two-door variety (Cabriolet, Convertible Coupe, Coupe Roadster, Convertible Victoria, etc.,) four-door open cars with roll-up windows, fixed windshields, and weathertight roofs were marketed under a variety of names. The majority of these cars were of prewar manufacture, but some were also built during the postwar period. This latter group includes models from Kaiser–Frazer, Willys–Overland, Lincoln–Continental and Mercedes–Benz. Some of which were offered as late as the 1960s.

The four-door convertible has always been an attention-getter due to relative scarcity and because such styling combines sportiness with the added appeal of extra passenger room. Nevertheless, the overall market for such models stayed quite small because of the impracticality of owning a large, family-type car with a somewhat impractical folding top. From an engineering standpoint, it is not an easy job to design a four-door convertible because of the difficulty of fashioning a reliable top-riser mechanism for a large, open car.

In addition, providing such models with an attractive appearance is a major challenge to the skill of even the most gifted stylist. As many old-car hobbyists have learned, replacing a large, folding roof can be an expensive and nearly impossible job to accomplish.

Due to factors such as these, production of four-door convertibles has never amounted to more than a trickle of cars leaving the auto industry assembly lines. Total production of open-bodied, four-doors during the years of peak popularity (1931–1935) accounted for only a .42 percent average market share in both the United States and Canada. The highpoint for sales of this style appears to have been 1931. Then a mere 19,082 Convertible Sedans were built by factories in both North American nations.

Covering the years 1936–1941, the output of four-door convertibles is simply lumped-into the "Roadster and Touring Car" category (which in itself was not very big). An indication of more specific trends for this period can be obtained by counting the number of 1938 Cadillac Convertible Sedans built in the company's five series that season. See Table 8-3. Also consider the production of Convertible Sedans by Ford Motor Company (the largest open-bodied producer) in the same year (Table 8-4).

Although similar figures are not available for all manufacturers or for the overall industry, these totals give a clear general indication of low-volume output in

Table 8-3. 1938 Cadillac Convertible Sedan Production

Series Sixty V-8	60 units
Series Sixty Special V-8	0 units
Series Sixty-Five V-8	110 units
Fleetwood 75 V-8 Series	58 units
Fleetwood 90 V-16 Series	13 units
	241 Total

Table 8-4. 1938 Ford Convertible Sedan Production

Model 78	0 units
Model 81A	2507 units
Model 91A	47 units
	2,554 Total

both the low-, upper-medium, and high-priced car segments of the market. In addition, it must be noted that many volume-producers such as Chevrolet, Graham, Hupmobile, Nash, and Plymouth were not even offering such a style in 1938. Other firms like Pontiac, Hudson, Dodge, and DeSoto built such models in very limited quantities—probably by actual customer order. It's likely that the 1935 output of 6890 was never again surpassed.

Convertible Sedans were relatively expensive offerings; this partially explains the low sales figures. The 1930 Cadillac Model 3905 Fleetwood All-Weather Phaeton (Figure 8-16) listed for $6,850 as a new car. That was nearly $1,000 more than the basic convertible coupe of the same make and vintage. This flat-windshield model would sell for about $200,000 today. There was also a V-windshield version which is now worth about $10,000 more. The car shown in Fig. 8-16 was originally owned by the Mayor of Jersey City, New Jersey.

Chrysler was another of the major convertible sedan producers in the prewar era. The 1931 Chrysler five-passenger Phaeton (Fig. 8-17) was a sleek, handsome-looking machine sporting a custom coachbuilt body.

Buick also produced many fine-looking, four-door convertibles, such as the 1933 Series 80 Phaeton Convertible that seemed like a bargain at a factory price of only $1,845. Today, such a car is valued at $30,000 in top condition.

While many convertible sedans are rated as full classics, only the larger, Series 90 Buicks are listed by the CCCA, VMCCA, and AACA. Other Buicks with custom bodies may be approved by the CCCA through owner application to the club.

Most early convertible sedans had front doors that were hinged in the so-called suicide style. They opened from the front to the rear. The term suicide door seems to stem from the type of hinging that would sometimes cause the doors to fly open due to flexing of the body at high speed. By 1938, Cadillac had devised a method of hinging the front doors to the cowl (Fig. 8-18), thereby eliminating the safety problem.

It was hard to build convertible sedan bodies with anywhere near the integrity of closed cars or even convertible coupes. In most cases, by the time such models were just a few years old the body would be bothered by many squeaks and rattles and proper panel alignment was then difficult to achieve. These are some additional reasons that four-door convertibles remained low-production automobiles.

Fig. 8-16. Convertibles like this 1930 Cadillac Model 3405 V-8 Convertible Sedan were popular. This one belonged to the mayor of Jersey City. (Michael A. Carbonella photo)

Fig. 8-17. Chrysler produced a line of sleekly styled four-door convertibles in their Imperial line. This is the 1931 five-passenger phaeton. The body is a LeBaron design.

Fig. 8-18. For 1938, Cadillac devised a method of hanging doors in a conventional manner with both front and rear doors opening to front of the car. (Micheal A. Carbonella photo)

According to automotive historian Robert F. Mehl, Jr.—the author of several authoriative articles about convertible sedans—the Lincoln Motor Car Company might have been the first American automaker to offer this body style.[1] The Lincoln that claims the honor is the Model 1056 LeBaron Custom Phaeton. It was shown at the Chicago Automobile Show in 1925.

Lincoln remained a leading producer of this type of car for many years during the classic car era. After 1934, the magnificent Model K Lincolns were built with new LeBaron semicustom factory coachwork that included a division window, rear-opening doors, and a flat-folding top. According to Mehl, "The division window could be lowered into a compartment behind the front seat, the center posts folded into the center and a small tonneau was thus formed."

For 1939, Lincoln introduced the Model 740 Lincoln-Zephyr convertible sedan as a surprising attempt to mate the features of a four-door convertible with the fastback Zephyr style body. With a price of just $1,790, this car drew 461 orders, but sales of the luxury-class Model K convertible sedans dropped. The Model 413A five-passenger LeBaron convertible sedan had a production run of only five cars. The Model 413B LeBaron WP Convertible Sedan (Fig. 8-19) found only seven buyers. Remaining examples of both of these cars are extremely rare. They sold for $5,800 and $6,000 when new and are valued at approximately $38,500 and $39,000 today. The "WP" designates the model "with

partition." In other words, the car with the rear tonneau.

The last of the full classic convertible sedans were the 1941 models offered only by General motors and Packard. Fewer than 2,000 four-door convertibles were sold that year. Of these, about 380 examples were made by Packard. The General Motors versions were built on the company's "torpedo" or "C") body shell. Buick division manufactured 508 cars in its Super Series and 326 in the Roadmaster Series. Oldsmobile sold the Custom Cruiser Convertible Phaeton in their Ninety-Eight Series. A total of 119 were made and just nine of these cars are known to survive today. The 1941 Cadillac Series 62 convertible sedan was one of the prettiest offerings of the season, and the company sold 400 copies at $1,965 each. According to Robert Mehl, Jr., some of these even had the new Hydra-Matic transmission option.

Although most people think of large classic cars when they picture convertible sedans, such body styles were also sold by companies in the low- and medium-price fields. For example, the 1936 Ford Convertible Sedan had a factory price of just $780 (Figure 8-20) and the 1937 Pontiac Convertible Sedan sold for $1,197 as a six and $1,235 as an eight.

LATE PREWAR CONVERTIBLES

In the period just prior to the outbreak of World War II, the convertible coupe represented the sportiest car available in the car lines of most manufacturers. With the move toward streamlining in this era, it seemed that the smoother and rounder character lines being used on American cars were perfectly suited to the open-bodied models. This was also the period in which the convertible was usually marketed with high-level trim and appointments, many extra-cost accessories, and improved seating configurations.

The 1939 Plymouth convertible coupe (Fig. 8-22) has square-shaped headlamps integrated into the fenders. This was one of the first production ragtops to sell with an hydraulic top-riser system. The bodies that evolved on most American cars in 1939–1940 would later be carried into the immediate postwar era with very little change except for new grille designs and bright metal trim.

Convertibles of this period are extremely popular with collectors and, though not extremely rare, they bring high prices in the hobby market due to their popularity. A good example is Ford's 1940 DeLuxe Convertible Coupe (Fig. 8-23). This V-8 powered model was sold to 20,850 buyers; that is a fairly high production total for any convertible. This car has always had appeal to collectors as well as to hot-rod enthusiasts. Such a car in Number 1 condition is worth about $25,000 today. With accessories such as a radio, an antenna, a cowl-mounted spotlight, grille-mounted driving lamps, and fender skirts, the value would go even higher.

One of the hottest-performing cars of 1940 was the Buick Century Convertible Coupe with its twin-carbure-ted Fireball straight eight, an engine that produced an amazing 141 horsepower. Note the absence of running-boards on this car and the optional sun visor and rear fender skirts. This car had a factory price of $1,431. The example shown in Fig. 8-24 is a Number-2 condition car and now would be valued at some $10,000.

EARLY POSTWAR CONVERTIBLES

The soft-top car did not make a quick reappearance after the close of World War II because the automakers were hard-pressed to get back into full-scale, peacetime production. Most companies started building coupes and sedans in late 1945 or early 1946. By the middle of the latter year, the convertible coupe began to show up again.

With the beautiful 1947 Cadillac convertible, the traditional styling created a most handsome automobile. Unlike the prewar years, this was now the only ragtop available from Cadillac. Designated the Series 62 Convertible Coupe, it sold for $2,741 and weighed 4455 pounds. Power came from the standard 346-cubic-inch flathead V-8 engine that developed 150 horsepower at 3400 rpm. A total of 6755 copies were made and survivors bring up to $15,000 at collector car auctions. These cars are bound to increase in price as the popularity of postwar cars continues to spiral upward.

Fig. 8-19. This 1939 Lincoln Touring Cabriolet is one of only a few such cars ever built.

Fig. 8-20. Low-priced convertible sedans were offered by several manufacturers. This is a 1936 Ford model.

Fig. 8-21. A medium-priced car builder, Pontiac constructed just 1266 convertible sedans in 1937. Most, like this example, had six-cylinder power. (Courtesy Crestline Publishing)

Fig. 8-22. Chrysler Corporation claimed that its 1939 Plymouth Convertible Coupe was the first to feature an hydraulic top-riser mechanism. (Michael A. Carbonella photo)

Fig. 8-23. One of the most popular prewar convertibles is the 1940 Ford Deluxe Cabriolet.

Fig. 8-24. Buick's 1941 Century Convertible Coupe featured a straight-eight engine with twin carburetion. It was a performance car in its day. (Michael A. Carbonella photo)

Packard continued to offer two different lines of convertibles after the war. The company's 1946–1947 models also had carryover styling that was much like that seen in 1941–1942. In 1950 the all-new 22nd Series line was introduced (Fig. 8-25). Convertibles were offered in the Super Eight and Custom Eight Series. The Super Eights were built on a 120-inch wheelbase and the Super Eights were built on a 7-inch longer stance. The official body style designation was Victoria Convertible Coupe and the factory prices were $3,250 and $4,295 respectively. The new Packard body styling was often referred to as the "inverted bathtub" or "pregnant elephant" school of design. In reality, however, these cars are both very impressive machines and also quite pleasing to the eye. Only 614 Super Eight ragtops were made and the total number of Custom Eight convertibles was a mere 85 units.

Another early postwar convertible that collectors love is the 1949 Buick Roadmaster (Fig. 8-26). It sold for $3,150 and accounted for 8095 domestic deliveries and an additional 149 shipments to foreign countries. Buicks of this era were distinguished by two characteristic styling traits: the "bucktooth" grille and chrome-trimmed "port holes" on the front fenders. The medium-low priced Special Series models had three port holes and the larger Buicks had four. A Special convertible was not available, but buyers were able to purchase ragtops in both the Super Series and Roadmaster Series.

While companies like Cadillac, Buick, and Packard tried to update the styling after 1949, Chrysler Corporation products followed a more conservative pattern preferred by company president W.T. Keller. Keller felt that American buyers wanted cars that were roomy enough to hold backseat passengers wearing hats. What resulted was the so-called box-on-a-box look that was not particularly suited to the sportiness of the convertible. This is characterized by the 1949 Plymouth Super DeLuxe convertible coupe (Fig. 8-27) that has a somewhat old-fashioned appearance. These Chrysler products were well-engineered automobiles, but could not be regarded as innovative cars in either technical or styling terms. They were out of pace with the preferences of postwar customers who favored lower, sleeker models with V-8s and automatic transmissions. To a large degree, this explains why Chevrolet and Ford sold 32,392 and 51,333 convertibles, respectively, in 1949 compared to just 15,240 ragtop sales for Plymouth.

Unlike the case of prewar cars, the greater rarity of the 1949 Plymouth convertible does *not* increase its value to collectors. For postwar cars, the general rule is the more popular a car was when new, the more popular it will be with hobbyists. According to the latest *Old Cars Price Guide* the three 1949 ragtops would be valued as follows: Chevrolet $9,000, Ford $13,500, and Plymouth $11,000. These are the value estimates for survivors in perfect condition.

Convertibles were usually priced at or near the top of a manufacturer's price scale in the early postwar years. The reason was that these cars were more expensive to build than coupes, sedans, or hardtops. Factors that added to the cost of making a ragtop were extra frame bracing (required to keep the body from flexing), hydraulic top mechanisms, the construction of roof bows, and the extra assembly time required to cut, trim, and fit a cloth top. In addition, most convertibles had special interior appointments such as genuine leather upholstery.

Standard equipment for a 1952 Packard 250 convertible (Fig. 8-28) included everything found in lower-priced models plus hydraulic valve lifters, an oil filter, an

Fig. 8-25. Typical of the "pregnant elephant/inverted bathtub" school of design is this 1950 Packard Convertible Victoria Coupe. (Michael A. Carbonella photo)

Fig. 8-26. Buck-tooth grilles and front fender port holes were postwar characteristics of Buicks. This is a 1949 Roadmaster ragtop. (Michael A. Carbonella photo)

Fig. 8-27. Chrysler's early postwar styling—as seen on this 1949 Plymouth convertible—was considered extremely conservative. (Michael A. Carbonella photo)

Fig. 8-28. Just over 1000 of these 1952 Packard 250 Convertibles were made. That makes surviving examples postwar rarities.

146

oil bath air cleaner, a trunk lamp, a tilt of rearview mirror, front and rear wool carpets, rear-seat armrests, and seats covered in a combination of genuine leather and washable, woven, leatherlike plastic material. This car was priced at $3,476. Only the luxury-class Patrician 400 sedan cost more. Packard made 1133 ragtops for the 1952 calendar year, model year figures aren't available.

Pontiac also placed its convertibles in the high-priced end of the market. In 1954, this was the all-new Star Chief line that incorporated an extra-long rear deck. Although Star Chiefs had the same wheelbase as other Pontiacs, an 11-inch long extension was added toward the rear of the cars to make them more appealing to buyers. The Star Chief convertible (Fig. 8-29) was the company's high-dollar offering with its base factory price of $2,630. This was the first year the convertible cost more than a Pontiac station wagon.

The 1957 Chevrolet Bel Air convertible has taken on cult car status with postwar car collectors. Some enthusiasts refer to the 1955-1957 Chevrolets as Classic Chevys. The values of the 1957 Chevrolet convertible have been skyrocketing over the last several years. In 1979, such a car in perfect condition was valued at $7,500. Today, the ballpark estimate has climbed to $19,000 with no end in sight! It seems that it won't be very long before this model is selling for as much as some of the smaller prewar classics.

If the 1957 Chevy is a classic of its day and age, the 1958 Oldsmobile Ninety-Eight convertible (Fig. 8-30) should probably be viewed as a classic example of bad taste. The highly sculptured body lines, wraparound windshield, quad-lens headlights, and other styling touches represent an ultimate expression of excessive gaudiness in automobiles. But then, these are all part of the reason that cars of this vintage stand as a symbol of American '50s culture.

SPECIAL RAGTOPS OF THE MID-1950s

Although the history of the convertible in the 1950s ended in a fit of styling excess, this was also a period that left us with a number of specialty ragtops that were truly beautiful and rare limited-production cars.

One of these cars was the 1953 Buick Skylark (Fig. 8-31). Technically referred to as the model 76X Buick Roadmaster Skylark Anniversary Convertible, it was specially designed by stylist Ned F. Nickles. It was based on a 1951 Roadmaster ragtop that he had modified for his own use. Legend has it that Nickles wanted to take his modifications a little further so he made some sketches that were seen by Buick general manager Ivan Wiles. Wiles decided to let Nickles modify a 1952 Roadmaster convertible to match the sketches. It became a pilot model for the 1953 limited-production car.

The Skylark was released at a price of $5,000, and 1,690 copies were sold. Interestingly, many were actually sold—at discount prices—during 1954. Not that people

didn't think they were beautiful, but it was difficult to sell $5,000 Buicks in 1953. About four years ago, I located an old Buick dealership in a small Pennsylvania town that still had a brand-new Skylark! They had never found a buyer for the car so it was simply kept around for dealer use in local parades. The odometer showed under 10,000 original miles. Today, a restored Skylark is valued at about $18,000 and that brand new car would be worth even more.

The 1953 Skylark (as well as the rarer 1954 models) are recognized as Milestone Cars. This label has been established by the Milestone Car Society (MCS), a group that has applied standards much like the CCCA's to formulate a list of highly collectable postwar cars. The MCS criteria are very strict and a committee vote is required to grant Milestone recognition.

Buick was not the only company to create limited-edition convertibles. Packard's 1953 Caribbean convertible is another example of a show car that made it to the assembly lines. It featured special body modifications by the Mitchell-Bently Corp. of Ionia, Mich. It's standard features include a full-leather interior, chrome-plated wire wheels, enlarged wheel openings with flared outer lips, full-length, full-width hood scoop, dechromed body look, special horizontal twin taillights, intergrated "fishtail" rear end, front and rear bright metal wheel opening trim moldings, continental tire kit and custom finish in one of four colors: Polaris Blue, Gulf Green Metallic, Matador Maroon Metallic, or Sahara Sand. The Caribbean convertible was priced at $5,210 and a total of 750 were made. They are worth about $13,000 restored to Excellent condition.

Pontiac got into the specialty convertible game in 1957 when the supercharged Bonneville convertible (Fig. 8-32) was released as a midyear addition to the line. Officially called the Style 2867SDX Star Chief Custom Bonneville Convertible Coupe, it had as standard equipment a Rochester fuel-injection engine, oil bath air cleaner, full-flow oil filter, outside rearview mirror, Hydra-Matic transmission, power brakes, electric wipers, windshield washers, dual exhausts, special exterior trim, custom wheel discs with tri-bar spinners, and four-ply whitewall tires. The Bonneville was released as a true limited-edition convertible for "dealer use only." A total of 630 dealers ordered the one car to which they were entitled. Today the cars are worth about $13,000 to $20,000.

Unlike the Buick Skylark and Packard Caribbean, the Bonneville is not recognized as a Milestone car. In the general collector's market, it is commonly undervalued. Nevertheless, specialized Pontiac enthusiasts will give above market prices to take possession of a good Bonneville that's in mint condition.

The Cadillac Eldorado Biarritz convertible of 1957-1958 (Fig. 8-33) is another of the specialty ragtops made during the mid-1950s. This car features special styling

Fig. 8-29. Extended rear deck styling is one reason why postwar Pontiac enthusiasts love the 1954 Star Chief convertible.

Fig. 8-30. Flamboyant trim and sculptured styling are traits of the 1958 Oldsmobile Ninety-Eight convertible. (Michael A. Carbonella photo)

Fig. 8-31. The 1953 Buick Skylark Convertible was released in commemoration of the company's 50th year in production. It is a recognized Milestone Car. (Michael A. Carbonella photo)

Fig. 8-32. The 1957 Pontiac Bonneville convertible was a mid year model sold on a one-car-per-dealer basis. Not all dealers ordered a copy; just 630 examples were built. (Courtesy Pontiac-Oakland Club International)

Fig. 8-33. Cadillac's Eldorado Biarritz convertibles are another early postwar-era specialty car. (Michael A. Carbonella photo)

and a long list of standard equipment. The engine was a special 365-cubic-inch V-8 with three two-barrel carburetors, which helped it develop 335 horsepower. The 1958 price tag for a Biarritz was $7,500 and production amounted to 815 units. For 1957, the respective figures are $7,286 and 1800 units. The top-condition value today is in the $15,000 bracket! Cars of both years are recognized by the MCS.

Not quite as exclusive as Skylarks, Carribbeans, Bonnevilles and Eldorado Biarritz ragtops, but nevertheless a "modern classic" is the 1955–1957 two-seat Thunderbird. Of the three-year grouping, the 1957 model (Fig. 8-34) features the most distinctive styling.

The first Thunderbirds were introduced to the public on February 20, 1954. Designed as America's first personal-sized luxury/sports model of the postwar era,

Fig. 8-34. Two-seat Thunderbirds are honored by the Classic T-Bird Club International.

the T-Bird was intended to fill the same market gap as cars such as the all-new Chevrolet Corvette, the Kaiser-Darrin, and the Nash-Healey. It was a clear attempt to give buyers a car with features and styling like imported sports cars that were then rising in popularity.

The Thunderbird was marketed with many optional luxury and convenience features. Buyers could select a host of extra-cost equipment such as power steering, power brakes, power windows, and power seats. Although the Thunderbird was a true convertible with roll-up windows and a top that disappeared, it was also innovative because the top was made of fiberglass and was completely removable rather than lowerable. A rayon ragtop was offered only as optional equipment and cost $290 extra.

Ford Motor Company was also responsible for another type of specialty ragtop. This is the distinctive Skyliner retractable hardtop, which wasn't a real ragtop at all. Instead of a cloth roof, the Skyliner features a removable top that is made of steel and retracts into the trunk of the car. The operation of the retractable roof is accomplished with the transmission lever placed in Neutral via a pull-out dashboard control. The trunk lid unlocks and an electric motor lifts it toward the rear of the car. Next, the rear package shelf panel disappears into the body. After being unlatched, the steel roof moves

toward the rear on four hinged "arms" that lower it into the trunk. The forward roof panel "flaps" downward, thereby reducing the length of the top so it will fit inside what is usually the luggage compartment. Then the trunk lid comes down again, completely covering the roof below it.

Like many people of the day, I remember reading about this car when it was new. Of course, it seemed like the answer to everyone's ultimate dream (a car that was both a hardtop and a convertible). The top lowering system was very complicated. It required six electric motors, switches, relays, lever-arms, rods, circuit breakers, and over 600 feet of electrical wires. This added up to a mechanism that was prone to trouble. In addition, the car was especially long and high at the rear, making it resemble a pickup truck. Then there was lots of extra weight and an especially high price tag to cover the cost of manufacturing the hardware. All of this meant additional problems in marketing the cars.

Ford produced the Skyliner for just three years before dropping the concept. The first edition appeared in the 1957 Fairlane 500 series as a V-8-only model. It had a base price of $2,942 and weighed 3,916 pounds. Production hit 20,766 cars. Model positioning for the 1958 Skyliner (Fig. 8-35) was the same. It sold for $3,138 and weighed 4094 pounds. A combination of styling

Fig. 8-35. Ford released the 1958 Skyliner retractable hardtop; the world's only true "hardtop convertible".

Fig. 8-36. The 1959 Corvette Convertible sold for $3,875 new and is worth about $19,000 in this shape today. (Michael A. Carbonella photo)

Table 8-5. Specifications and Values.

Year	Body Style	Original Price	Production Total	1983 Value (Excellent condition)
1953	Conv-Rds	$3,498	300(*)	$35,000
1954	Conv-Rds	3,934	3,640	33,000
1955	Convertible	2,934	700	29,000 (**)
1956	Convertible	3,120	3,467	27,000
1957	Convertible	3,465	6,339	27,000 (***)
1958	Convertible	3,631	9,168	20,000
1959	Convertible	3,875	9,670	19,000

Notes:

*Most of the 1953 Corvettes were sold to well-known personalities.

**A handful of 1955 models seem to have been built with six-cylinder engines. They would be worth $2,000 more in 1983.

***Optional fuel-injection adds $2,000 to the 1983 value of 1957 models; $1,500 to all post-1957 models.
Sources:

Specifications: Standard Catalog of American Cars 1945–1975
Ballpark Values: Old Cars Price Guide, Summer 1983

Fig. 8-37. The 1959 Cadillac has become an American cult car. This is the Model 62 version. Even more desirable and costly is the Eldorado Biarritz of the same year. (Courtesy *Old Cars Weekly*)

excesses and a poor economy held sales to just 14,713 units.

For 1959, Ford entirely redesigned the standard cars, including the Skyliner. The result was a handsome-looking machine that looked squarer and bigger than the models of the two previous seasons. In actuality, however, these cars were slightly smaller and the overall design seemed better-suited to the hardtop-convertible concept. The Skyliner still came only with V-8 power. It was based on a 118-inch wheelbase and measured 208.1-inches overall. With a price of $3,346 and weight of 4064 pounds, it was also the least popular version; only 12,915 copies were sold.

The Milestone Car Club recognizes all 1957–1959 Ford Skyliners as milestone cars. Collectors consider the last year models the most desirable. Excellent-condition cars at auction prices run about $13,000. That compares to around $11,000 for first-year editions and $10,500 for 1958 models.

When considering specialty convertibles of the first postwar decade, another car that deserves mention is the fabulous Chevrolet Corvette (Fig. 8-36). The original 1953 Corvette was based on the EX-122 Chevrolet show car (which appeared in the company's traveling Motorama during 1952). It was conceived of as an economy sports car with a sleek, fiberglass body with futuristic styling. Features included a six-cylinder engine with three two-barrel carburetors, floor-mounted transmission controls, and bucket seats for two passengers. By 1955, V-8 power was adopted. The Corvette's styling was updated in 1956 and it was turned into a better-performing car—a year later—with the release of an optional, fuel-injected engine. For 1958, some extra chrome trim was added and the 1959 model looked much like a cleaned-up 1958. All 1953–1957 models are classified as milestone cars, but Corvette lovers consider all of the years as "modern classics." Almost everyone in the old-car hobby agrees with them. Table 8-5 gives specifications and ballpark values for the 1953–1959 models.

Another of the more popular ragtops of the 1950s is the beautiful 1959 Cadillac convertible (Fig. 8-37). It has become a postwar cult car. With its gaudy "drawer-pull" grille, rocketshiplike tailfins, skirted rear fenders, and bullet-shaped taillights, this car seems to characterize the flavor of the period in which it was built. To Cadillac collectors, the limited-edition Eldorado ragtops are the most appealing version, but any 1959 "Ca-doo" open-bodied model is certain to be a hit today. In top condition, the luxurious Eldorado Biarritz convertible sells for up to $16,000, and even the Series 62 counterpart is now into the five-figures bracket.

Footnote

[1]*Best of Old Cars*, Volume 2, 1978. Krause Publications, Iola, WI 54945. Page 360.

9. The 1960s

Convertibles from the '60s are hot items in the current collector-car market. Hobbyists, collectors and investors are now buying these models by the dozen. This growing interest in '60s convertibles was readily apparent in Apache Junction, Arizona when Art and Betsy Grandlich sold the vehicles from their Grand Old Cars Museum. Famous as the largest, privately owned display of open cars in the United States, this collection included approximately 150 ragtops. The major portion were postwar and '60s models. By the end of bidding, every last one of the cars had a new owner.

Similar results were registered at the Lazarus Automotive Museum's April-In-Rockford Auction. Out of 500 cars included in this sale, an extremely large number were '60s ragtops. About half of the cars changed hands. One consignor brought 40 convertibles to the show and sold them all! Again, the majority were 1960s models.

Body style trends of the early 1960s were toward two-door hardtops, but convertible production was also at its peak. Ragtops accounted for 4.8 percent of all assemblies in 1961, 5.9 percent in 1962, 6.6 percent in 1963, and 6.3 percent in 1964. That drop for the later year started an irreversible trend of falling popularity.

In 1964, the Ford Mustang and the Pontiac GTO appeared. The Mustang—an instant and remarkable success—popularized the sports/personal car to millions of buyers. The GTO—originally an optional equipment package, but later a full-fledged model—kicked-off the short, but sweet, history of high-performance "muscle cars." Such machines were factory-built hot rods created by installing big, powerful V-8s in mid-sized bodies.

In 1965, the year of fastback rooflines, disc brakes, perimeter frames and three-speed automatic transmissions, more ragtops than ever before (or after) were made. The total was 507,337 cars. Nevertheless, the convertibles share of the total market dropped to 5.7 percent. *Wards 1966 Automotive Yearbook* noted, "While the convertible is obviously plateauing out in automotive demand, the spectacular acceptance of vinyl-covered tops on sedan (closed) models commencing with the '65 model year outwardly is borrowing from convertible sales."

This factor, combined with the increased popularity of air conditioning, continued to hurt ragtop sales. The convertible's market share went to 4.9 percent in 1966, 4.4 percent in 1967, 3.4 percent in 1968, and 2.7 percent in 1969. There was little reason to want a convertible when hardtops with a vinyl-covered roof had a very similar appearance and when air conditioning allowed for cool, year-round driving in any climate. These were the two main factors leading to the convertible's decline.

Many people have incorrectly assumed that Federal Motor Vehicle Safety Standards (FMVSS)—adopted in stages from 1966 on—actually outlawed convertibles. This isn't true. The only FMVSS regulations that remotely relate to this matter are Standard No. 212—windshield mounting retention in crash required (effective 1970)—and Standard No. 216—Roof crush resistance, minimum strength requirements set (effective 1973). The latter standard might have *discouraged* convertible manufacture, but it did not forbid it.

Hundreds of different convertibles were sold during the 1960s. In addition, thousands of regular production options (RPOS) allowed buyers to tailor a car to their personal taste. Special Production Options (SPOs) were also available in some cases; these are considered very rare. The SPOs include everything from special-color paints to factory-built, experimental racing engines.

Counting all the various models and options combinations is a virtual impossibility. They would run into the millions. However, it is very important to understand that '60s car enthusiasts sometimes consider a car with certain options to be comparable to a one-of-a-kind item. If the options are very desirable ones—such as an aluminum-block Corvette motor—collectors will pay much more than market values for the car. Knowledge of different models, RPOs and SPOs is essential to the collector who specializes in 1960s ragtops.

The Chrysler 300-G convertible for 1961 (Fig. 9-1) is a good example of a low-production, full-sized '60s ragtop. Like other Chrysler Letter Cars (specialty models identified by a letter after the 300 designation), the G was intended to be a limited-edition performance car. A long list of equipment, usually considered optional, was standard on this model. It included a special wedge-head V-8 engine. heavy-duty suspension, swivel-type bucket seats, padded dashboard, power accessories, tachometer, and low-back-pressure exhaust system. Only 337 Chrysler 300-G convertibles were assembled and, according to records maintained by the Chrysler 300 Club International, Inc., about 61 of these cars (18.1 percent) still survive today. Because of this special status and extreme rarity, collectors will pay up to $6,000 for this car today.

Optional equipment will raise the value even higher. For instance, the Chrysler Air-Temp air-conditioning system adds over $500 to the price. Even more desirable and costly would be a ragtop with the year's special 400 horsepower short ram engine. Installed in only a handful of production units, this motor is extremely scarce and gives the cars equipped with it premium value. Air-conditioning would be considered an RPO, but the short ram V-8 was an SPO.

Most '60s ragtop collectors agree that General Motors products (Pontiacs and Chevrolets) were the styling pacesetters of the early 1960s. Ford products of the same years were more slab-sided and relied more heavily on the use of bright metal trim (Fig. 9-2). Meanwhile, Chrysler—the third major automaker—remained behind the times by sticking with tailfins and more radical styling motifs. This showed in low sales figures for Chrysler, Dodge, and Plymouth convertibles from 1961–1963.

The 1961 four-door Continental ragtop received the Industrial Design Institute's annual bronze medal award for outstanding design. Few other automotive

Fig. 9-1. The 1961 Chrysler 300-G convertible is a low-production, full-sized model. Chrysler stayed with tailfins and 1950s styling motifs longer than other automakers because of designer Virgil Exner's styling preferences. (Photo courtesy Bob McAtee)

Fig. 9–2. Ford products adopted a slab-sided look in the early '60s. The Galaxie 500 sunliner convertible for 1962 sold for $3,033. Production hit 42,646 units.

designs have been accorded this recognition. In 1962, there were mainly small changes in the basic styling, minor alterations to the bumpers, grille and trim, and a very slight increase in size (Fig. 9-3). Minor changes were also made on 1963 models.

The Ford Falcon convertible is a very good example of a compact that is now rising in collector appeal. This model evolved as Ford's answer to the wave of foreign car buying during the late 1950s. Caught by surprise in the 1957–1959 period, American automakers (except Rambler) were not able to market compact models until after 1959. The Falcon was introduced October 8, 1959 as a 1960 model, but a convertible was not offered in this series until 1963 (Fig. 9-4).

When the Falcon ragtop appeared, it was offered with three levels of trim and equipment. The Futura convertible was the most conventional version. The Falcon Sports convertible came with extra features such as bucket seats and wire wheel covers. The Falcon Sprint convertible had both of these features, plus a spunky V-8 and heavy-duty chassis parts pirated from the midsized Fairlane series. The Sprint was, essentially, the next best thing to a true imported sportscar. In fact, it was derived from special models built to compete in the famous Monte Carlo rally.

Falcon ragtops were an immediate hit. In 1963, Ford sold 18,942 Futuras, another 12,250 Sports and 4602 soft-top Sprints—a total of 35,794 compact convertibles. It was an excellent beginning to a trend that didn't last too long. Sales slid downhill after 1963.

Only 21,088 Falcon convertibles of all types were

made in 1964 when completely new styling appeared on this line. There were only minor trim changes in the 1965 Falcon convertibles (Fig. 9-5), but production fell to just 6615 units. Some of the blame was found in the general decline in ragtop sales after 1964 and some was due to the mid-1964 introduction of the Mustang.

Prices for Number 1 condition Futura convertibles are currently in the $3,500 to $4,500 range. Sport convertibles run around $500 higher. Sprint convertibles are even more valuable; prices in the $5,000 to $6,000 range are getting more common with each passing auction.

Chevrolet's answer to the growing compact-car market was the more radical Corvair, with its four-wheel independent suspension and air-cooled, rear-mounted engine. Introduced October 2, 1959 as a 1960 model, the Corvair first included everything from Club Coupes and sedans to Lakewood station wagons and van-style trucks (introduced in 1960). The ragtop Monza appeared in 1962 and it sold 16,569 copies. By 1963, production of this model jumped to an amazing 44,165 units, of which 7472 had the sports-performance Spyder option.

The 1963 Corvair Monza Spyder was just this side of a true, all-out sports car, and Corvair lovers are likely to insist that even this is an understatement. They will argue—probably quite fervrently—that the Monza Spyder ragtop was more of a real sports car than the 1963 Corvette!

Corvair convertibles are extremely popular in the collector car market. In top condition, a base Monza ragtop will bring $4,500 to $5,500. The last Corvair

Fig. 9-3. The last four-door convertibles were offered by Lincoln–Continental from 1961–1967. Stylist Elwood P. Engel is credited with this classic design. (Courtesy Ford Motor Co.)

convertibles of 1969 bring the top values for standard models; only 521 were made. Spyder convertibles or '65 ragtops with high-performance engines and in perfect shape sell for $5,600 to $6,000 and up.

"Senior" compacts and intermediate mid-sized convertibles are also quite popular with '60s car enthusiasts. If the true compacts in ragtop form seemed like Americanized versions of European sports models, the mid-sized convertibles seemed to represent a modern form of the hot rod. They did not, of course, look like the fenderless, antique roadsters that started the hot-rodding craze in California after WWII. Yet, in a technical

and emotional sense they were much the same type of vehicle when equipped with the optional, high-performance V-8s. They were trim-sized, lightweight machines with outstanding power-to-weight ratios.

The 1963 Buick Wildcat convertible was one of the first high-performance intermediates. Sized between the compact Buick Special series and the full-sized Electra 225, the Wildcats sat on a 123-inch wheelbase. Standard equipment on the convertible included front bucket seats, center console, and a floor-mounted, turbine-drive, gear-selector stick. Power was supplied by a 401 cubic-inch V-8 with 10.25:1 compression and a four-

Fig. 9-4. Compact-sized convertibles made an important contribution to ragtop history in the 1960s. This 1963 Falcon convertible marked the introduction of this body type in Ford's compact line.

Fig. 9-5. Falcon ragtops were offered for only three years. This 1965 version reflects the square, angular look that characterized both 1964 and 1965 Falcon convertibles.

barrel carburetor that added up to 325 horsepower at 4400 rpm.

The 1963 Wildcat ragtop was actually considered a luxury sports model. It was one of the earliest midsized cars with a real performance image. Being a Buick product, it was still a bit bigger and more expensive than the later intermediate-sized muscle cars. The Wildcat ragtop had a factory price of $3,961.

In contrast, the 1964 Pontiac Tempest LeMans convertible (Fig. 9-6) was just a little smaller and more affordable. It had a 115-inch wheelbase and was priced at $3,081. Bucket seats were $134 extra and the 326 cubic-inch V-8 was a $167 option. But when the Tempest was so-equipped, it had almost the same characteristics as a Wildcat with a price some $500 lower.

By mid-1964, a low-cost equipment package known as the Grand Turismo Omologato (or GTO) option was released for the LeMans convertible, coupe, and hardtop. The GTO was the car that changed the midsized market. Instead of going toward the luxury/sports field, it was geared to all-out performance. It began a complete shift in midsized model buying trends. The GTO was the first of what soon became known as muscle cars, and all such models—especially convertibles—are now highly collectable. In top shape, the 1964 GTO ragtop is valued at approximately $8,500 today. It was recently selected by *MONEY* magazine as one of the best '60s cars in which to invest.

For 1965, there were only small changes in the GTO convertible (Fig. 9-7). In 1964, the GTO had been a totally new type of car, and the demand for the car outpaced production. Only 6,644 ragtop examples were made. By 1965, the assembly lines were geared up and a total of 11,311 convertibles were built.

By 1964–1965, the four basic types of '60s convert-

Fig. 9-6. Popular since the day it was introduced, the trim 1964 Pontiac LeMans convertible was available with many options that gave it almost the same features as a Buick Wildcat (for about $500 less). This car became the basis for the original GTO, America's first muscle car. (Courtesy Pontiac Motor Division)

ibles had been established. There were full-sized, compact, midsized and pony-cars ragtops.

From 1965–1969, there were changes in styling and technology. The 1966 Chevrolet Impala convertible (Fig. 9-8) for example, exhibits more rounded lines and contours than most cars of the 1962–1964 period. A popular new treatment was the so-called Coke-bottle shape that refers to the kick-up of the upper rear fenders in back of the doors. This type of styling evolved in 1963–1964, but became more prominent in the full-sized 1965 models from General Motors. By 1966, most cars from GM and Ford had adopted the rear fender kick-up, along with some Chrysler products. American Motors followed the trend during 1967.

Chevy convertibles of the 1965–1966 vintage were relatively slow sellers as new cars. The company's sales of full-sized ragtops fell from 81,897 units in 1964 to 72,760 in 1965 and 47,064 in 1966. Open models were getting increasingly rare after 1964 and this could be very good news for wise enthusiasts. Why? Because these cars are growing in collector appeal, but can still be bought at lower prices. In good shape, they sell for around $1,000 less than a 1964 Chevy convertible. The rarity factory suggests that this relationship may soon be reversed. This might be the perfect time to buy into 1965–1966 Chevy ragtops if investing is your goal.

As rounder body contours and curvier character lines returned to favor after 1965, there was also a movement back to some of the styling motifs of the past. For example, skirted rear fenders regained popularity on higher-priced, full-sized cars. Use of bright metal trim was slightly increased. Some models such as 1966 Pontiac Bonneville convertibles (Fig. 9-9) received a new frontal treatment with a prominent bulge running the center of the hood. This was a direct throwback to the early 1950s as far as basic design elements, although the rendition was done in a subtler way. Instead of using bright chrome moldings under the lower body "skeg," the Pontiac stylists fashioned the trim of a brush-finished type of metal that was broken with delicate horizontal grooves.

Following the Pontiac lead, almost all manufacturers began marketing intermediates with muscular engines. Another very popular model was the Chevelle Malibu with the Super Sport equipment package. The 1966 Malibu SS convertible was a potent street machine. Only 19,614 Chevelle convertibles were made in 1966 and just a fraction were Super Sports.

The 1966 Thunderbird convertible (Fig. 9-10) has an optional fiberglass rear tonneau with built-in headrests. This feature first appeared, in 1962, when cars equipped with the tonneau were considered a separate model known as the Sports Roadster. Only 1427 Sports Roadsters were built in 1962 and they are rare and valuable today. The 1963 Sports Roadster was also a separate model selling for $5,563 compared to $4,912 for a regular

Fig. 9-7. As was the case in 1964, the second Pontiac GTO was actually an options package that turned the LeMans ragtop into a high-performance machine. This 1965 convertible is a very popular collector car today.

Fig. 9-8. Beginning in 1965, General Motor's "big" cars took on more rounded lines and popularized the so-called Coke-bottle shape. This 1966 Chevrolet Impala SS convertible had a base factory price of $3,199 (with V-8 power).

Fig. 9-9. What might be called a "neo-classic" styling motif was seen on many 1965–1969 models. This 1966 Pontiac Bonneville ragtop features fender skirts and a hood having a longitudinal center bulge. (Courtesy Mike Carbonella)

Fig. 9-10. The last year for the Thunderbird convertible was 1966. This one has a 1964 Thunderbird option—the fiberglass rear seat tonneau. This was not genuine factory equipment for 1966 models. The same is true of those fender skirts. Nevertheless, both of these parts from 1964 will fit the later ragtops.

Fig. 9-11. Adding to the value of this 1968 Ford Torino GT convertible is that it features a rare option (428-cubic-inch Cobra Jet engine). It served as the Official Indianapolis 500 Pace Car for the year. (Courtesy Indianapolis Motor Speedway Photo)

convertible. The '63s are even rarer because only 455 were made. After 1964, the Sports Roadster was dropped as a model, but the tonneau cover was made an option priced at $269. It came in eight colors.

When Ford dropped the Thunderbird convertible, Pontiac tried to fill what looked like a market gap by introducing a Grand Prix convertible for 1967. This was the only year that a ragtop was available in this series, and just 5856 copies were built and sold. This gives the car extra value and the *Old Cars Price Guide* estimates it to be worth $5,500 in top shape. That ties it with the 1967 GTO convertible as the most expensive Pontiacs of that year (without considering options).

There are many special considerations that collectors must consider when buying and selling '60s ragtops. Wire wheel covers and a fiberglass tonneau on a 1964 Thunderbird convertible would raise its value from around $6,500 to nearly $9,000. On other models fiberglass hardtops, bucket seats, four-speed manual transmissions, fuel-injection, air-conditioning, power accessories, and special radios can have considerable influ-

ence over how much a car is worth in the collector's market. High-performance engines can mean a $500 to $3,000 premium. For some motors of this type, the cylinder heads alone bring nearly $1,000.

In some cases, a certain car will have special historical significance. For example, a 1968 Ford Torino convertible—complete with a 428 cubic-inch Cobra-Jet engine—served as the official pace car (Fig. 9-11) at the Indianapolis 500 Mile Race that year. This car, if located today, would have a great deal of extra value.

Some collectors of '60s convertibles also consider full-sized luxury models to be in a class of their own. Cars such as the 1969 Cadillac have great appeal in the hobby market because they embody a degree of luxury—combined with impressive size—that cannot be purchased for any price in the market today. All Cadillac, Chrysler-Imperial and Lincoln–Continental convertibles fall into this category. There are also some Chrysler, Oldsmobile, Buick, Pontiac, Mercury, and Dodge ragtops that are on the fringe of being luxury-class cars.

10. Pony-Car Ragtops

T he Ford Mustang was the first of a herd of models that have come to be known as Pony Cars. Others in the pack include Plymouth Barracuda, Mercury Cougar, Chevrolet Camaro, Pontiac Firebird, and Dodge Challenger. It doesn't take much guessing to figure out that the term pony car sprung directly from Ford's new, sporty, small car with its bucket seats, floor shifter, long hood, and short rear deck.

Writing in *MOTOR TREND* magazine in March, 1969, Road Test Editor, Bill Sanders said, "Ford had a better idea and the Mustang was born back in April, 1964. Driving hasn't been the same since. The Pony Car was followed by fish, cats and birds . . . In four years, this menageri has proved itself strong enough to dominate over 10 percent of the total car market." Of the 10 percent market shares that Sanders referred to, the production of pony car ragtops was a relatively miniscule total. Some Pony Car ragtops, with specific equipment features, are exceptional rarities in the collector car market.

MUSTANG

Of the 441,601 factory-produced pony car ragtops built in America from 1964 through 1973, 291,042 were Mustangs. That equals 65.9 percent of the total—a rather amazing figure. Not counting any aftermarket conversions (including the factory-authorized 1983 convertible sold through Ford dealers), the Mustang ragtop was offered for *10* years. That's twice as long as Barracuda and Cougar, more than three times as long as Camaro or Firebird, and five times as long as Challenger!

The earliest Mustang convertibles were originally considered 1965 models by Ford even though they were sold in the spring and summer of 1964. There are slight differences between these cars and those of the normal 1965 model year, which began October 1, 1964. Because of this collectors retroactively began separating 1964½ models from true 1965s.

The 1964½ convertibles are considered to be rarer and more desirable. Only 28,833 of the early cars were built, compared to 73,112 of the later ragtops. In addition, those early cars with the optional 260 cubic-inch V-8 are also more popular with collectors. That engine wasn't offered in the true 1965 models (Fig. 10-1).

Something to keep in mind is that a 1964½ Mustang convertible was used to pace the Indy 500. The company choosen for this honor is required to build at least 38 replicas of the actual pace car. Undoubtedly, any of these cars surviving today (if documented as genuine) would be worth in the $20,000 range. Otherwise, Number-1 condition 1964 ragtops bring up to $12,000. One car with extremely low original miles and the right optional equipment has sold, at auction, for over $21,000! Not bad appreciation for a 19-year-old car that cost $2,614 when new!

Fig. 10-1. Officially a 1965 Ford product, collectors know how to spot 1964½ Mustangs. Higher prices are paid for them. Only 28,833 of these early ragtops were made—all prior to August 1964.

The 1965 Mustang ragtop cost the same as the 1964½ type (although it gained 25 pounds in weight). While 73,112 copies were built, 5,338 were luxury-level cars and 2111 were assembled with front bench seats. Cars of this vintage that are in excellent shape fetch around $10,000 to start. Pony interiors and performance V-8s add extra dollars.

For 1966, the Mustang convertible was changed very little. The sticker price jumped to $2,750 and sales fell slightly to 72,119 units. Of these, 12,520 were luxury ragtops and 3190 had bench seats. Ford sold more Mustang ragtops than full-sized Ford convertibles! Sales of four-speed manual transmissions were down to 7.1 percent of output.

Collector values for 1966 models are around the same as those for 1965s—with one big exception; 1966 was the first year that a Shelby-Mustang convertible was built by former race driver Carroll Shelby's California-based, Shelby-American Corporation. The Shelby-Mustang was the result of a factory-supported aftermarket competition conversion program. The Shelby-Mustangs were true racing cars. Most were built to take sedan-class racing in the Sports Car Club of America's (SCCA) Trans Am racing series. A total of six Shelby-Mustang *ragtops* were built during 1966. These cars are worth about $30,000 today!

Ford received stiff competition in the Mustang market for 1967. Previously, only Plymouth's fastback Barracuda could loosely qualify as a pony car (early Barracudas were small and sporty, but they did not have the long-hood/short-deck look of true pony cars). Now there were Cougars and Camaros to contend with—and Firebirds after the middle of the 1967 model year.

To combat the new competitors, a major—but not drastic—restyling was part of the 1967 Mustang story.

Convertible sales took a dip. Ragtop production peaked at 44,808 units (including 4848 luxury editions and just 1209 cars with bench seats).

According to the Summer 1983 *Old Cars Price Guide*, a 1967 Mustang convertible, in excellent (Number-1) condition, is worth about $5,500. There would be a 5 percent premium for GT equipment and another 10 percent increase for high-performance powerplants. That's around $6,300 for a convertible with just the right equipment.

The 1968 Mustang convertible looked much like the 1967 model. The most apparent of several, minor trim changes was that the crossbars—formerly used to support the emblem in the grille—disappeared. The chrome horse now seemed to be "floating" on the front of the car. The factory base price jumped considerably, to $2,814. Production dropped to 25,376 ragtops, including 3,339 with DeLuxe trim.

Collector values for base 1968 Mustang convertibles peak at about $5,500. The GT option adds a 5 percent premium and the 427 or 428 motors are worth another 10 percent. Especially desirable are "California Specials" with a custom-trim package sold only on the West Coast. This rare option is worth another 10 percent bonus.

Shelby-Mustang convertibles came as two different models in 1968. A total of 404 GT-350s (302-cubic-inch V-8) were built and are now worth around $19,000 in top shape. The 428-powered Shelby GT-500 Series (Fig. 10-2) generated 402 convertible sales. These cars are valued at approximately $25,000 when found in excellent condition.

A larger, smoother-looking Mustang was the news for 1969. The convertible was again offered in the 6 or V-8 series, each of which could be enhanced with numerous options. The prices for a 6-cylinder ragtop began at $2,832 while stickers for V-8s were from $2,936 up.

Fig. 10-2. All Shelby-Mustang convertibles are high-dollar collectibles. This style was introduced in 1968 and is worth about $25,000 with the 428 cubic-inch engine.

There was a big drop in total sales. Only 14,746 open-bodied Mustangs were made, including 3439 with DeLuxe interior features.

Collectors haven't focused as much attention on 1969 Mustangs as on the earlier models. However, you can be sure this will change in the future. Right now, it's possible to find ragtops of this vintage—in excellent shape—for around $4,000.

The 1969 Shelby GT-350 and GT-500 (Fig. 10-3) models are specially equipped with roll bars, heavy-duty suspension components, and either a 290-horsepower 351 (GT-350) or 335-horsepower 428 (GT-500). These cars were based somewhat closer on stock models, but they were still specially modified for enthusiast buyers. Production amounted to 194 GT-350 convertibles and 335 GT-500 ragtops. Values for examples in top shape run $16,600 and $17,000.

Collector values for cars built during 1970 through 1972 are uniform. The factory-built models bring top prices of about $5,000 at auctions. The Shelby-Mustang ragtops were last in 1970 (after which production ceased). Assemblies were made on 315 GT-350 convertibles and 286 GT-500 ragtops. Because the former are slightly more common than '69s, they bring about $100 less in top shape. On the other hand, the slightly rarer 1970 GT-500, in excellent shape, will go about $500 higher than its 1969 counterpart.

The 1973 model was the last Mustang convertible built in the pony-car years. By the time it was introduced, collectors had already begun scooping up the early ragtops. Some wanted "first" and "last" editions, so sales took a leap. Even though Ford built nearly twice as many 1973 Mustang convertibles than the three previous years, they are more highly valued. In top condition, expect to pay at least $5,500 to $6,000 for a 1973 model.

Fig. 10-3. After 1969, Shelby-Mustangs started to look more like regular factory models. The GT-500 convertibles, like this one, are worth $17,000 in top shape.

PLYMOUTH BARRACUDA

Although the first Plymouth Barracuda appeared in the showrooms only a month after the Mustang's introduction, there was no convertible in this line until 1967 (Fig. 10-4). In that season, the Barracuda was redesigned and a ragtop was added.

The 1967 Barracuda convertible came in two series. The 6 sold for $2,779 and came with Plymouth's larger, 225-cubic-inch engine (which gave 145 horsepower at 4000 rpm). Prices for the V-8 series began at $2,860. A 273-cubic-inch, 180-horse-power-base engine was used, while a 383 cubic-incher with four-barrel carburetion and 280 horsepower was optional. These cars were handsomely styled, but never found great popularity in the mass market. Only 4228 first-year-ragtops were made. Despite their rarity, top values in the collector market peak at a modest $4,000 for 1967 Barracuda convertibles.

Plymouth retained the Barracuda convertible for 1968. Below the hood the 6 was unchanged and a 318 cubic-inch motor with 230 horsepower became the base V-8. Price increases—to $2,907 for the 6 and $3,013 for the V-8—helped to offset the appeal of a more powerful V-8 engine option. Production fell to a mere 2840 ragtops. These, being slightly rarer than '67s, command higher collector values. The Old Cars Price Guide gives a top price of $4,500 for the 1968 ragtop. In addition, cars with the Formula S option receive a 10-percent value premium.

In 1969, Barracuda convertible production slipped to a mere 1442 cars. They were much the same as the previous models, with minor alterations to the trim. Base factory prices were $2,976 for the 6 and $3,082 for the V-8.

The Formula S package was offered only for the Barracuda 383 convertible this season. It cost $198 extra. Of more interest to enthusiasts was the special 'Cuda high-performance package. The 'Cuda 340 cost $309.35 above the cost of a base V-8 while the 'Cuda 383 was a $344.75 package. Only the less powerful package was offered for convertibles.

Due to the rarity factor, collector's prize 1969 Barracuda ragtops even more highly than '67s or '68s. Prices of $5,000—for examples in top condition—are about average. There are rumors that a few Barracudas with the famed Chrysler Hemi V-8 were made this year. In the unlikely event that you found a ragtop with this motor, you could expect it to be worth as much as 40 percent more than standard Barracuda ragtops.

In 1970, Barracuda convertible sales increased a bit when the ragtop was offered in three series. Accounting for 1554 customers was the base edition priced at $3,034 with a V-6 and $3,135 with a V-8. A new entry was the luxurious Gran convertible coupe (with leather bucket

Fig. 10-4. Introduced on November 6, 1966, a new convertible was one of three models in the Barracuda lineup for 1967. Until 1970, the small, sporty Plymouth looked somewhat different from other American pony cars. (Courtesy Chrysler Corp.)

seats). It sold for $3,160 as a 6 or $3,260 as a V-8, and claimed a mere 596 sales. Available only with a 335 horsepower high-performance V-8 was the 'Cuda 383 convertible—base-priced at $3,433. It generated just 635 sales.

The base 1970 ragtop is worth about the same as its 1969 counterpart in the collector's market. Gran Barracuda convertible coupes and 'Cuda convertibles go somewhat higher. Again, there would be a steep premium for a Hemi-powered ragtop. Its extremely doubtful—but not impossible—that such cars were made in the Barracuda line.

The Barracuda convertible clung to life in the base and 'Cuda series during 1971, which was the body style's last year on the market. Production totaled 1014 "straight" Barracudas and a low 374 'Cudas. These cars retained the new, long-hood/short-deck look introduced on Barracudas the previous season. There were just minor updates to the appointments and trim. New graphics treatments—including some really outlandish paint schemes—added some sparkle to the new Plymouth ponies.

As the last Barracuda ragtops, these cars warrant a slightly higher collector value than the 1970 models. Recent auctions suggest a difference of around $500 between the two years.

All Barracuda convertibles are rare cars. Only 12,683 examples were made over the five years of production for this model. Many of these cars have unusual options or special engines that make them nearly one-of-a-kind items. Plymouths, however, do not have as large a base of enthusiasts as Mustangs and Camaros. Cars with many options will usually be worth considerably more to specialized, one-marque collectors than they bring in the general market.

MERCURY COUGAR

Ford's Mercury Division introduced its Mustang-based pony car in 1967. A convertible was added in 1969 when the Cougar was redesigned. Like the Mustang, the 1969 Cougar received a slightly larger and smoother body. The base Cougar ragtop sold for $3,365 and an XR-7 edition sold for $3,578. Production amounted to 5,796 and 4,024 units respectively.

Most Cougar convertibles were on the tamer side of the high-performance scale. They stressed luxury over all-out speed. Top collector value estimates run $3,000 for the standard 1969 ragtop and $3,400 for an XR-7. Add about 5 percent for bench seats or 15 percent for the Cobra Jet 428 (*note:* It's possible that no ragtops were made with these options).

Value estimates for 1970 Cougar and XR-7 convertibles run $1000 and $1,100 higher than for the '69s. This is probably related to a production decline because only 2322 base ragtops and 1977 open-bodied XR-7s were made. There was a new, and very desirable, extra-cost engine—the 375 horsepower Street Boss 429. In addition, the Drag-Pack and Ram-Air options also were available. A convertible with any such equipment would be a very rare automobile worth far in excess of going auction prices for standard versions.

In 1971, the Cougar became an all-new type of car. With a 112-inch wheelbase and 170-inch overall length, it seemed little like a real Pony Car. The base Cougar ragtop sold for $3,681 and just 1723 copies were made. The XR-7 was priced at $3,877 and found a mere 1717 buyers. Collector values are $4,000 and $4,100 respectively. The late Cougar ragtops are unusual-looking cars and seem just strange enough to interest collectors in higher potential prices.

There were no major changes in Cougar convertible styling beyond 1971. The grille had a criss-cross pattern in '72 and a vertical look the next year. Trim was modestly changed from one season to the next. There were 1240 sales of 1972 Cougar ragtops plus 1929 XR-7 models. This jumped to 1284 Cougars and 3,165 XR-7s in 1973, the last season for the body style. Collector values follow the pattern of being stronger for "last-year" cars. The *Old Cars Price Guide* suggests excellent condition prices of $4,100 for 1972 Cougars, $4,300 for 1972 XR-7s, $4,200 for 1973 Cougars, and $4,500 for 1973 Cougar XR-7s. Both models seem to represent an excellant long-term investment.

CAMARO

Camaro convertibles were offered for only three years and represent an extremely worthwhile collector car. When Chevrolet joined the pony car revolution in 1967, the company was aiming directly at the Mustang market. This meant covering all bases from the grocery-getter type car to the quick-takeoff/stoplight racer. It also meant offering a ragtop in both 6 and V-8 series. Factory prices were $2,704 and $2,809 respectively.

The first Camaro convertible featured a manually operated top, built-in arm rests, and dual courtesy lamps. Base engines were a 140 horsepower, 230-cubic-inch 6 and a 210-horsepower, 327-cubic-inch V-8. Final production hit 25,141 ragtops. That's enough to ensure great popularity, but still low enough to make this car relatively scarce.

Ultimate scarcity in the Camaro convertible field really depends on which building blocks the original owner ordered when purchasing a car. Specific optional equipment installations add immensely to collector appeal and values of these models.

Perhaps the most interesting thing about Camaro ragtops is that, out of the three production years, this model was selected twice as an Indianapolis 500 pace car. In 1967, the actual pace car was an RS/SS-396 convertible. It had a "bumble bee" stripe around its nose, twin "power bulge" hood, and special lettering on the sides. About 100 replicas of this car were made. The majority of them were SS-350 models with Powerglide automatic transmission. These cars were supplied to officials and members of the motoring press. No effort was made to market similarly trimmed Camaros to the general public. Some of the replicas were sold as used cars to those who used them during the race.

Collectors consider both the pace car and the authentic replicas very special. Out of the 100 copies built, those that survive are valued extremely high. There are few actual sales of these cars, however, and this makes it difficult to estimate a fair market value.

There were few changes in 1968 Camaros. The main way to tell the two years apart is to look for vent windows on the 1967 models. The rear side marker lamps used with 1968 models are not found on the '67s. New federal safety regulations brought this change. Convertible sales tapered off to 20,440 cars.

In top shape, a 1967 ragtop is worth about $5,200 and a 1968 convertible is worth about $5,000. The Rally Sport and Super Sport packages both add approximately 10 percent to these values, and the 375 horsepower 396 cubic-inch engine is also good for an additional 10 percent premium.

The last Camaro convertibles were made in 1969. There was an all-new, lower and longer body. Once again, option package selections had a great affect on final appearance. The Rally Sport Group now included a blacked-out grille with hidden headlights. A functional hood scoop could be ordered with Super Sport-equipped models. There were many other new high-performance options as well.

The second Camaro Indy pace car convertible appeared in 1969. The car used to start the race was really something special. It was a Super Sport ragtop with the 396 Turbo-Jet V-8, and the new Super Scoop hood design. It featured the Rally Sport trim package, special dual orange racing stripes running lengthwise across the hood and deck, white body finish, and a special red interior. Following standard practice, about 100 original replicas were provided to dignataries and the press corps. These were SS-350 models with many less options.

Somewhat later, Chevrolet decided to make the pace car trim package a regular options group that the public could purchase when ordering a new Camaro ragtop. This was called RPO Z11 and, technically, included only a set of special pace car decals selling for $36.90. Many other options were mandatory when this package was ordered.

According to experts, about 2,000 of these packages were sold. Cars equipped with them are worth approximately $2,000 more than other RS/SS Camaro ragtops built in 1969. More specifically, according to *Old Cars Price Guide*, a 6-cylinder convertible of this vintage has a top price of $4,500, and the base V-8 adds some 5 percent more to this price. The Pace Car replicas, in top shape, are worth approximately $7,000. The *Price Guide* also notes a 10 percent addition for RS or SS equipment (20 percent for both), a 10 percent premium for the 375-horsepower Turbo-Jet engines and another 10 percent for the L-89 aluminum heads. Of course, the engine and trim option value additions would not apply individually to the pace cars because they were mandatory on this model.

FIREBIRD

The Pontiac Firebird was based on the Camaro, but was not nearly the same car in either a physical or technical sense. The Firebird had distinctive Pontiac styling motifs such as a split grille design and slat-type taillights. In addition, the rear suspension was setup differently to give a lower automobile with firm-riding qualities.

The base 1967 convertible sold for $2,903 and came with the 230-cubic-inch, 165-horsepower OHC-Six. The Sprint convertible cost $3,019 and had a 215 horsepower OHC-6. The base V-8 convertible (Fig. 10-5) used a 250-horsepower version of the 326-cubic-inch engine and was priced at $2,998. The Firebird 326 HO (high output) convertible (Fig. 10-6) sold for $3,062 and had 285 horsepower (thanks to a four-barrel carburetor and other special engine parts). The fifth Firebird ragtop had a 400 cubic-inch, 325-horsepower motor and a $3,177 window sticker (Fig. 10-7). Production of all five models, in convertible form, hit 15,528 cars.

Average collector values for Firebird convertibles haven't gone through the ceiling yet. The base 6 is estimated to be worth $3,900. Add 10 percent for the standard 326 V-8 or the Sprint Six. Add 15 percent for the Ram Air 400. That means that even the top model shouldn't cost more than $4,485 or perhaps $5,000 with

lots of extra convenience options. Pontiacs simply do not bring high prices in Collector car auctions.

Changes in 1968 Firebirds paralleled those for Camaros of the same year, with a new engine substituted for good measure. As for styling, the big differences were the disappearance of vent windows and the addition of rear side marker lamps. Two chassis engineering advances were a switch to bias-mounted rear shock absorbers and multileaf rear springs. Under the hood, a new 350-cubic-inch V-8 replaced the old 326.

A total of 16,960 assemblies were counted for the ragtop. Collector values start at a top price of $3,700 for a 6. For optional equipment, add the same premiums listed for the '67s.

Like the Camaro, the Firebird was restyled and enlarged a bit for 1969. This was the last year of convertible production, and the base price for the 6-cylinder version was $3,045.

Pontiac introduced its high-performance Trans Am package on March 8, 1969. It was the most highly refined RPO-created Firebird to come from the company up to this point. Special Trans Am Features included the Ram Air 400 engine; heavy-duty three-speed transmission with floor shifter; 3.55:1 rear axle; fiberglass-belted tires; H-D shocks; H-D springs; 1-inch stabilizer bar; power front disc brakes; variable ratio power steering; engine exhaust louvers; rear deck air foil; black textured grille; full-length body stripes; white and blue finish; woodgrained steering wheel; and special I.D. decals.

For 1969 only, both coupes and convertibles were offered with the Trans Am option. It was the only year

Fig. 10-5. The Firebird came in a quintet of different prepackaged versions advertised as the Magnificent Five. All could be ordered as convertibles. This is the '67 Firebird 326 ragtop. Note the front vent windows used only on this model.

Fig. 10-6. A Firebird 326 H.O. convertible can be identified as a 1968 model by absence of front vent windows (or ventipanes) and addition of triangular rear side marker lamps. Rally II spoke wheels are a popular option that can increase collector values.

Fig. 10-7. A new frontal treatment—with Endura rubber bumper—characterized the last-year Firebird convertible. Twin scoop hood was used on all 1967-1969 Firebird 400 models. (Courtesy Pontiac Motor Division)

Fig. 10-8. This 1971 Challenger convertible was the first Dodge ever used as an Indy Pace Car. The R/T option was dropped this year and only 2,165 Challengers were made in a single series. (Courtesy IMS Official Photo Dept.)

that a Trans Am ragtop was available. Only eight Trans Am convertibles were ever made. Of these extremely rare cars, half had four-speed manual transmissions and the others had Turbo-Hydramatic Drive. All used the L-74 Ram Air III V-8. They listed for $3,770 without add-on options and might be the rarest Pontiac ragtops ever built in regular production.

The 1969 Firebird convertibles (non-Trans Ams) are worth more to collectors than those of the earlier years. In top shape, the standard 6 brings $4,500. Add 10 percent for a base V-8 or Sprint Six. Add 15 percent for the Ram Air IV engine. Add 20 percent for any Firebird 400 convertible with the Ram Air III engine.

Trans Am convertibles are a different story. Because only eight copies were made, values for these cars are extremely high. Such a ragtop, in excellent, Number-1 condition, would be worth about $25,000 if you could even find one for sale!

CHALLENGER

Dodge was the latecomer in the pony-car field. The company's Challenger appeared in 1970. It was based on the Plymouth Barracuda, but wasn't strictly a badge-engineered car in that Dodge gave the Challenger a 2-inch longer wheelbase. The Barracuda body shell was nicely adopted to it.

Originally, two Challenger convertibles were offered. The base model came with one of two standard engines. The first was a 170-cubic-inch, 101 horsepower "Slant Six" used in only 13.4 percent of all Challengers. Base V-8 was the 318-cubic-inch job with 320 horsepower. There was also an R/T convertible that included special trim and a 383-cubic-inch, 330 horsepower engine at $335 extra. Other options included nine engines ranging from a 225 6 (145 horsepower) to the 426 Chrylser Hemi with 415 horsepower.

In midseason, the company released a V-8-only, high-performance series called the Challenger R/T. It included a 383-cubic-inch V-8 with a four-barrel carb and 335 horsepower, plus a twin scoop fiberglass hood, special wide tires, and the complete works. Its base price was $3,535.

Sales of 1970 Challenger convertibles certainly didn't skyrocket. Only 3173 ragtops were built in the regular line, while R/T deliveries of this body style peaked at a mere 1070 units. This type of rarity gives the basic ragtop a top price in the $4,600 range today, while the R/T goes about $200 higher.

The second year of Challenger production was also the last for building convertibles in this series. They came only as a base 6 ($3,105) and base V-8 ($3,207). The R/T version was dropped. Sales reached only 2165 units before ragtop assemblies halted.

One of these rare 1971 Challenger convertibles (Fig. 10-8) served as an official Indy 500 pace car. During the prerace ceremonies, this car was involved in an unfor-tunate accident. The driver, a local Dodge dealer, lost control of the vehicle as he was returning to the pits after the parade lap. The car rammed into the photo grand-stand and a number of photographers were injured. Dodge did not release a regular pace car option after that.

Collector values for the 1971 Challenger convert-ibles are hard to pin down because very few of these cars are actually sold each year. They seem slightly less popular than the 1970 models and are probably worth about $3,300 when they are in top shape without extra-cost options.

11. Super Rarities

art of honing your skills as a car collector requires setting personal standards and drawing fine lines between the desirability of different automobiles. By specializing in convertibles, you have automatically taken a first step in this direction. With few exceptions, production figures will show that convertibles of a specific year, make and model are the rarest body style in a certain manufacturer's lines. The next step you have to make is distinguishing between rare ragtops and those made in large numbers. To a degree, your guidelines for doing this will be arbitrary because the field of collecting allows considerations for relative scarcity. For example, Mustang enthusiasts will often speak of the 1964 1/2 model as a rare convertible because its production of 28,833 units was the lowest figure for early examples of the marque. At the same time, Camaro collectors will talk about their rare 1969 pace-car option where approximately 5000 cars were built. Those who like Buicks will note the 1954 Skylark's low output of 836 units. And there are cars such as the 1961 Chrysler Imperial convertible; only 429 copies were built.

Estimated prices that collectors might pay for the four ragtops previously listed (in top shape) are $8,000, $7,000, $15,000, and $6,500 respectively. The scarcest model ('61 Imperial) isn't the most valuable. The commonest of the group ('64 1/2 Mustang) is second highest in value. Collecting convertibles strictly according to rarity isn't recommended. Comparing Camaros to Imperials is like judging apples against oranges.

In spite of this, there *does* exist a line beyond which the rarity factor takes on added significance in determining the collector value of a car. This is the point at which a certain convertible was so scarce, originally, that collectors will pay an unreasonable premium to own one.

When a convertible gets to be one of ten (or less) similar vehicles built, it seems to move into the class of being a super-rare machine. At about the same point, it seems that logic in pricing will often be tossed to the wind.

Many six-figure classics from the 1930s (Fig. 11-1) were cars built in extremely low quantities. In many cases, no others like them were made. You are not going to find such cars for sale these days for less than $100,000. Prices in the $200,000–500,000 bracket have become the rule rather than exception. Such cars simply are not out there in the general buying-and-selling market today.

In many cases, super-rare postwar ragtops will be difficult to recognize because they look nearly the same as other regular production cars built in much greater numbers. For example, some Chrysler 300 letter car enthusiasts believe that only one 1960 convertible (Fig. 11-2) was ever built with a very rare transmission option. With the exception of the special gear-shifter installed in this car, it looks just like regular Chrysler 300 con-

Fig. 11-1. Claimed to be the largest two-seat convertible in the world, this custom-built 1937 Cadillac V-16 roadster measures over 6 meters long. Wearing coachwork fashioned by the Swiss bodybuilder von Hartmann, it is a-one-of-a-kind vehicle. You won't find a super-rare car like this one for sale in an affordable price range. (Courtesy Veedol Autoparade)

vertibles of the same vintage. Yet, this car is said to be worth one and one-half times as much as the others!

Does this mean that any convertible with unique assortments of optional equipment is valuable? The answer is no. There has to be something really special about the equipment for it to make the car a super-rarity.

In his book *My Years With General Motors*, Alfred P. Sloan, Jr. (a former GM chairman), explained that even some very insignificant equipment features could have been rarely used on certain models. He points out that Chevrolet had so many different choices of colors, upholstery, trim, and options available for its 1959 models, that it was conceivable for the company to go through the year without building any two cars exactly alike.

For 1960, Chrysler wanted to recapture a performance image. To do this, they offered the French-built Pont-A-Mousson, four-speed manual transmission, as a special order option, to those who had raced Chrysler 300s in the past. Prices for this gearbox were steep because extensive floorpan modifications were required for installation. The cost was about $800 extra.

In January, 1979, Bruce Hoover and George Cone, of Illinois, purchased a *convertible* that carried the rare transmission. Documentation received with the car says that it was delivered originally, in this form, to George Kuehm of Milwaukee, Wisconsin on April 25, 1960. The dealer who sold the car was the Edwards Motor Company of Milwaukee.

The original selling price for this super-rare ragtop was $6,200. Today, it is considered to be worth in excess of $25,000. That is twice what a similar model with Torqueflite automatic transmission is valued at in the same condition. And the only difference between the two is the engine, transmission, gearshift controls, and turn-signal mechanism.

Only eight examples of the 1969 Trans Am were ever made (half with four-speeds and half with automatics).

The car shown in Fig. 11-3 belongs to Charles F. Adams, who works for D'Arcy-MacMan & Masius, Pontiac's advertising agency in Bloomfield Hills, Michigan. To my knowledge, three other '69 Trans Am convertibles are in the hands of collectors. According to *Old Cars Price Guide*, they are worth about $25,000 in top condition (compared to $4,500 for a regular Firebird ragtop of the same vintage).

The chances that you'll find cars similar to this Chrysler and Trans Am on the streets or in a used car lot or in a junkyard are slim, but not impossible. Afterall, it's the quest of hidden treasure that keeps most car collectors deeply involved in their hobby. Everyone of us hopes to unearth that super-rare ragtop owned by a seller who doesn't know what he has.

I have to admit that looking for cars made in quantities smaller than ten might get a bit discouraging for the average collector. Table 11-1 shows postwar convertibles known to have production totals lower than 1000 units. In Table 11-1, some of the figures marked * are estimated production totals and a few marked ** are two-year combined totals. Series production for many convertibles (i.e., Dodge, Packard, pre-1955 Pontiacs) aren't available.

IDEA CARS

Another super-rare type of postwar convertible is the idea car that was—usually built by a manufacturer as a factory experimental prototype. Sometimes they were made for other purposes such as publicity campaigns, film use, or parade cars. The majority of such vehicles were built either for display purposes (at auto shows) or for testing new styling and engineering concepts. Some were commissioned by companies related to the auto industry, but not directly involved in marketing cars.

Fig. 11-2. This 1960 Chrysler 300-F, now owned by George Cone, is considered a super-rare car by Chrysler 300 enthusiasts. It is the only example of this rare body style known to have a super-rare and desirable four-speed transmission.

Fig. 11-3. Only eight Trans Am convertibles were ever built by Pontiac Motor Divison. Like this car owned by Charles Adams, they were all 1969 models finished in white with blue stripes. (Courtesy Ted Cram)

Table 11-1. Super-Rare Postwar Convertibles.

NOTE: The Chrysler parade phaetons were supplied to the cities of New York, Los Angeles and Detroit. In 1955, these cars were updated to 1955 specifications. The N.Y.C. car is known to survive today).

SUPER-RARE POSTWAR CONVERTIBLES

UNDER TEN EXAMPLES BUILT

1960 Chrysler 300 w/Pont-A-Mousson four-speed--one (1) built
1958 Chrysler Windsor--two (2) built
1952 Chrysler Imperial Parade Phaetons--three (3) built
1957 Lincoln-Continental Mark II--two (2) built
1969 Pontiac Trans Am--eight (8) built

UNDER FIFTY EXAMPLES BUILT

1946 Crosley Phaeton--12 built
1954 Dodge Coronet--50 built
1948 Ford Sportsman--28 built
1948 Hudson Commodore Six--49 built (*)
1952 Hudson Hudson Commodore Six--20 built (*)
1952 Hudson Commodore Eight--30 built (*)
1953 Hudson Super Wasp--50 built (*)
1971 Pontiac GTO "The Judge"--17 built

UNDER ONE-HUNDRED EXAMPLES BUILT

1961 Chevrolet Impala Super Sport--exact total unknown
1958 DeSoto Adventurer--82 built
1959 DeSoto Adventurer--97 built
1960 Edsel Ranger--76 built
1949-1950 Frazer (phaeton)--62 built (**)
1948 Hudson Super Six--86 built (*)
1948 Hudson Commodore Eight--65 built (*)
1949-1950 Kaiser (phaeton)--55 built
1949 Packard Custom 8--60 built
1950 Packard Custom 8--85 built

UNDER FIVE-HUNDRED EXAMPLES BUILT

1968 AMC Rebel 550--377 built
1954 Chrysler Windsor DeLuxe--500 built
1957 Chrysler 300C--484 built

1968 Shelby-Mustang GT-350--404 built
1968 Shelby-Mustang GT-500--402 built
1968 Shelby-Mustang 500KR--318 built
1969 Shelby-Mustang GT-350--194 built
1969 Shelby-Mustang GT-500--335 built
1970 Shelby-Mustang GT-350--315 built
1970 Shelby-Mustang GT-500--286 built

UNDER ONE-THOUSAND BUILT

1968 AMC Rebel SST--823 built
1952 Buick Special DeLuxe--600 built
1954 Buick Skylark--836 built
1971 Buick Skylark GS/GS 454--902 built
1972 Buick Skylark GS350/455--852 built
1949 Chrysler Town & Country--1,000 built
1950 Chrysler New Yorker--899 built
1953 Chrysler New Yorker DeLuxe--950 built
1954 Chrysler New Yorker DeLuxe--724 built
1955 Chrysler New Yorker DeLuxe--946 built
1956 Chrysler New Yorker DeLuxe--921 built
1958 Chrysler New Yorker--666 built
1959 Chrysler Windsor--961 built
1959 Chrysler New Yorker--286 built
1960 Chrysler New Yorker--556 built
1961 Chrysler New Yorker--576 built
1951 Chrysler Imperial--650 built
1958 Chrysler-Imperial--675 built
1959 Chrysler Imperial--555 built
1960 Chrysler Imperial--618 built
1962 Chrysler Imperial--554 built
1963 Chrysler Imperial--531 built
1964 Chrysler Imperial--922 built
1965 Chrysler Imperial--633 built
1966 Chrysler Imperial--514 built
1967 Chrysler Imperial--577 built
1969 Corvair Monza--521 built
1949 Crosley Phaeton--645 built
1949 Crosley Hot Shot Roadster--752 built

1958 Chrysler 300D--191 built
1959 Chrysler 300E--140 built
1960 Chrysler 300F--248 built
1961 Chrysler 300G--337 built
1962 Chrysler 300H--123 built
1965 Chrysler 300L--440 built
1961 Chrysler Imperial--429 built
1968 Chrysler Imperial--474 built
1953 Corvette Roadster--300 built
1950 Crosley Phaeton--478 built
1951 Crosley Phaeton--391 built
1957 DeSoto Adventurer--300 built
1958 DeSoto Fireflite--474 built
1959 DeSoto Firedome--299 built
1959 DeSoto Fireflight--186 built
1970 Dodge Challenger R/T--296 built
1963 Ford Thunderbird Sport Roadster--455 built
1965 Ford Falcon Sprint--300 built
1965 Ford Falcon--124 built
1951 Frazer Phaeton--130 built (*)
1946 Hudson Commodore Eight--140 built (*)
1947 Hudson Commodore Eight--361 built (*)
1950 Hudson Commodore Eight--426 built (*)
1951 Hudson Super Six--282 built (*)
1951 Hudson Pacemaker--500 built (*)
1951 Hudson Commodore Six--211 built (*)
1951 Hudson Commodore Eight--181 built (*)
1952 Hudson Wasp--220 built (*)
1946 Lincoln-Continental Cabriolet--265 built
1948 Lincoln-Continental Cabriolet--452 built
1950 Nash Rambler--221 built
1952 Nash-Healey--254 built
1954 Nash-Rambler--378 built
1953 Oldsmobile Fiesta--458 built
1968 Oldsmobile Cutlass "S"--410 built
1969 Oldsmobile Cutlass--234 built
1954 Packard Carribean--400 built
1955 Packard Carribean--500 built
1956 Packard Carribean--276 built
1969 Pontiac GTO Judge--108 built
1970 Pontiac GTO Judge--168 built

1952 DeSotoo Firedome--850 built
1955 DeSoto Firedome--625 built
1955 DeSoto Fireflight--775 built
1958 DeSoto Firesweep--700 built
1959 DeSoto Firesweep--519 built
1970 Dodge Coronet 500--924 built
1970 Dodge Polara--842 built
1958 Edsel Pacer--914 built
1946 Ford Sportsman--723 built
1949 Hudson Commodore Six--656 built (*)
1949 Hudson Commodore Eight--596 built (*)
1950 Hudson Pacemaker DeLuxe--660 built (*)
1950 Hudson Commodore Six--700 built (*)
1951 Hudson Hornet Six--551 built (*)
1954 Kaiser-Darrin--435 built
1947 Lincoln-Continental--738
1950 Lincoln Cosmopolitan--536
1951 Lincoln Cosmopolitan--857
1958 Mercury Monterey--844 built
1958 Mercury Park Lane--853 built
1966 Mercury S-55--669 built
1967 Mercury Cyclone--809 built
1970 Mercury Monterey--581 built
1946 Oldsmobile Custom--874 built
1950 Oldsmobile "76"--973 built
1949 Packard--671 built
1950 Packard Super 8--614 built
1953 Packard Custom--750 built
1969 Plymouth Sport Satellite--818 built
1969 Plymouth 440 GTX--700 built
1970 Plymouth Gran Convertible--596 built
1970 Plymouth 'Cuda--635 built
1970 Plymouth Road Runner--824 built
1970 Plymouth Satellite--701 built
1971 Plymouth Gran Convertible--374 built
1957 Pontiac Bonneville Convertible--630 built
1971 GTO--661 built
1964 Studebaker--703 built

(*)Indicates estimated total.
(**)Indicates two year total.

Some are modified production models and others have the "car of the future" treatment.

Some of these cars such as the Pontiac Parisienne (Fig. 2-6) were designed and built by the auto companies. Others like the 1952 Chrysler-Ghia C-200 (Fig. 11-4) were constructed by custom body shops for both the auto companies and private owners. Several have been found and restored by modern collectors. The normal practice within the auto industry was to order them destroyed after they were used.

Table 11-2 shows some of the show cars from the early prewar or postwar period that were open-body cars (convertibles, roadsters or pheatons). An asterisk is used to indicate those that are known to survive today.

In case you think that *your* low hobby budget automatically precludes the idea of ever purchasing an idea car, consider that a hobbyist once called me to check on a car he had found in a junkyard. According to him, this car carried no serial number or body tag (a sign of a factory show car) and it was a 1962 Pontiac Grand Prix convertible (a model never sold by the factory). Without inspecting the car, I couldn't tell him if it might be the original Grand Prix X-400 show car, but *could* have been.

INDY PACE CARS

There are several factors to consider when Indy pace cars are for sale at auctions, through hobby publications, or in the private market. Is the car being offered an *actual* Pace Car? Is it one of the 38 to 100 actual replicas that appeared at the track for race day? Is it simply a pace-car option package offered through dealers? All three types of cars would have some extra collector value, but it would vary in relation to how unusual the car really is.

There is only one Official Pace Car each year and it goes to the winner of the 500. A collector getting such a

Fig. 11-4. Show cars and experimental prototypes might be the postwar counterparts to Duesenbergs and Bucialis. This "idea car" is the 1952 Chrysler-Ghia C-200 convertible. (Courtesy Chrysler Corporation)

Table 11-2. Show Cars.

OPEN-AIR "IDEAS"
Listing Convertible/Roadster/Phaeton Experimental, Prototype, Show, Custom and Competition Type Automobiles

1937 Buick "Topper" Movie Car (*)
1941 Buick "Y" Job (*)
1953 Buick Wilcat Roadster
1942 Cadillac Dual-Cowl Phaeton
1953 Cadillac LaSalle Roadster
1954 Cadillac LaEspada Convertible
1940 Chrysler Newport Phaeton (* 2 of 6 remain)
1940 Chrysler Thunderbolt (* 1 of 6 remain)
1942-1946 Chrysler Derham Phaetons
1952 Chrysler Ghia C-200
1952/1955 Chrysler Imperial Parade Phaetons (*)
1953 Chrysler New Yorker Thunderbolt
1955 Chrysler Firesweep Roadster
1955 Chrysler Falcon Roadster
1961 Corvair Sebring Spyder
1962 Corvair Super Spyder (update of 1961)
1963 Corvair Monza SS Roadster
1964 Corvair "Black Widow" (*)
1957 Corvette Sebring SS Roadster (*)
1961 Corvette Cerv I (*)
1962 Corvette Cerv II (*)

1964 Dodge Charger Roadster (*)
1955 Gaylord (by Brooks Stevens) (*)
1961 Ford Mustang I Roadster
1963 Ford/Mustang Torino Roadster
1953 Oldsmobile Starfire Convertible (*)
1954 Oldsmobile F-88 Roadster
1962 Oldsmobile X-215 Roadster
1941 Plymouth Interceptor Roadster
1954 Plymouth Flightsweep I
1960 Plymouth XNR Roadster
1953-1954 Pontiac Parisienne (*)
1956 Pontiac Club De Mer Roadster
1957 Pontiac Bonneville Prototype (*)
1961 Pontiac Tempest Monte Carlo (*)
1962 Pontiac GP X-400 Convertible
1963 Pontiac X-400 Convertible
1964 Pontiac Flamme GTO Convertible
1965 Pontiac (Banshee) XP-833 (*)
1966 Pontiac (Banshee) GM-X
1966 Pontiac La Grand Conchiche
1967 Pontiac Saint Moritz

NOTE: Asterisk indicates that at least some examples of this idea car(s) are known to survive today. Certainly, there are some omissions, hundreds of show cars were probably built.

Table 11-3. Postwar Indy Pace Cars.

1948 Chevrolet Fleetmaster Convertible
1949 Oldsmobile 88 Convertible
1950 Mercury Convertible
1951 Chrysler New Yorker Convertible
1952 Studebaker Commander Convertible
1953 Ford Crestline Convertible
1954 Dodge Royal Lancer Convertible
1955 Chevrolet Bel Air Convertible
1956 DeSoto Fireflight Convertible
1957 Mercury Turnpike Cruiser Convertible
1958 Pontiac Bonneville Convertible (Tri-Power)
1959 Buick Electra 225 Convertible
1960 Oldsmobile Ninety-Eight Convertible
1961 Ford Thunderbird Convertible
1962 Studebaker Lark Daytona Convertible
1963 Chrysler 300 Pacesetter Convertible
1964½ Ford Mustang Convertible
1965 Plymouth Sport Fury Convertible

1966 Mercury Comet Cyclone GT Convertible
1967 Chevrolet Camaro RS/SS Convertible
1968 Ford Torino GT 428-Cobra Jet Convertible
1969 Chevrolet Camaro RS/SS Convertible
1970 Oldsmobile Cutlass 4-4-2 Convertible
1971 Dodge Callenger Convertible
1972 Hurst-Oldsmobile Convertible
1973 Cadillac ElDorado Convertible
1974 Hurst-Oldsmobile Custom T-Top
1975 Buick "Free Spirit" Custom T-Top
1976 Buick LeSabre T-Top
1977 Oldsmobile T-Top
1978 Chevrolet Corvette T-Top
1979 Ford Mustang II T-Top
1980 Pontiac Trans Am Turbo T-Top
1981 Buick Regal Custom Targa-Top
1982 Camaro Z-28 T-Top
1983 Buick Riviera **CONVERTIBLE**

NOTE: The true convertible! Indy 500 paced by a real ragtop in 1983, for the first time in ten years.

Fig. 11-5. This rare 1933 Chrysler Imperial served as the Indy 500 Pace Car in 1933. It is an eight-cylinder Custom Imperial roadster. (Courtesy IMS Official Photo Dept.)

Fig. 11-6. Cord paced the Indy 500 in 1930 with this super-rare Model L-29 cabriolet. (Courtesy IMS Official Photo Dept.)

Fig. 11-7. Eddie Rickenbacker, the famous WWI pilot, was the owner of the Indy Speedway for a time. Rickenbacker can be seen in the back seat of this Buick Roadmaster Phaeton, the 1939 Official Pace Car. (Courtesy IMS Official Photo Dept.)

Fig. 11-8. The 1940 Chrysler Newport Dual Cowl Phaeton paced the Indy 500 in 1941. It was originally built as an "idea car" and became the first nonproduction model to ever pace the race. (Courtesy IMS Official Photo Dept.)

Fig. 11-9. Studebaker was a fairly popular choice as Pace Car years ago. This rare Commander ragtop did the honors on May 30, 1952. (Courtesy IMS Official Photo Dept.)

Fig. 11-10. After 1974, the T-Top replaced the convertible top on Indy Pace Cars. This is the 1978 Corvette Pace Car.

Fig. 11-11. Despite what it says on the side of this Buick ragtop, it was not the Official Indy Pace Car in 1975. The actual Pace Car was a 1975 Buick Free Spirit with a custom T-Top roof. Nevertheless, 40 of these specially trimmed LeSabre convertibles—all white with white notch back seats—were produced and turned over to the Indy Festival Committee. (Courtesy Buick Motor Division)

Fig. 11-12. Here's another approach to customizing a Buick Pace Car to give both soft and hardtop features. It's the 1981 Indy pacemaker, a custom Targa-top Regal with Speedway Corporation President John Cooper behind the wheel. (Courtesy IMS Official Photo Dept.)

car would have both a one-of-a-kind item and a personality car. Taking title to one of the limited number of replicas used on race day would be the second-best possibility for the collector. Though 38 replicas are required, there are sometimes 100 or more built.

Purchasing a car with a factory-installed pace car package would be third choice. In this case, the car is probably one of just a few thousand. Remember, values don't follow rarity in a direct sense.

Trying to authenticate one of the replicas used on race day is probably next to impossible. Evidence would have to be supplied by the seller. Also, check the physical signs. See if the lettering is a decal or hand-painted. If painted, the car could be a copy.

If you are thinking of buying a car purported to have a mass-produced Pace Car package, it should have the right equipment features. Check sources of factory literature to see what the option included. With some models, there will be codes—in the serial or body tag numbers—to identify the options the car has.

The Indianapolis Motor Speedway Official Photo Department, P.O. Box 24152, Dept G, Speedway, IN 46224 can provide 8-×-10 black-and-white glossies of most Indy Pace Cars (Fig. 11-5 through 11-12) for just $3 each, plus a small handling charge. In addition, color photos of some cars are available at higher prices. Ron McQueeny, head of the Photo Department, can supply an ordering form and list of available Pace Car pictures.

A list of all postwar pace cars is given in Table 11-3. Late in 1982, Buick Motor Division announced that a special, one-of-a-kind Riviera convertible would serve as the official pace car for the 67 running of the Indianapolis 500, May 29, 1983. This car was the first true convertible used to pace the 500-mile race since 1976.

12. Ragtop Alternatives

From the convertible's inception until about 1964, few body styles posed a real threat to the ragtop's enviable position. No other type of car could offer a comparable blend of sports car excitement and family practicality at anywhere near the same price. The touring car fitted with a California-type hardtop (Fig. 12-1) was a common sight by the mid-1920s, particularly on medium-priced automobiles like Studebakers and Buicks. This type of top was generally fashioned of lightweight wood paneling, protected and decorated with a leatherette covering. This prevented rain and snow from swelling the wood or entering the car. It also imparted a rich, luxurious appearance such as seen on Broughams and Victorias of the day. These tops were sometimes sold separate from the car as an extra-cost factory (or dealership) option. Sometimes the touring car with such a top was officially listed as an individual model.

California (or Cape) tops were a mixed blessing. You could not simply lower the top when the weather was nice; it had to be detached and then re-installed. Carmakers knew that there had to be better ways to let the sun in on good days and keep the rain out on bad ones. Some foreign cars—even in the early 1930s—had a sliding roof. Around 1939, General Motors tried this in America. They called it the sunshine top (Fig. 12-2). Today we have sunroofs that do the same job.

If the seeds of the ragtop's decline were planted in the '30s they pollinated during the '60s when car makers launched what seemed like all-out efforts to reduce the crop of ragtops. Convertibles were getting expensive to build, harder to sell, and more difficult to justify. Buyer's preferences were moving in several different directions at once (none of which enhanced the convertible's chances of survival). Car owners wanted luxury, convenience, a "whisper-quiet" ride, and more and more practicality. Convertibles were by at times inconvenient, noisy, and impractical machines. Between 1960 and 1983, many leaps were made toward better styling and marketing.

Accessories. For some 1964 GM convertibles, a rare factory option—a detachable fiberglass top—was released. Priced at $500, few of these detachable tops were ordered. As with the old California tops, nobody wanted to lug such an item around or be bothered with putting it on and taking it off. Yet, this component was much lighter and durable than previous types of detachable tops and might have caught on if convertible sales hadn't gone on a downslide shortly after its introduction.

Vinyl Tops. As *Ward's Automotive Yearbook* noted in 1966, "In styling, public demand for the vinyl-covered top, simulating the convertible in appearance, increased sharply." A year later, the same source noted, "Some of the industry's two-door hardtop strength (up 3.6 percent for 1966) stemmed from the vinyl roof innovation which dented soft top convertible assembly for the second straight year."

Sunroofs and T-Tops. Around 1970, the sliding

Fig. 12-1. This early Studebaker touring car features a detachable California style hardtop.

roof marked a big revival in the U.S. auto market. Convertibles were rapidly being dropped and the sunroof provided a way to let sunlight and fresh air into the interior of a closed car. A number of the industry's supplier firms—as well as aftermarket parts producers—were pushing this new option.

In addition, American cars were starting to compete more directly with imports for sales. Sunroofs had long been a popular feature of many imports. Technological improvements overcame most problems and drawbacks traditionally associated with sunroofs. Furthermore, sun roofs had always seemed better suited to small cars, and domestic models were growing smaller.

By 1975, the market for cars with T-Tops was becoming a strong growth area. The T-Top (Fig. 12-3) was simply a safer alternative to open-air driving and it also gave the Detroit supply firms a new option to sell.

Because of all these reasons, plus the thread of Federal Motor Vehicle Safety Standard No. 216 (roof-crush standard) being passed into law, the sales of

Fig. 12-2. General Motors introduced the Sunshine Roof on some four-door models in the Buick, Cadillac, LaSalle, Oldsmobile, and Pontiac 8 lines. (Courtesy Crestline Publishing)

184

Fig. 12-3. Sunroofs came into vogue in the early 1970s, and were then followed by the T-Top. This option was included as part of the $550 Golden Anniversary Package offered for 1975 Pontiac Grand Prixs.

convertibles dropped drastically from the peak of the mid-1960s. During 1965, the two-door hardtop took over the number 1 spot as America's leading auto body style, passing up the four-door sedan. The extra sales needed to achieve this gain came directly from the convertible marketplace. Hardtops with vinyl roofs and air-conditioning continued to steal away ragtop buyers throughout the '60s. Convertible deliveries declined almost steadily from 1966 on (Table 12-1).

By 1973, it was time to face the fact that a convertible was no longer the best compromise between open and closed car advantages. Even though a limited market still existed for the ragtop's emotional appeal, there were various influences that made marketing this body style seem like a dead issue.

Although a few new models (i.e., Grand Prix, Camaro, Firebird, and Mercury Marquis) were introduced in the late 1960s, and other ragtops were re-shuffled (i.e., the Pontiac Gran Ville replaced the Bonneville), it was clear that the convertible's days were numbered. American Motors built its last ragtop in 1968, Chrysler in 1971, Ford in 1973, and General Motors in 1976. After that, most people were sure that the history of the domestic-built convertible was over.

Table 12-1. Ragtop Sales Decline: 1966-1976.

Year	General Motors	Ford	Chrysler	AMC Motors	Total
1966	238,339	140,995	34,508	6,033	419,875
1967	215,137	84,882	31,424	3,867	335,310
1968	200,187	58,220	27,191	1,203	286,801
1969	164,075	49,035	21,665	—	234,775
1970	91,286	24,093	14,772	—	130,151
1971	55,313	16,924	3,553	—	75,790
1972	58,306	13,804	—	—	72,110
1973	43,320	11,853	—	—	55,173
1974	27,983	—	—	—	27,983
1975	29,978	—	—	—	29,978
1976	14,000	—	—	—	14,000

13. Premature Obituaries

T he fanfare surrounding Cadillac's close of open-car production, on April 21, 1976, brought a number of immediate reactions. In the used car market, values for convertibles in good condition began to soar. At the same time, foreign manufacturers still building open cars steadily increased pricing on such models. The Alfa Romeo Convertible Spider Veloce 2000 jumped $3,200 in four years, the Mercedes-Benz 450 SL Coupe-Roadster climbed $10,692 during the same period, and the Volkswagen Cabriolet went from $4,545 to $6,800 between 1976 and 1980. Entrepreneurs in California and Florida adopted another approach towards filling the gap in the market for ragtops by rushing into the production of kit cars or fully assembled replicas. Other firms turned to the practice of converting two-door closed cars into soft-top convertibles. All three types of custom-built vehicles—kits, replicas and conversions—are often referred to as hand-crafted automobiles.

KIT CARS

The history of the kit car dates back to at least the 1920s when mail-order cars could be purchased by mechanically inclined buyers looking for automotive bargains. These cars are often called Sports Customs and the National Sports Custom Registry, Inc., 1306 Brick St., Burlington, Iowa 52601, is the best source of information about them.

In the late 1960s, with the large growth of interest in antique autos, classics and special-interest cars, a new type of kit car began to evolve. These kits had fiberglass bodies patterned after vintage European sports cars (i.e., Jaguar SS, Bugatti, Frazer–Nash, and MG-T models). They were designed for the Volkswagen Beetle platform and used the air-cooled VW "Bug" engine mounted at the rear. Of all the kits, those resembling the 1952–1953 MG-TD (Fig. 13-1) proved most popular. Such kits were offered by dozens of manufacturers and thousands were sold.

Although offering fun driving and an affordable means of owning a classic-looking open car, the early vintage sports-car kits were not true convertibles. They were technically roadsters. Like authentic examples of the roadster body style, they featured only side curtains for weather protection. This generated the desire to have kits of a more substantial type with roll-up windows and weathertight tops. Several companies then introduced kits fashioned after two-seat Thunderbirds (Fig. 13-2).

Kit cars—whether they look like vintage sports models or Thunderbirds—should not be confused with replicas. While they might be patterned after original classic sports cars, the kits require the buyer/owner (or his builder) to handle the assembly job. This entails securing an engine and, in most cases, the platform, chassis, or running gear.

Fig. 13-1. This is a modern kit-car. The fiberglass body is patterned after the 1953 MG-TD and designed to fit the Volkswagen beetle chassis. Assembly may be handled by the homebuilder (buyer) or by an outside contractor (body shop).

Fig. 13-2. This Classic Thunderbird kit car is a true convertible with roll-up windows. A fiberglass body is used with VW beetle running gear. The detachable hardtop is an option.

One of the more sophisticated kits offered recently is the E.R.A. Cobra (Fig. 13-3) made by E.R.A. Replica Automobiles, 608-612 E. Main St., New Britain, CT 06051.

According to *The Complete Guide To Kit Cars*, there are about 100 companies producing 130 different kits today. This fully illustrated, 196-page magazine is published by Auto Logic, Inc., P.O. Box 2073, Dept. PG, Wilmington, DE 19899. It lists the names and addresses of all companies and gives specifications, technical data, product reviews, and assembly advice. The same firm also prints a monthly newsletter covering new offerings in the field, plus *The Official Replicar Value Guide*.

REPLICARS

Dozens of ragtop replicars are also available today. This branch of the hand-crafted automobile industry has greatly progressed since 1958 when American Air Products, Corp., of Fort Lauderdale, Fla brought out its Merry Olds. This bicycle-tired machine—patterned after the famous curved-dash Olds—seems to have been the first replicar. Two years later, Greg-Sun Klassic Kars, of Glendale, California offered a smaller replica of the 1902 curved-dash Olds called the Merry Runabout.

More directly related to the modern replicars was the well-known Glen Pray 8/10 Cord. This car was 80 percent as large as the original 1936 Cord Model 810 speedster on which it was based. The 8/10 model designation was a natural. It used an air-cooled Corvair engine.

From the early 1970s on, the replicar business started to boom. Auburn replicars (Fig. 13-4) and Cords were available from various markers. There were Stutz boattail speedsters, Porsche speedsters, Duesenbergs and Mercedes–Benz copy cats. In 1981, Exxacta Cars, Inc., of Clearwater, Florida made a protype 1953 Corvette replicar (Fig. 13-5) called the XC-53. It featured a new Chevrolet Monte Carlo drivetrain, original Corvette styling, and Turbo-Hydramatic transmission.

An off-shoot of the replicar, that *looks* like an original model is the exoticar that merely resembles a generic kind of classic. Undoubtedly, the most famous and successful exoticar is the Excalibur (Fig. 13-6) designed by Brooks Stevens and built by his Milwaukee, Wisconsin-based Excalibur Motor Car Co. It has been in continuous production since 1965 and averages about 100 sales per year.

Fig. 13-3. Available in kit form only, the E.R.A. Cobra—at a price of $14,800—comes in street and competition models. The latter version is shown here at Limerock Race Park. (Courtesy JVS Enterprises)

Fig. 13-4. This Auburn look-alike is a replicar, marketed in fully assembled form, patterned after the Classic boattail Auburn speedster. It is shown here at the 1982 Street Rod Nats in Minneapolis.

CONVERTERS

Making closed cars into ragtops dates back to the days when open-bodied speedsters were all the rage. Thousands of coupes and sedans, especially those of the Model T Ford variety, were turned into sporty little roadsters (boattailed or otherwise) in the 1920s. During the classic car era of the '30s, custom coachbuilders continued this practice, turning it into an art. After the close of World War II, such shops all but disappeared.

An excellent example of a first-class ragtop con-version is the Cadillac LeCabriolet from Hess & Eisen-hardt (Fig. 13-7). Long recognized as a producer of custom-built luxury cars, Hess & Eisenhardt (H&E) has been in business for over 100 years. The company is best known for its funeral cars and armoured limousines (the latter produced for several U.S. presidents and other heads of state). The Cadillac-based LeCabriolet con-vertible was first introduced in 1979.

According to George L. Strike, president of H&E, "This (conversion) is not a garage operation. We have a fully staffed engineering department which designs our

Fig. 13-5. The XC-53 Corvette-styled replicar was scheduled for marketing in 1982 by Exxacta Cars, Inc. of Clearwater, Fla. Chevrolet Monte Carlo running gear was used under this one-off prototype.

Fig. 13-6. Brooks Stevens' designed Excalibur series of exoticars holds the record for longevity and sales in this segment of the handcrafted auto market. The first Excalibur production models appeared in 1966. (Courtesy Excalibur Motor Car Co.)

convertibles. They work closely with Cadillac to make sure that what we do is compatible with their designs. Le Cabriolet begins as a Coupe DeVille, America's favorite luxury car. When we are finished, there is little doubt in anyone's mind that it is a bonafide convertible in the factory sense. It is not just a matter of cutting off a hardtop and replacing it with a convertible top."

The H&E engineers actually produce their own electro-hydrauilic top mechanism. The geometry of the Le Cabriolet top is that of the straight foldback variety. The roof of the standard Coupe DeVille is removed and portions of the body sides are built up and molded to provide a finished look. The convertible features power-operated rear quarter windows, a large and spacious trunk, tempered rear window glass heat-sealed into the fabric top and a rear window defroster. The top is padded inside and, when folded, is protected by a taught-fitting boot.

Fig. 13-7. The Cadillac Le Cabriolet convertible is a quality crafted conversion built by Hess & Eisenhardt, a firm that has long specialized in making limos and professional vehicles. (Courtesy D.J. Edleman, Inc.)

Fig. 13-8. Two-passenger Chrysler LeBaron convertible appeared in early 1982 calendar year with a $10,995 price tag. A luxury edition Mark Cross designer model is also available. (Courtesy Chrysler–Plymouth Public Relations)

The 1979 Le Cabriolet had retail prices beginning at $25,977 f.o.b. Cincinnati, Ohio and was marketed through about 75 select Cadillac dealers with GMAC financing available to qualified buyers. According to Strike, the company could accommodate up to 500 orders per year and had scheduled 300 assemblies for 1979.

Hess & Eisenhardt also offered similar conversions for the Buick Electra 225 and Oldsmobile 98 Regency at $22,000 each.

Not all convertible conversions are done to the same standards as the H&E models or are backed by the same type of reputation for quality. There are wide variations in basic designs as well as in the quality of construction. The normal cost charged for such work is $3,400 to $6,000 above the price of the basic closed car. Some exceptionally detailed jobs will run as high as $10,000 for just the conversion work where major body-panel modifications are required. Even the least expensive acceptable conversions will be in the $3,000 + bracket.

DETROIT JUMPS BACK IN

Chrysler Corporation was the first of the major automakers to jump back into the convertible market. Chrysler marketing executives noted the success that the custom converters were enjoying with ragtop sales and, in 1980, suggested that the all-new Dodge Aries/Plym-

Fig. 13-9. Seen here at its Chicago Auto Show introduction, in February 1983, is the Chrysler LeBaron Town & Country convertible with its simulated wood-grain exterior trim.

Fig. 13-10. This preproduction Dodge 400 convertible appeared at 1981 auto shows sporting a "rumble seat" and custom white vinyl with red plaid cloth interior. The Dodge Aries K-Car is the basis for this model.

Fig. 13-11. The Mustang GTL ragtop is being promoted as a high-performance car to fill the market gap between the various competitors. With the LeBaron and Riviera positioned in the luxury-class bracket and the Dodge 400 in the economy-price class, the Mustang has the super-car field to itself. (Courtesy Ford Motor Company)

Fig. 13-12. As on the Cavalier, the Pontiac Sunbird's soft-top conversion is by American Sunroof Corp. of Lansing, Mich. Although sales introductions have been delayed, this unit was displayed at the Chicago Automobile Show in February, 1983.

Fig. 13-13. Buick Rivera convertible appeared as a mid-1982 entry aimed strictly at the personal-luxury class buyer. A full list of standard features is included with the $25,000 price tag. Buyers can choose a V-6 or V-8 with no difference in price. (Courtesy Buick Motor Division)

Fig. 13-14. The Pontiac 2000 Sunbird convertible is based on the original J-Car platform with a spunkier fuel-injected, 1.8 liter four providing power. (Courtesy Pontiac Motor Division)

outh Reliant K-Car platform was well-suited to such a transformation. A number of aftermarket customizing firms were asked to supply bids on what it would cost to modify the K-Car into a ragtop.

Dave Draper, the president of Cars & Concepts, of Brighton, Michigan, made a successful bid to have the work done by his 400 employees on a special assembly line. The cars scheduled for the conversion were called the Chrysler LeBaron (Figs. 13-8 and 13-9) and the Dodge 400 (Fig. 13-10). They began life as Plymouth Reliant/Dodge Aries two-door coupes assembled at the company's St. Louis, Missouri assembly plant with bare metal roofs and without windows. They were then shipped to Cars & Concepts to be made into ragtops. More than 21,400 copies were sold.

For the 1983 model year, Chrysler announced that future assemblies would be switched to an in-house operation. All 1983 K-Car ragtops were to be built entirely at the St. Louis plant. At the same time, Ford and GM announced they would re-enter the convertible market with models fashioned by several different outside contractors. They were to be based on the Ford Mustang (Fig. 13-11), Chevrolet Cavalier (Fig. 13-12), Buick Riviera (Fig. 13-13), and Pontiac 2000 (Fig. 13-14).

14. How To Make A Convertible

Almost every automobile enthusiast has dreamed of making a favorite car—one not offered as a ragtop—into a convertible. It seems like it would be a simple job to hack the roof off a closed car and transform it into an open-air cruiser. Unfortunately, that isn't true in most cases. Back in the good old days, when every auto manufacturer built and sold ragtops, convertibles were usually the second heaviest type of basic body style in a car line (next to station wagons).

The considerable weight of the convertible was mostly attributable to the fact that open car bodies required extra structural support. In many cases, additional frame cross members or body-to-frame attachment braces were used to provide this support. This can be seen by comparing the 1958 Pontiac convertible frame with the frame used on other models (Fig. 14-1). Four extra body-to-frame mountings (Nos. 2, 3, 4, and 5) were required to give the ragtop's lower body structure a great deal more rigidity.

Without these extra attachment points, the convertible's sheet metal could not withstand the flexing and vibrations caused by the car making turns, riding over bumps, climbing inclines, etc. On closed-body cars, the steel/wood roof super structure gives the needed integrity that a car requires for normal road use. Lacking this type of rigid top structure, the open car must incorporate an alternative means of achieving body integrity. This entails beefing up the frame or attaching the sheet metal more firmly.

The extra frame members and body supports add to the weight of the car. In addition, design engineers might have to add hydraulic or hydroelectric systems to a convertible (Fig. 14-2) to allow for power top operation. The parts can include a heavy hydraulic pump, booster spring, regulator panel, and pivot plate bracket (Fig. 14-3). Even small hardware such as striker supports, control-link adjusting plates, braces, hinges, and attaching bolts must be figured in as added weight.

If you wanted to turn your dream car coupe or sedan into a ragtop, you would have to add on these parts yourself. In effect, you would be re-engineering the vehicle. If you didn't do this and simply sliced the top off, your "convertible" wouldn't last very long. The body panels would start to rattle and would eventually shake loose. When this happened, you'd start to see the car sag. The doors and other body panels would loose proper alignment. In extreme cases, the body will partially or completely collapse and turn a dream into a nightmare.

This is not to say that no one has ever built a homemade convertible. It can be done. All sorts of hand-crafted automotive creativity has surfaced over the years. I recently spotted a homebuilt 1956 DeSoto four-door convertible for sale in *Old Cars Weekly*. Chances are

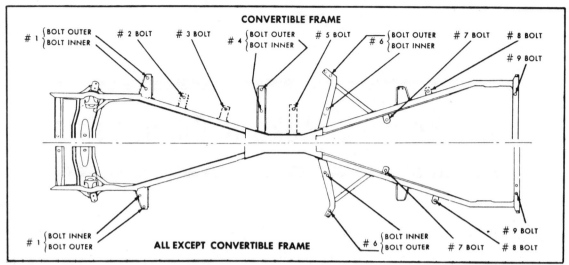

CONVERTIBLE FRAME

#1 {BOLT OUTER / BOLT INNER}   #2 BOLT   #3 BOLT   #4 {BOLT OUTER / BOLT INNER}   #5 BOLT   #6 {BOLT OUTER / BOLT INNER}   #7 BOLT   #8 BOLT

#9 BOLT

#1 {BOLT INNER / BOLT OUTER}   **ALL EXCEPT CONVERTIBLE FRAME**   #6 {BOLT INNER / BOLT OUTER}   #7 BOLT   #8 BOLT

#9 BOLT

Fig. 14-1. Open car bodies require extra structural support to compensate for not having a roof. Shown here are the designs of the two frames used on 1958 Pontiacs. Note that the convertible frame (above horizontal centerline) has four more body-to-frame mounting "arms" than the frame used on all other body styles (below horizontal centerline). This allows use of five extra fastenings—bolts Nos. 2–5—to more rigidly join the frame and ragtop sheet metal. (Courtesy *Pontiac Service Craftsman News*)

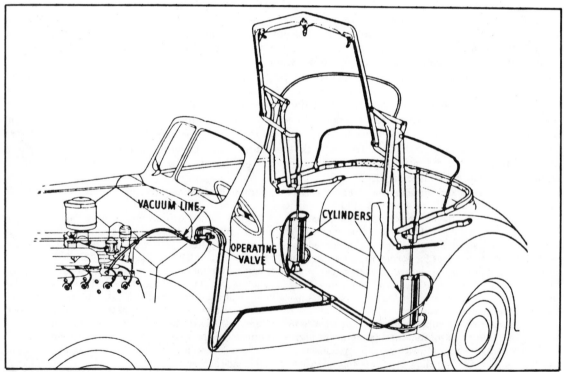

VACUUM LINE   CYLINDERS   OPERATING VALVE

Fig. 14-2. Adding greater weight to convertibles are components such as hydraulic lines, top motors, and controls. Engine vacuum is used to operate the top on this 1940 Ford so vacuum tubing is required. (Courtesy *Ford Factory Service Bulletin*)

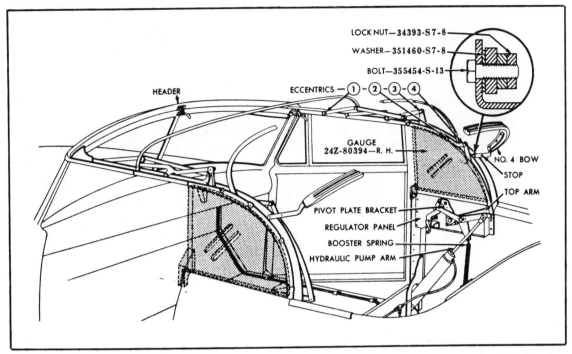

LOCK NUT—34393-S7-8
WASHER—351460-S7-8
BOLT—355454-S-13

HEADER
ECCENTRICS—①-②-③-④

GAUGE
24Z-80394—R. H.

NO. 4 BOW
STOP
TOP ARM

PIVOT PLATE BRACKET
REGULATOR PANEL
BOOSTER SPRING
HYDRAULIC PUMP ARM

Fig. 14-3. This is the convertible top-riser system and attachment hardware used on an early 1950's Pontiac. Home builders would have to custom-engineer parts like these—a very difficult job. (Courtesy *Pontiac Service Craftsman News*)

good that people will keep making cars of this sort as long as the automobile survives. There's an even better chance that amateur conversions such as this one won't last very long unless the car has been completely re-engineered, from the frame-up, according to professional standards. For many of us "shade tree" mechanics, this is simply an impossibility. We do not have the time, place, or equipment to handle such a big job.

HOW THE PROS DO IT

After bidding successfully for the job of making the first Chrysler K-Car convertibles, Cars & Concepts president Dave Draper knew that some changes would need to be made. His company had formerly concentrated on the aftermarket installations of T-Tops, fiberglass wheel-lip flares, simulated convertible tops, and special striping and deck-spoiler treatments. Handling some 12,500 ragtop conversions for Chrysler seemed a much bigger task.

Draper sat down with his many engineering and manufacturing specialists to discuss how the work could best be handled. The result was the creation of a miniature assembly line inside the Brighton, Michigan factory. It was patterned along the same separate-work-station system long used successfully by Detroit manufacturers. It stretched over 300 feet long and comprised 18 different stations where various tasks could be performed in logical sequence.

The cars were shipped in from Chrysler's St. Louis assembly plant. They had bare metal roofs, no windows, no back seats no sun visors, and they also came without seat-belt anchors and a few pieces of standard interior trim.

As with any restoration job, the first step in the construction process was somewhat destructive. Parts were removed from the cars and carefully attached to a conveyor above the worker's heads. These components included the deck-lid cover, interior door-panel trim, windshield moldings and wipers, front seats, and the upper dashboard panel. The windshield (with mirror) was also removed.

Floorpan modifications came next. The brackets—that normally held the gear shifter in place—were cut out of the center console and structural reinforcements were added, below the floor, to form torque boxes. The windshield pillars were beefed up by pop-riveting reinforcing plates to them. Once riveted, a urethane plastic bonding material was used as a no-welding-needed final attachment agent.

Still more reinforcement of the floorpan was re-

Fig. 14-4. Blueprints for building Sport Custom ragtops can be found through advertisements in national hobby magazines such as *OLD CARS WEEKLY, HEMMINGS,* or *CARS & PARTS.* The National Sport Custom Registry, 1306 Brick St., Burlington, IA 52601, can also provide information. This Sport Custom chassis, seen at a Florida show, appears to be available in kit form.

quired. This was achieved through use of five preformed assemblies that link together to form a new, box-sectional "spine" for the open cars. The five sections were installed in the following order and manner: (section 1) a member placed across the rear seat area of the floorpan, running widthwise; (section 2 & 3) two members, each being placed along the dogleg area on either side of the car (they ran lengthwise and were attached to the ends of the first member); (section 4) a member placed over the area usually called the transmission tunnel and spreading across the toeboard region, widthwise; (section 5) a member placed down the center of the floor pan, running lengthwise and joining the fourth member to the front-center area of the first one.

Fig. 14-5. Beginning its life as a stock 1936 Ford convertible cabriolet, this custom/rod designed by Ken "Posies" Fenical is a radical approach to open-air individuality. It drew lots of attention at the '83 Street Rod Nats in Minneapolis.

The overall affect of the design of this formed structure added both longitudinal and lateral support to the front, rear, and center of the floorpan in the passenger compartment area. With this accomplished, the side window frames were sawed off at the belt line level and, wherever bare metal became exposed, an anticorrosive sealer was applied.

Next came replacement of the forward edge of the rear package shelf with a newly designed section that was riveted into position. It was placed between the remainder of the original shelf and the rear seatback supports. Before sawing off the roof pillars completely, a pair of temporary braces was crisscrossed inside the car. Bolted to the inner rocker panels and braced against the upper third of the windshield posts with turn-buckles, these provided for tight adjustments.

The A-pillars were then sawed off about 6 inches from the roof. Then a jig was set up against the body to allow marking for saw cuts through the B and C pillars. The roof was then removed after the necessary cuts were made.

A new inner quarter panel, designed to flow water out of the car, was installed. The only welding in the entire procedure took place at this state. A strong, three-piece windshield header was attached to the stubs of the A-pillar. Added next were door jamb reinforcements (lower windshield frame area), rocker panel drainage troughs, inner door panel stiffeners, and door-hinge reinforcements.

New, custom-designed window glass was added to the doors along with more hardware to ensure positive door latching and door-glass weather sealing at the upper front corner.

On the LeBaron convertible, a fiberglass panel was used in place of the normal rear seat. The Dodge 400 had its short-cushion rear seat added later (when the inner liner, radio speakers, and trim were being installed).

Additional hardware attachments made next included the installation of dual, Dodge Omni-type door mirrors, guide-pin blocks for the windshield header, and external A-pillar clips and trim. Then the original gear selector assembly was re-installed on the new (section number 5) center support member. Supports for the convertible top motor, the motor itself, and tubing and parts for the hydraulic pressure system were added next. This was followed by re-attachment of the door trim panels.

With the car starting to come together again, acoustical insulation was now bonded to the floorpan, new carpeting was installed, and the final interior trimming was accomplished. After adding two new struts to beef up seat belt mountings, lap and shoulder harnesses custom-designed for the convertible were installed. Then a new console was screwed in place.

Before adding the convertible top mechanism, new sun visors and top latches were attached to the windshield header. The preconstructed top assembly (built on a separate jig) was next lowered in place with the hinge mechanisms bolted to mounting brackets previously installed at the inner rear quarter panels. Tacking strips holding the fabric were then screwed tight up against the body. The hydraulic rams were added next.

Final assembly details were comprised of adding exterior trim, a new body panel between the top and the deck lid, a vinyl strip to cover the upper rear top seam, snap fastener moldings for the convertible top boot, and the original bucket seats (on new guide rails). Finally, a protective cover was placed over the ragtop and the car was readied for final destination shipping.

HOMEBUILDING ALTERNATIVES

Completely homebuilding a one-of-a-kind convertible (according to professional standards) just isn't the world's most practical idea. There are a few alternatives that you can follow if you're absolutely determined to make something a little different that's still safe to drive.

You can go the kit-car route discussed in Chapter 13, or you might want to look around for plans for building sports/custom type automobiles (Fig. 14-4). Publications such as *Old Cars Weekly*, *Hemmings Motor News*, and *Cars & Parts* frequently carry advertisements from individuals who have formulated blueprints for making such machines. In most cases, they have used parts from a variety of production models in combination with homemade bodies and running gear.

The Sports Custom Registry, 1306 Brick St., Burlington, Iowa, can help provide information about the most successful efforts of this type. The Registry can help you find the plans and materials you'll need to build a really distinct ragtop that is safe to drive.

Hot-rodding and customizing existing convertibles can be another way to achieve ragtop individuality. Some hot-rod ragtops (Fig. 14-5) are quite unusual. Other customized convertibles are less radical, but they are still different enough to standout in a crowd of car enthusiasts.

For example, several years ago a 1966 "Chrysler 300" convertible showed up in several auctions. It drew second and third looks from lots of people who realized such a model had never been factory built. This car was actually a New Yorker convertible. The owner had simply added 300 letter car trim and an Imperial bumper and grille to make it look just like the original item The factory-built Chrysler C-300 hardtop was actually a New Yorker body with an Imperial bumper and grille, plus other custom touches.

No, it wasn't an authentic Chrysler 300 letter-car ragtop. That car really upset quite a few Chrysler purists. But it sure looked nice. Too bad the company didn't build originals just like it. Being based on another convertible, it was safe to drive and lots of fun to use.

15. It's Up to You

Y ou now have the essential information needed to get started. From this point on, it's up to you to find and buy a convertible, get it fixed up, and then get yourself involved in the many events and activities that the collector-car hobby offers. Whether you just like to drive your car or want to show it off at car shows, you will find some appealing aspect of the automotive sport (Figs. 15-1, 15-2, and 15-3). Maybe it's buying and selling, vintage racing, or driving on a coast-to-coast tour. The activity itself isn't as important as the enjoyment that you get from it. When a convertible is involved, everything is going to seem even that more exciting.

The real excitement will start on the day that you get your ragtop licensed for road use. This may happen quickly or the big day might come after you finish restoring a car that you've been working on for weeks, months or years.

Your use of the car might be seasonal, occassional, or extremely limited—most likely based on its value, degree of restoration or original condition, and its age. Here are some possibilities:

- ☐ Outdoor antique auto shows.
- ☐ Indoor antique auto shows and new car shows.
- ☐ Tours (ranging from short trips to coast-to-coast journeys).
- ☐ Vintage racing (vintage road racing or bracket drag racing).
- ☐ Gymkanas and rallys.
- ☐ Car club picnics.
- ☐ Displays at racing tracks.
- ☐ Parades and parade laps (at racing events).
- ☐ National car club conventions.
- ☐ Making a movie (such as when film companies rent cars).
- ☐ Hill climbs.
- ☐ Car games and contests.
- ☐ Drive-in nights.
- ☐ Nostalgia parties (1950s or Roaring '20s style, etc.).
- ☐ Cruises.

In the last few years, there has been a transition away from the static type of activity such as simply displaying a car at a show. There has been much greater emphasis placed on doing things with older cars. People are collecting more modern cars that are better suited for use on modern highways and several large-scale events have been organized, by individuals or groups, due to growing interest in the old-car hobby.

Indoor New Car Shows. More and more old-car owners are participating in new car shows, either individually or as members of clubs. For example, the promoters of the annual Chicago Automobile Show allow car clubs in their area to set up booths to attract new members to their club.

Parade Laps at Race Tracks. Auto racing of all types has always been one of America's largest spectator sports. Now many tracks—especially the southern stock

Fig. 15-1. Members of the Pontiac-Oakland Club International prepare a 1970 Pontiac Bonneville convertible for the club's annual car show. This event is held once a year in different cities throughout the United States.

Fig. 15-2. Some hobbyists, especially those on the East and West Coasts might have the opportunity to join in the making of a film by renting their cars to a movie studio. This '39 Cadillac appeared in the movie *The Godfather*.

Fig. 15-3. During race weekends at Road America, Elkhart Lake, Wisconsin, owners of certain kinds of cars can participate in show-and-shine and parade lap activities. Owners of Corvette convertibles can also take part in the Corvette Corral.

car speedways—are becoming conscious of the fact that people are interested in the history of American racing. They are therefore staging parade laps, prior to major races, with owners of older ragtops taking a lap around the course.

Filmmaking. Most film companies have consultants who are responsible for locating cars used for background scenes. They often advertise in car club magazines or local newspapers to find the cars they need. Owners are usually paid from $25 to $150 per day for use of their cars, plus having the opportunity to see their vehicle used in a film.

Drive-In Nights. This type of activity is really picking-up steam today. All across the country, old-fashioned drive-in restaurants are coming back into popularity. Working through clubs or local advertising, hobbyists are promoting shows at these drive-ins where on a certain night dozens of '50s and '60s cars converge at

the restaurants in order to bring back a glimpse of the past.

Nostalgia type Parties. "Flapper" parties and "sock hops," old-car owners are invited to join in the fun and help recreate a nostalgic atmosphere.

Cruises. The weekend cruise is a social phenomena that started in California. Such cruises remain popular there (Hollywood Boulevard on Friday nights) and are catching on all across the country.

Whether it occurs while taking part in organized hobby activities or simply when taking a ride on a warm summer night, you're going to realize that ownership of a ragtop suddenly makes driving lots of fun again. There is definitely something special about driving an open-air car. You are going to feel the convertible mystique each time you slide behind the wheel, turn the ignition key, and push the button that lowers the top to a brand-new world of driving pleasure.

Index

Index

OTHER POPULAR TAB BOOKS OF INTEREST

Basic Body Repair & Refinishing for the Weekend Mechanic (No. 2122—$13.50 paper)

Convertibles: The Complete Story (No. 2110—$20.50 paper)

Car Design: Structure & Architecture (No. 2104—$20.50 paper)

Car Interior Restoration—3rd Edition (No. 2102—$7.25 paper)

All About Electric & Hybrid Cars (No. 2097—$9.95 paper; $16.95 hard)

Supertuning Your Firebird Trans-Am (No. 2088—$9.95 paper)

The New Mazda Guide (No. 2082—$13.50 paper)

The 1960s Supercars: A Repair and Restoration Guide (No. 2077—$13.50 paper)

The Complete Handbook of Automotive Power Trains (No. 2069—$9.95 paper)

Dreamboats & Milestones: Cars of the '50s (No. 2065—$11.95 paper; $18.95 hard)

Formula Vee/Super Vee—Racing, History, and Chassis/Engine Prep (No. 2063—$6.95 paper)

Boss Wheels—End of the Supercar Era (No. 2050—$7.95 paper; $9.95 hard)

The Ford Mustang—1964-1973 (No. 2048—$8.25 paper; $9.95 hard)

The Coach Trimmer's Art (No. 1213—$12.95 hard)

Vanner's How-To Guide to Murals, Painting & Pinstriping (No. 1032—$5.95 paper)

101 Vantastic Ideas to Improve Your Van (No. 1018—$4.95 paper)

How to Convert Your Car, Van, or Pickup to Diesel (No. 968—$7.95 paper)

Step-By-Step Guide to Brake Servicing (No. 818—$8.95 paper)

Step-By-Step Guide: Carburetor Tuneup & Overhaul (No. 814—$8.95 paper)

Customizing Your Van—2nd Edition (No. 2112—$11.50 paper; $16.95 hard)

The RV/Truck/Van Conversion Guide (No. 2109—$12.95 paper)

Propane Conversion of Cars, Trucks & RVs (No. 2103—$9.95 paper; $14.95 hard)

Automobile Restoration Guide—3rd Edition (No. 2101—$8.25 paper)

Choosing the Right Car for the 1980s (No. 2095—$10.25 paper)

Morgans: Pride of the British (No. 2083—$29.95 hard)

The Triumph Spitfire (No. 2079—$6.95 paper)

Troubleshooting Old Cars (No. 2075—$9.25 paper; $13.95 hard)

Rebuilding the Famous Ford Flathead (No. 2066—$7.25 paper; $9.95 hard)

Studebaker: The Complete Story (No. 2064—$39.95 hard)

The Complete MG Guide—Model by Model: 2nd Edition (No. 2056—$4.95 paper)

The Giant Book of 4 × 4's & Off-Road Vehicles (No. 2049—$10.95 paper)

Modern Diesel Cars (No. 2046—$7.95 paper; $9.95 hard)

The Complete Guide To Car Stereo Systems (No. 1121—$7.95 paper)

Automotive Air Conditioning Handbook—Installation, Maintenance & Repair (No. 1020—$9.25 paper)

Fixin' Up Your Van On a Budget (No. 982—$10.25 paper; $13.95 hard)

Do-It-Yourselfer's Guide to Auto Body Repair & Painting (No. 949—$7.95 paper; $10.95 hard)

How to Repair Diesel Engines (No. 817—$10.95 paper; $15.95 hard)

TAB   TAB BOOKS Inc.

Blue Ridge Summit. Pa. 17214

Send for FREE TAB Catalog describing over 750 current titles in print.